"Nigel Roberts has written a glittering memoir of his walk in the Himalayas—within which is a story of family tragedy, perseverance and love, told with vast insight and grace."

> —**Meg Rosoff**, winner of the Astrid Lindgren
> Memorial Award and author of *How I Live Now*,
> *Jonathan Unleashed* and *The Great Godden*

"Nigel Roberts' book is a deeply moving and beautifully-written memoir, both an adventure and a literary homage to a classic of travel writing, *The Snow Leopard*."

> —**Roger Crowley**, historian and author of
> *1453*, *Empires of the Sea* and *Spice*

"I am honored to have read your manuscript. It is excellent. I greatly admire your research. Your Nepal history provides a superb overview, and your frequent quotes from the past and present greatly add to the text. Your evocative writing retrieved many memories of the brilliant and cold landscape, of blue sheep courting, and of digging up caterpillar fungus. I hope that your important historical record will be translated into Nepalese and Chinese, and that the government departments concerned will make positive changes to give greater protection to their natural treasures."

> —**George Schaller**, field biologist, conservationist
> and author of *The Year of the Gorilla*,
> *The Serengeti Lion* and *Stones of Silence*

THE LEOPARD AND THE MOON

A JOURNEY IN DOLPO, NEPAL

NIGEL ROBERTS

In Memory of Tess and Mandana
For my wife Sarah, and my grandson Alex

"Though nothing can bring back the hour
Of splendour in the grass, of glory in the flower;
We will grieve not, rather find
Strength in what remains behind;
In the primal sympathy
Which having been must ever be;
In the soothing thoughts that spring
Out of human suffering".

William Wordsworth, *Ode: Intimations of Immortality*
from Recollections of Early Childhood[1]

CONTENTS

AUTHOR'S NOTES

A note on dialogue

In *Specimens of the Table Talk of Samuel Taylor Coleridge,* this advice:

> *"A poet ought not to pick nature's pocket: let him borrow, and so borrow as to repay by the very act of borrowing. Examine nature accurately, but write from recollection; and trust more to your imagination than to your memory".*[1]

A convention in many memoirs and travel books is the reproduction of dialogue without any sort of caveat, implying that the words on the page are an exact reproduction of the words that were spoken. This, of course, is most unlikely, except in cases where the author has recorded the conversation. So too in this book: with those few exceptions, I do not claim the dialogue is exact.

. . . on altitude

Most altitudes were recorded by the Delorme InReach Explorer Handheld Satellite Navigator I carried in Dolpo, which uses the Global Positioning System (GPS) to fix both location and altitude, measuring the latter in feet. I used my own readings because the maps and guidebooks covering the west of Nepal lack any consistency.

...on transliteration

There is no universally accepted way of transliterating Nepali. I have left place names (e.g. Phoksundo) and commonly-used terms/names (e.g. Limbu) as they are commonly found, and in normal font; otherwise I have italicized Nepali words and phrases, and have attempted to clarify the length of ambiguous vowels (in particular the long "a", which is shown as ã), and to indicate consonants carrying an aspirated h, such as chh (छ), bh (घ), kh (ख), dh (ध), th (थ) and jh (झ). Nepali, like Hebrew and Arabic, also infers vowels between certain consonants: thus the word for "strong" transliterates literally as *"bliyo"*, but is pronounced *"boliyo"*; the choice of whether to fill the gap with an "a", an "o", or sometimes a "u" can vary by region, or with a person's pronunciation.

...and on history

There are many references to Nepalese history and politics in this book. For those interested in an overview, I have added a brief annex on Nepali political history.

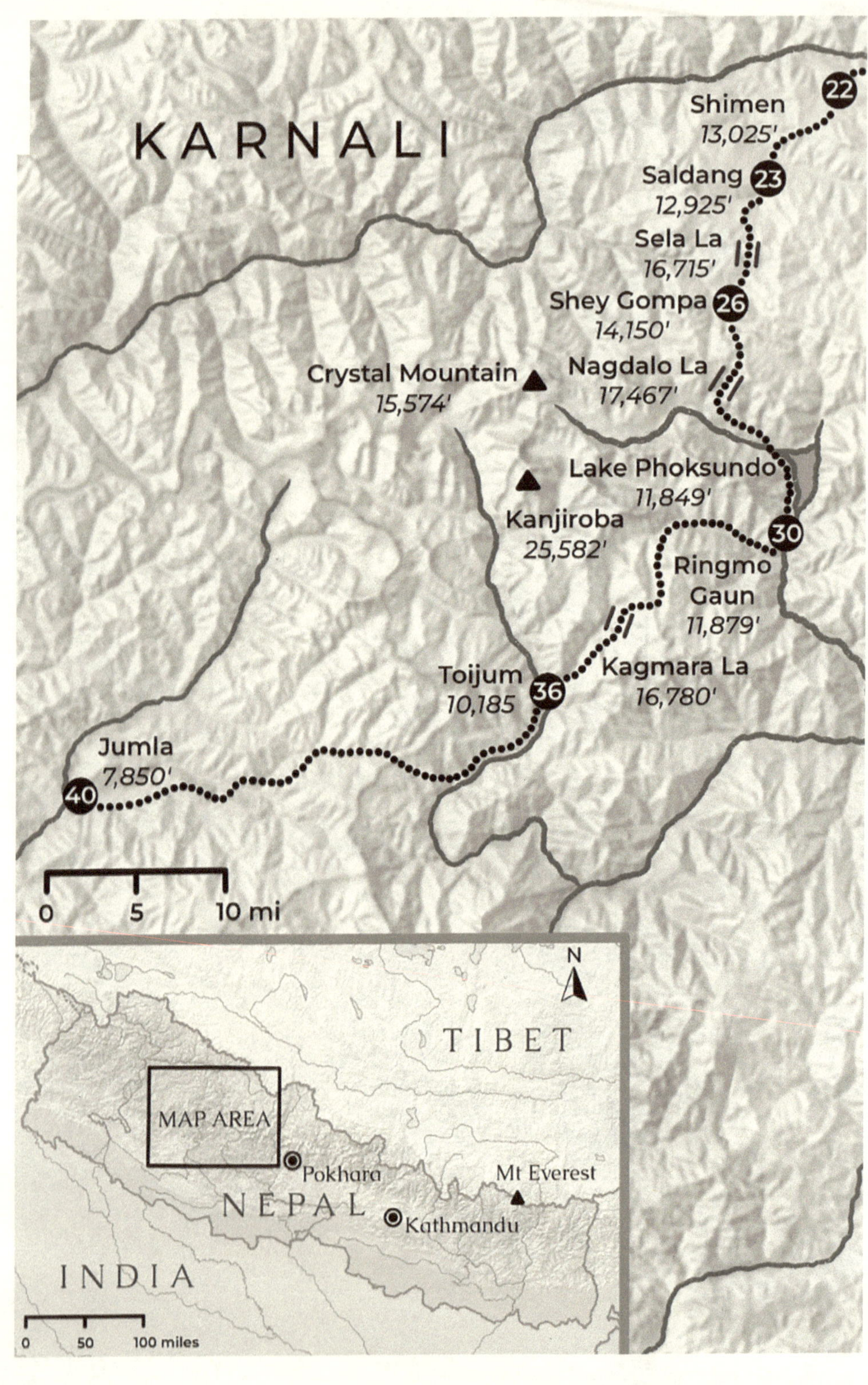

KARNALI
Shimen
13,025'
22
Saldang
12,925'
23
Sela La
16,715'
Shey Gompa
14,150'
26
Crystal Mountain
15,574'
Nagdalo La
17,467'
Lake Phoksundo
11,849'
Kanjiroba
25,582'
30
Ringmo
Gaun
11,879'
Toijum
10,185
36
Kagmara La
16,780'
Jumla
7,850'
40
0   5   10 mi
N
TIBET
MAP AREA
Pokhara
Mt Everest
NEPAL
Kathmandu
INDIA
0   50   100 miles

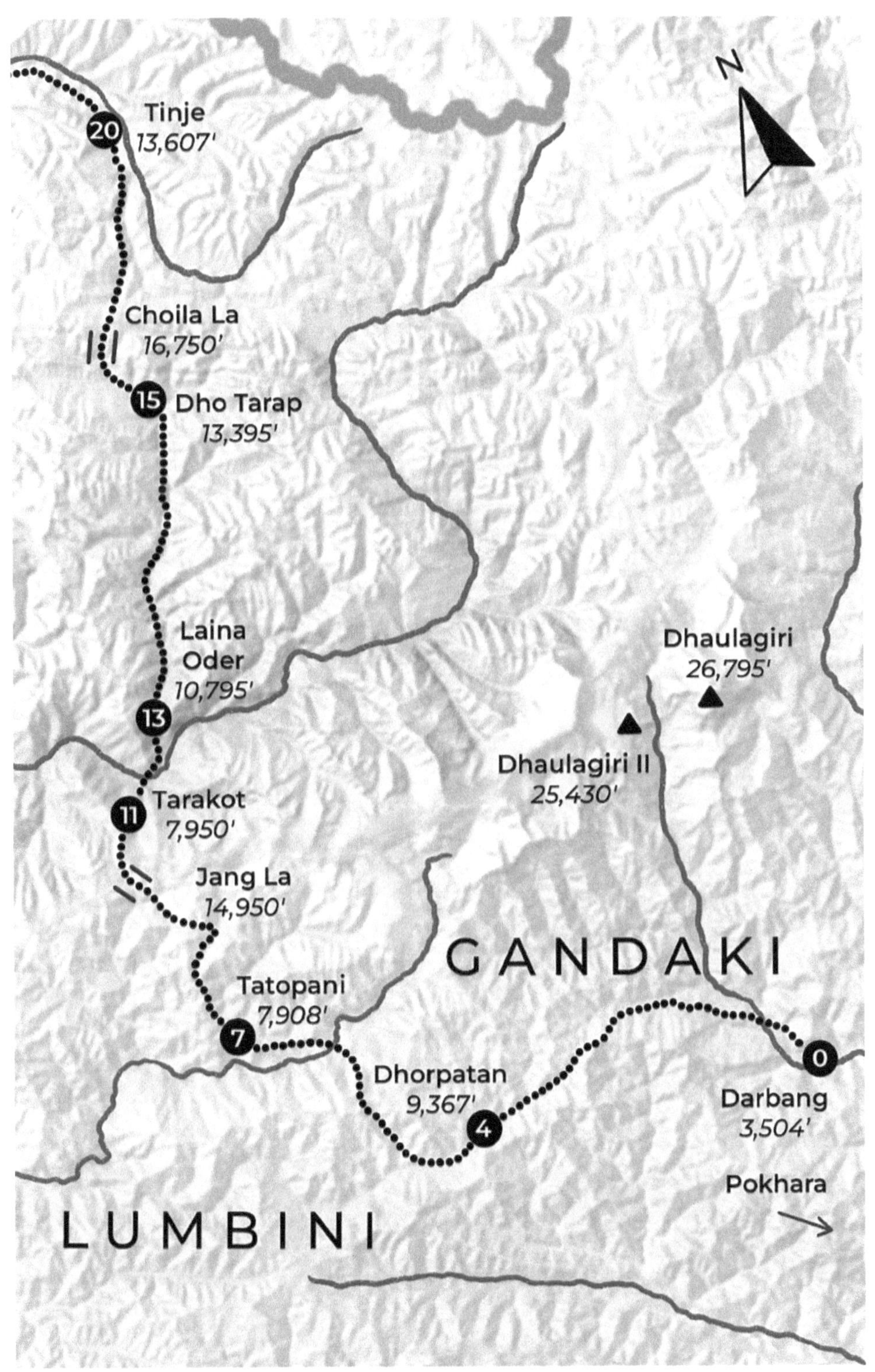

N
Tinje
13,607'
20
Choila La
16,750'
15 Dho Tarap
13,395'
Laina Oder
10,795'
13
Dhaulagiri
26,795'
Tarakot
7,950'
11
Jang La
14,950'
Dhaulagiri II
25,430'
GANDAKI
Tatopani
7,908'
7
Dhorpatan
9,367'
4
Darbang
3,504'
0
Pokhara
LUMBINI

Matthiessen's and Schaller's trip

...as shown in the maps published in *The Snow Leopard*

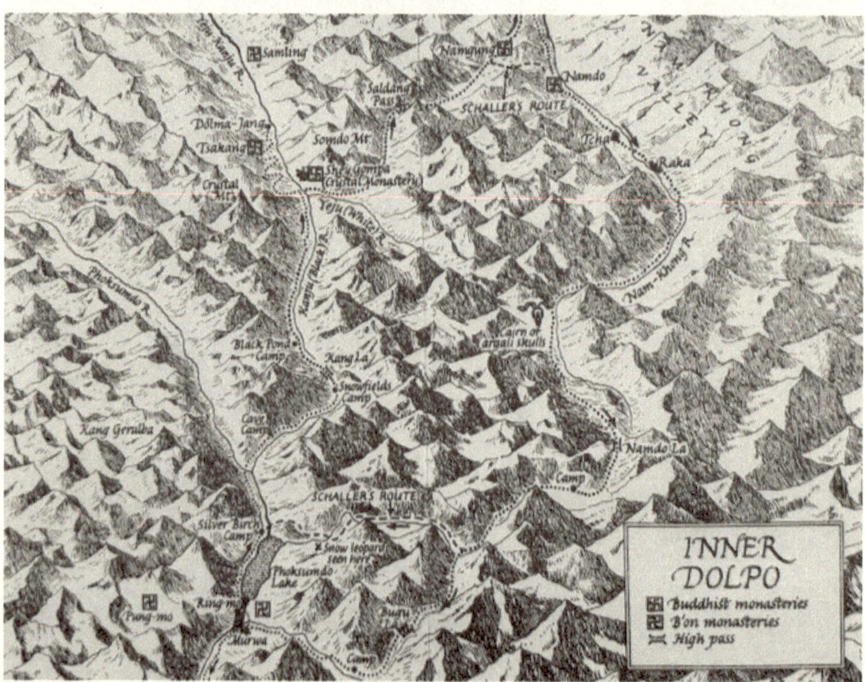

ACKNOWLEDGMENTS

This is my first book; getting here needed a lot of encouragement, and I want to thank three people in particular. Meg Rosoff, the well-known author, plowed her way through five successive drafts, and made me believe it was worth my persisting. Melanie Viets edited the book with great insight, helping to shape the narrative and persuading me to discard passages I was attached to but which didn't belong here. My wife Sarah, who has always believed that I could write, has consistently encouraged me through the nine years it took me to finish the book.

I also want to thank George Schaller. With some trepidation, I sent him the manuscript in early 2022, highlighting for him only those parts that mentioned him. He read the whole thing—in a single day. He suggested a number of corrections, which I have incorporated. He also kindly read the final version earlier this year.

Others who have read parts or all of the manuscript and have offered valuable insights are Karl French (on behalf of The Literary Consultancy), and my friends Roger Crowley, Kalyan Bhakta Mathema, Kedar Bhakta Mathema, Tara Niraula, Doug Porter and Peter Womack. Tara has also checked, and corrected, my errant Nepali transliteration. Katie Barry added a stringent final copy edit, Valerie Ann Nemeth advised me on copyright issues, Melissa Nash created the map of my journey, and David Wogahn and Manon Wogahn of AuthorImprints guided me through the publication process with skill and patience.

Finally, I want to thank my grandson Alex, who read one particular section that matters a lot to us both.

This is a book that focuses on my life, and those of my wife Mandana and our daughter Tess. It is also a book about Nepal and the changes I have witnessed there. Although it falls outside the scope of my 2016 journey to Dolpo, a 2020 trek to the east of Nepal with two of my old comrades from the Britain-Nepal Medical Trust, Dr. Nigel Padfield and Paul Hamlyn, is worth mentioning. It is rare that you have an opportunity to revisit a place that meant so much to you, but which you have not seen for forty years; if you do, the material changes will strike you much more forcefully than if you had lived there constantly, or returned often.

We found the eastern hills transformed, by roads and by the remittances that have flowed in from Nepali workers in India and the Gulf. People are clearly better off and healthier than they were in the 1970s—and yet we all felt a deep sense of loss. As the population increases, and as global connectivity reaches up to the doorsteps of the high Himal, the landscape and the cultures that once astounded us are vanishing.

Loss, of course, implies possession, and Nepal was never ours to possess: but it possessed us, and in this there is some small claim to ownership. Part of our sadness was knowing that we had helped propel these changes; part of it was our own advancing age, and the nostalgia that recollections of what William Wordsworth called *"our noisy years"* inevitably bring.[1] Though I plan another trip to the eastern hills in 2026, my two friends may never go there again.

PROLOGUE

August 12, 2016—British Airways 143, London to Delhi

The cabin lights are dimmed. The map on my inflight display tells me
we are over Sochi, on the Black Sea. Here, in a Boeing 777, time, place
and my life are suspended. Here there is no context; just me, some anonymous fellow passengers, and the turning earth. All obligations are on
hold.

Alongside this suspension, a reluctance to arrive: a reluctance both
general, and specific to Delhi, where arriving means pitching into the
airport at midnight with its hard benches, stale air and foul coffee, and
hours of fretting over transit baggage while I wait for my connecting
flight to Kathmandu. I have neglected to pack the essentials into my
carry-on luggage. If those bags do go astray, I could lose some stuff I
really need—solar panel, Bluetooth keyboard, blood pressure medicines.

But such anxiety is foolish. The system works; Sarah and I navi-
gated it last year. You surrender your passport to slim strangers without
uniforms or insignia; they inspire little confidence. But they do at last
return, complete with your new luggage tags. There is hesitation; tips
are appreciated, without demands or deference.

So I stop fretting, and I return to the map. We have reached the
Caspian: and there too is the real thing, in the twilight below the port
wing. I can see lights in the Elburz mountains. I look intently at the

darkening sea that marks the border of Central Asia, remembering how my daughter and I once splashed about in the surf there, all those years ago.

Wide awake, I return to my book: *Goodbye Darkness*, William Manchester's moving account of a 1978 visit to his old Pacific battle-grounds. I've only a few pages left. The book is shot through with a recurrent dream, in which two versions of the author climb a devastated hill in Okinawa: *"the scrawny, Atabrine-yellow, cocky young Sergeant of Marines who had borne my name in 1945,"* and *"the portly, balding, Brooks-Brothered man who bears it today. They met on the crest, facing each other in the night like mirror and object."*[1] In these dreams, the younger Manchester demands to know why the America he fought for has fallen so short of its ideals, and why older men like him have lapsed into mediocrity. In the final iteration of the dream, today's Manchester finds himself alone on the hilltop. *"The old man grasped what had happened. Embers would never again glow in the ashes of his memory. His Sergeant would never come again. He turned away, blinded by tears."*[2]

As we leave our active years behind us, the need to hold mirror to object becomes more insistent. For a long time, like most men of my generation, I put my work first; that was where I looked for purpose, identity and affirmation. Now, though, having lost whatever influence I once had, I find myself relatively indifferent to what I did or did not achieve, or how I am remembered by my colleagues. Those accounts feel settled. Far more clamorous are questions about my family, about those who were closest to me and who are now gone. Questions about what I did, what I failed to do, and why I didn't do better.

Why I didn't do more for my first wife Mandana, who died in March 2014, worn down by the most tenacious of bipolar disorders. She tried every kind of medication, but nothing worked for long—so she drank and took various drugs, from Ativan to opiates, to dull the pain. At the age of sixty, she collapsed in her bathroom. The autopsy found codeine and heroin in her blood.

Why I didn't do better with my daughter Tess, who died in September 2010. Like Mandana, Tess was afflicted with bipolar disorder. She drank too, and it didn't help much. She was twenty-five, a new mother, when she fell from a high balcony. Under *"cause of death"*, her autopsy report states *"suicide"*.

That I failed them is clear; why I did so is more opaque. How much can be traced to my upbringing, an upbringing shaped by a war fought by my parents' generation, by a colonial childhood in Africa, and by English boarding schools—experiences so alien to most of those I have come to live among? And how much can be explained more simply, by the person I let myself become?

Tess left a son, Alex; he lives in Virginia with his father and his paternal grandmother. Four years ago I bought a house nearby, and I help bring him up. This will be the longest I have spent away from him. I am uneasy about this separation.

I am on my way back to Nepal, a country I first visited in 1974. I spent the best years of my young adult life there as a volunteer, and later returned with Mandana and Tess as the World Bank's representative in Kathmandu. Mandana's time in Nepal was one of hope and occasional relief, her depression and addictions less suffocating than they later became.

I will be hiking the route taken by Peter Matthiessen in *The Snow Leopard*. In 1973, Matthiessen was invited by his friend George Schaller to accompany him to the remote district of Dolpo, where Schaller hoped to solve a long-standing, somewhat obscure biological mystery: whether the elusive Himalayan Blue Sheep was, in reality, a goat. Schaller also wrote about their trip in the last section of his great book on the Himalaya, *Stones of Silence*. There are still no motorable roads in those parts of Nepal. When I reach Jumla, the end of Matthiessen's route, I plan to meet my new wife, Sarah, and go north to Lake Rara. The whole journey is something over five hundred miles and will take about eight weeks—presuming I last that long.

In the first three pages of *The Snow Leopard*, Matthiessen explains what he hoped to gain from his journey. There is the pull of the Himalayas, and of Dolpo in particular, something he had been drawn to twelve years earlier, in 1961, when he first saw *"those astonishing snow peaks to the north"* from Kathmandu. He quotes Buddhist Lama Anagarika Govinda's *Way of the White Clouds*:

> *"...to close that distance, to go step by step across the greatest range on earth to somewhere called the Crystal Mountain, was a true pilgrimage, a journey of the heart. Since the usurpation of Tibet by the Chinese, the Land of Dolpo, all but unknown to Westerners even today, was said to be the last enclave of pure Tibetan culture left on earth... "*[3]

Then there was the possibility of seeing a snow leopard—for Matthiessen the naturalist, *"reason enough for the entire journey."*[4] As readers of his book know, he did not see one, though George Schaller did: and in this lies a subtle spiritual irony.

There was also a third reason: a few paragraphs later he mentions the Buddha he bought in Kathmandu and placed by his wife Deborah's bedside when she lay in hospital in New York in the winter of 1971, dying of cancer. His journey would give him space to remember, to grieve, and to reprove himself for how he had treated her—and it is this that struck me most forcefully when I first read his extraordinary book. He wrote, in part, for absolution.

As for my journey, I harbor no such spiritual ambitions; nor am I seeking absolution. Indeed, I am not entirely sure what I expect. So much of me is invested in Nepal, and a trek like this will bring back days when I was still innocent of family responsibilities, as well as a time in Tess' and Mandana's lives when happier futures still seemed possible. I hope the journey (or rather, writing about the journey) will preserve something of Tess and Mandana: few now remember them, except fleetingly, and the distractions of daily life are eroding even my own memories.

1

DID YOU MAKE ME?

June 17, 2016—The Plains, Virginia.

Two months earlier. Max, my eighteen-pound Israeli cat, is sitting on my chest. It's breakfast time. Sun fills the bedroom. We have no curtains: we live on the edge of a forest, without near neighbors.

Like an incubus, Max is drawing out the tail of a dream. I see Tess staring into a fireplace. We are in my father's old house outside Edinburgh. It's almost twenty years ago; she's in her teens. Lowering Scottish skies outside, the fire a honeycomb of red embers. A strong smell of oranges. Tess turns her face, but does she even see me? Then the corner of her mouth moves, and she raises her eyebrows. She's happy I'm there. This is a good way to wake up.

In the bathroom another cat lies on the bathmat, a much smaller stray from the streets of Cairo. He used to be fierce, but he's old now, his black coat shot through with white needles. He likes to lick the water off the floor of the shower. I open the door for him, turn the shower on briefly, then step back. Once he's finished drinking, it's my turn. We have three old cats, eunuchs all. Sarah is away in Mali, so it's my job to get up and feed them.

It's a warm, humid day. I walk down our steep driveway to the postbox. Most of the mail is junk, and I throw the magazines, coupons and charity requests into a bear-proof dustbin. There are two things worth keeping, and their simultaneous arrival has me laughing. One is a letter from the UK Department for Works and Pensions, which has taken months to get here. It states *"We have decided that you are entitled to a UK State Pension at the weekly amount of £118.71 from 26 March 2016."* The second is a padded envelope containing the Delorme InReach Explorer satellite phone I've ordered for my trip to Nepal. Most of the route has no landlines, internet, or cellphone connections.

Yesterday I bought a couple of good rucksacks—a Deuter Aircontact 65+10-liter main backpack, and a Gregory Zulu 20-liter day pack. I'm stuffing one rubber dry bag with first aid and basic medicines (anti-diarrheal, etc.), and a second with a four-month supply of all the pills I take for blood pressure and heart health. Back in 2012 a stent was placed in my heart's left anterior descending (LAD) artery, which was 70 percent blocked. My cardiologist thinks I'm nuts to go on this trip, though I don't see quite why. I've told him I'll just turn around and come home if it gets too difficult.

I also have a hip problem, and I've just been to see an orthopedic specialist, Dr. Brantley Vitek. His waiting room is filled with pictures of Washington Redskins football players: he is an expert in self-inflicted bodily trauma.

He laid me flat on a bench and pushed, pulled and twisted my legs thoughtfully.

"This is straightforward," he said, staring through the window into blue air. "I could order an MRI, but I'm pretty certain this is a torn labrum. Labrum? The cartilage around the hip socket. It's like a gasket."

"You mean an O-ring?" I asked. I could see the space shuttle *Challenger*, exploding in an orange fireball above Cape Kennedy in 1986, the guilty Morton Thiokol right-hand booster shanking out of the spreading white cloud. Everyone knew what an O-ring was after that.

"Yes, but perhaps more like the raw pastry that spills over a pie dish. The labrum's torn, on the rim. A small tear, from your symptoms."

"Will there be any permanent damage if I—overdo things a bit?"

"The damage *is* permanent," he replied. "The cartilage won't regenerate. If you do too much, you'll get some inflammation. Over time it could deteriorate. But it may not. I could operate on you, but I'll be honest. It's pretty much a waste of time at your age. I don't want to take your money for no reason."

"Okay. If I rest it, will it heal?"

He looked at me without expression. He was handsome, a clean-cut man, shaved head, violet eyes—pleasant to look at. He was being careful with me; I needed things repeated, like so many patients do.

"No, you're too old. For any cartilage regeneration."

"I see . . . will it get worse? Will it seize up? How about a cortisone injection?" I'd already told him I was going to hike in the Himalayas.

"We could do that. You'd have to make another appointment. It's best I do it with ultrasound, so I can find the exact spot. But it won't last. You're better off taking ibuprofen. You can live with it."

"Sure, but can I do an eight-week hike with it?"

He smiled, as if this wasn't worth answering.

—·—

There's a knock on the door, and I go downstairs.

"Hi, I'm the Great Zucchini," says the man at the door.

I look at him, waiting for my reactions to catch up. He is a large man, his hair chopped about and untidy. But he looks sane, and his manner is friendly enough.

"Eric, if you prefer," he adds.

Then I remember: he's the magician. I booked him a year ago when I was planning a summer party for Alex. Since then, I've abandoned the idea. Alex has moved schools, and I'm not in touch with his new classmates. His grandmother has also given me grief about hosting another party; it's unnecessary, she says, it's spoiling him. She quite often gives me grief. "*I will NEVER understand you and frankly do not care to,*" she wrote recently. *"From day one you have been a thorn in my side, yes… day ONE. Sadly being around you from time to time is going to be a necessary evil… I do not need or want you in my life."* The proximate cause of this was me making some phone calls while Alex was in his taekwondo class, rather than watching him perform. *"If you are going to have him during 'parental' times, you need to step up to parental levels of responsibility… and take the advice/instruction when given from the people raising him. That is not optional…"* And so on.

I tell the Great Zucchini the party's off, that I should have let him know. He's been paid, though, so it's no big deal for him.

"How old is your son? Alexander, right?" He is pointing at a couple of Nerf guns on the lawn.

"He's eight now," I answer. I enjoy it when people mistake me for Alex's father; I like to think they're telling me I look younger than I am.

We chat a while; I offer him coffee, but he declines. It's rare here for strangers to accept such hospitality. Virginians are very conscious of each other's personal space. You see this in the stores when you bump into someone, or someone accidentally cuts in front of you. Lots of apologies.

After a while the Great Zucchini leaves. I pick up the Nerf guns and lug them upstairs to Alex's room in the attic. A white cat streaks down past me—Casper, the coprophiliac. I wave the Zombie Strike SlingFire Blaster vaguely at him, but I imagine something much worse. He shits everywhere.

As I get to Alex's room, I think how much I've paid to fix this house up, and how our three cats seem intent on tearing it apart again, scratching up the chairs and the carpets, vomiting on the woodwork, leaving feathers and mouse entrails inside the cooling ducts. And for some reason I'm reminded of what Mandana told me after the Taliban blew the enormous statues of the Buddha at Bamiyan to smithereens back in 2001. What did the Dalai Lama say? We should thank the Taliban. They have taught us a valuable lesson in impermanence.

I should be thanking my cats, then, not cursing them.

The walls of Alex's room are Prussian blue, with matching furniture from The Land of Nod. The doors and window frames are fire-engine red. The room is full of toys, along with mementos I bring back from the countries I visit. There's a painted wooden figure of Tintin and Snowy from Kinshasa, some rocks from Mount Everest, a brass sculpture of a Masai woman and her baby.

Alex calls these things his "collection." He likes me to get them, though he doesn't pay them any attention once they're here. One day, perhaps. The same goes for the 1:35-scale plastic farm animals I've kept from my own childhood. I tried them first on Tess, and again last year on him. Neither was interested. They're back in their old Britains Limited cardboard box (Farm Buildings—Cowshed, 1 Only, 501F), wrapped in toilet paper.

I take a bagel out onto the porch and settle down to re-reading *The Snow Leopard*. Thinking of Alex, I turn to one of the book's most affecting passages.

Peter Matthiessen joined George Schaller less than two years after his wife died. He had four children, three of whom he describes as "*away at school and college,*" mentioning them only once by name. The youngest—Alex as it so happens—stayed behind in Matthiessen's house, which had been "*lent to a family of his friends.*"[1] Early in the journey, before leaving Kathmandu for Dolpo, Matthiessen received a letter from Alex.

> *Dear Dad,*
>
> *How are you, I am fine. I was very sad, I was even crying, because I didn't write to you. But I feel a lot better since I'm writing to you now. The cat and the dog are great but I'm going to be so sad when they die. School is doing pretty well. I hope you can make it back for Thanksgiving. Did I spell that right. Yes □ No □*

I hope your mountain boots are still good. I hope you are having a very good time.

Love,
Alex

Save my letters and bring them home so I can see if they got to you. Hugs and kisses. By by a millyon times for now. Love

Your sun,
Alex

I think of the parting with my sun on the day that school had opened, just a month before, on a clear morning of September, of monarch butterflies and goldenrod, late roses, shining pine needles, of flights of cormorant headed south along the coast in a dry east wind. Alex asked how long I would be gone, and when I told him, blurted out "Too long!" I had driven him to school, and he was upset that he might be seen in tears. "That's much too long," he wept, and this was true. Hugging him, I promised to be home before Thanksgiving."[2]

This, then, was a guilty journey. Peter Matthiessen knew he shouldn't have gone when he did. Toward the end of the book, beset by anger and disgust at himself, he admitted this. *"I have neglected my children and done myself harm, and there is no way back."*[3]

I find Matthiessen's persona austere, demanding—intimidating even. His understanding of the natural world and of Zen Buddhism outrank anything I will ever achieve. In the subtext to his journey, though, I feel some companionship. He didn't need to point to his failings; he can't have thought it would bring him any credit with his family and his friends, let alone readers who didn't know him.

I am leaving my Alex to go on this journey. I have spent much of the last five years with and around him. Since I moved to The Plains, he has been a constant presence in this house. Although my work has required frequent travel, I've made sure I limit each trip to less than two weeks so I can be home for him every other weekend.

He comes less often now than he once did—his grandmother, who controls these matters, argued that he was becoming confused about where his "real" home was. Going away for four months, though, is still a big step.

When I first told him of my plans, he was thoughtful.

"Why, Papa?"

"There's a place I want to visit in the mountains. For many years now. There aren't any cars there—you have to walk. I'm getting older, and soon I may not be strong enough."

"Is it where my Mama lived when she was a baby?"

"It's near there."

"Is it important for you?"

"It is, yes."

"Then you can go," he said. I was surprised, and felt a lot better. But I was also sad. I can sense the connection between us weakening.

Thinking of this, I put *The Snow Leopard* aside, and fetch my laptop. I bring up the diary I have kept for the last four years. It's about our time together, and some of it is intense.

> *"September 2–3, 2012. Alex was volatile at bedtime on this two-day visit. On the first night all was going well until he asked "Did you make me?" I said no, and he became furious. I then said I had made his Mummy so yes, in a way I had made him. He said no, my Mummy and Daddy made me, and he started to hit me about the face and to say, "I won't live here anymore. I won't visit you when I am older. You are not my friend. I will unmake myself. I will cover myself in booboos" (he also said that he would shoot me, for good measure). He was angry and spiteful until he finally fell asleep in my arms.*

The next morning he awoke and said, "You made me," and told me he was sorry for being angry.

We had a nice day. We went to Ikea up on I-495, where I needed to buy a dining table; he got tired but held up well. Then he wanted to go and visit his Mummy's old apartment in Falls Church. He has asked to do this before and I'd put him off—but today I thought I should take him. I was nervous. We went on the swings outside; he remembered them. We rode the elevator. He wanted to knock on the door, but I said other people lived there now, and we couldn't do that. He asked where his old things were. I reminded him they were at his Daddy's condo.

Fortunately he lost interest, and we left. Later he asked me if his Mummy was at the apartment. This was heartbreaking. He hasn't wanted to go back again—though he did recently ask if we could visit a public playroom where Tess used to take him (to my frustration, I was unable to remember the address or to find it).

That night he was tired and went to bed without any fuss. I let him sleep and then retreated to my bed.

He awoke the next morning, found me missing, and lost his temper. Again, he said he would "unmake" himself, and that he would "destroy" my house (knowing that I was restoring it, inter alia, for him). Again, he calmed down after a while, and was once again very affectionate."

I'd forgotten how angry he used to get. He's more settled now. He's jumpy as a whippet sometimes, but the energy is different.

By the end of the day, the moisture has drained from the air. It's a cool and cloudy night. A couple of days ago there was hail up the road in Middleburg, big enough to bust windscreens and leave scores of cars looking like they had smallpox. I have the windows open, and the frogs are throbbing away down in the pond.

The three cats have already staked out their places on the bed, and I have to maneuver between them as I go under the duvet. They are purring like a distant cloud of cicadas.

July 11, 2016—The Plains, Virginia.

I'm driving along Zulla Road in the day's last light; the summer air is thick with insects. Out above our warm world, a half-moon shines through a halo of ice-crystals, shading the oaks and hickories that line this empty old Virginia thoroughfare.

The house sitters have arrived. Today I took Alex back home; I won't see him again until November. He spent yesterday with me. We swam at the Freedom Aquatic Center, watched *The Secret Life of Pets* in Gainesville, and stopped at a graveyard on the way home: he wanted to collect some new sticks. This old cemetery is an orphan, its church long gone, the green surrounded by housing estate access roads. We had a stick fight among the headstones while cars whizzed past on both sides. Then we went to Starbucks for his bacon and gouda sandwich, and once home worked a bit on the sequel to his first (self-published) book. That one was called *Alex and Papa and the Squid Lady*; this, imaginatively, is called *Alex, Papa, the Knights and the Squid King*. We wrote the first book in about three hours, but he hasn't found the same rhythm this time around.

"Read me the beginning again," he said, fidgeting about on the sofa.

"Okay . . . *After their famous victory over the squid lady, Alex and Papa lived quietly together with the one-eyed alien and the old man—*"

"Put little one-eyed alien."

> "*. . . little one-eyed alien and the old man. After a while, though, they decided they needed some more knights. The trouble was, the—little—one-eyed alien kept eating his armor and the old man kept falling asleep. Alex and Papa alerted the other two—*"

"I never said alerted."

"No, but it's fine here."

"… and they said, "Alright, let's look near the squid lady's cave and see if there is anyone there." And so they did. They all put on their swimming trunks and jumped into the cold pond."

"What about the Indian?"

"He comes later."

"Papa, I don't want to do this now." I was disappointed, but didn't say anything. Was I so impatient at his age? We went out and played soccer instead.

At sunset, I sat on the front steps with the cats. Alex was chasing fireflies; we'd been doing his reading practice. He's still reluctant, but much improved. We started C. S. Lewis' *The Magician's Nephew*, and he lasted ten minutes with minimal fidgeting. There were some unfamiliar words there, too: "Lewisham," "grubbier," and "attic stairs." But I could see that he's losing interest in the English books I've been getting for him.

Pale, indecisive thunderclouds hung overhead. A single loudmouth sang up in the woods—a rusty, impatient chirruping. Two silent airliners furrowed their way through the high air, reminding me how cold I'm going to be in a few weeks' time.

"What do they eat, Papa?" asked Alex. He was out of breath, his hair sweaty; he had a dozen fireflies in his jam jar. He has bright caramel eyes, like his mother.

"We need to get you to bed," I said.

"Later," he replied dismissively (he also has his mother's contrary spirit). "What about grass?" I began to sense that loss of control again; everything needs negotiation.

"I really don't know. I think it's best to let them go."

He thought about this. "How about I keep them on my pillow tonight? We can let them go tomorrow."

I was bending towards this when he reversed. "But you know, their families might not like that." So he unscrewed the perforated lid, and left the open jar on the back step.

It was 10 p.m. before he was settled into his bed. Instead of the fireflies, three Ninjagos on the pillow. I was lying beside him, waiting for him to drop off. Half-asleep, he said "Papa, why did you send my Mommy to boarding school?"

This wasn't a neutral question; some negative remark lay behind it. Nonetheless, it was fair.

"I didn't want to. Things at home were very difficult. Manani wasn't well. She would get really angry with your Mama." Manani was his name for Mandana.

I waited, but he didn't reply.

"I hated sending her away," I added, but he was already asleep.

As I went downstairs, I remembered Tess at Allhallows School, eleven then, begging us not to leave her after a weekend exeat. And I remembered the sapping mixture of pain and relief as we drove back to our hotel in Lyme Regis.

As I took Alex home today, we got talking about why I-66 is being widened, and how more people are moving into the area.

"They should all have fields and trees and grass around their houses, because we need grass to breathe," he'd said, as if I might not have known this.

"You're right," I replied. "But these developers, they build as many houses as they can on the land they buy. All stuck together. They don't care about trees and grass."

"No, they do their best," he replied, impatient with me. "Even in New York, each apartment has a place with trees and grass, and everyone can go there. Did you know that? It's a fact. We should be happy about that. Right, Papa?"

I wasn't sure what he meant, but I could see his mind was set, and anyway, what did I know about this? I had always thought my daughter—

and now my grandson—would come to me for advice, stories, glimpses of the distant worlds I've lived in, as I once did with my grandfather Louis when he took me out in his Saab Sport on his sales trips. But the world has accelerated since then, fraying such continuities of interests and values.

I kept quiet, and soon we turned into his grandmother's development in Manassas. Before we left my house—"our house," as I always say when I'm with him—he was depressed about going back, and upset that I was leaving; he'd kept on asking me how many hours we still had. Once I stopped the car, though, he wanted to get away. "Alex, wave goodbye to your papa," his grandmother said from the front door. "Bye Papa," he said quickly, running up the stairs. He didn't look back.

I drove off, feeling as if it were me who'd been left behind.

2

RELUCTANCE

July 28, 2016—Harleston, Norfolk, England.

Sarah's vacation is over; she went back to Mali yesterday. We won't meet again until she joins me in Nepal in October. When I saw her off at Heathrow, I felt deflated and detached; I'm always like this before one of us travels. It's as if I've already gone—my way of avoiding the pain of separation, I suppose. It helps me, but it must seem cold, particularly to someone as open-hearted as Sarah.

I'm in Harleston for a couple of weeks before I leave for Kathmandu; we own a tiny old house here. I bought it ten years ago, close to my father's place in the village of Pulham St. Mary.

Today I'm driving to nearby Banham Zoo. They have snow leopards. Given Peter Matthiessen's frustrating experience, I figure this is my best chance of seeing one.

It's holiday season. A lot of camper vans are parked outside, and the place is awash with kids. The leopards live in a large jumble of rocks, behind a chain-link fence. They hide most of the time, but one comes out and lounges in the sun for a bit. Even under these straitened circumstances, she is arresting—not much bigger than a Labrador, but bulked up by her fur and her vital, springy tail. A small head, and large, unblinking yellow eyes, glaring at the pests swarming about her cage.

I grew up among her African cousins, and her fierce grace takes me back to my childhood in Nyasaland (now Malawi). We moved there from a ration-straitened Britain in 1953, when I was two—my father escaping the penury of the post-War Bar for a job as a colonial prosector.

—·—

Wild animals, red earth, white light: my earliest memories.

We lived on the edge of the capital, Zomba, sharing the mountain foothills with leopards and hyenas. Bedtime stories came from Geraldine Elliot's *The Long Grass Whispers*—stories of Kalulu the wise rabbit, Kamba the clairvoyant tortoise, and Njati the water buffalo with the filthy temper.

At night, those leopards would cough in the nearby bush.

"Did you hear the lion, Denys?" asked my mother one morning at breakfast.

"No. What lion?"

"On the verandah. I could hear his claws clicking. I bet he was looking for Seamus." Seamus was one of a series of dachshunds; none of them lasted long.

Before I was five and first went to school, I spent my time with my mother, our servants, and other British tiddlers. We were skinny, hyperactive and unruly, tiny princes and princesses living grand lives in the sun of the East African plateau. My mother was always attentive, yet I sensed some emotional distance: and, as children so often do, I assumed I must be a disappointment to her. It was only much later that she told me how surprised she was that a child—her child, too—should prove to be such acceptable company. "Children are a bore, really," she said. "Even one's own. I mean, most of them can't have a sensible conversation until they're at least twelve. That's an awful long time to wait, if you ask me."

She was quite lonely in Africa. Not because of any alienation from the country or its African inhabitants, for whom she held a lasting affection.

She didn't think much of her more pompous British compatriots: but the real problem was her relationship with my father. Their marriage was a mistake, and had quickly left both these intelligent, decent people adrift in their own lifeboats. They were friends, had always been friends, but their inner lives were lost to one another, and they looked elsewhere for whatever seemed missing. My parent's difficulties weren't apparent to me during my childhood. They were kind and affectionate, though they seemed preoccupied; and at times I felt invisible.

My father's job took him on circuit; he would usually fly to distant towns "in a Beaver." For years I imagined him entering the stomach of a large and friendly rodent, a bit like the Catbus that zips around the sky in Hayao Miyazaki's touching animé cartoon *My Neighbor Totoro*. When he was away, my mother and I would misbehave. We would go on long drives to see the scary hippos in Lake Nyasa. There was a place there where she ordered gin and tonic (for me), and smoked.

"Best you learn to drink now," she said. "It'll stop you overdoing it later. Far too many people are alcoholics, Nigel. Even Nea, I'm afraid, but don't tell anyone I said so." Nea was her mother.

Our African servants were more relaxed and funnier than the British, and with them I always felt welcome. They did what I asked with good grace—parading round the garden as my militia, with branches for rifles, teaching me how to catch snakes with a forked stick. I liked their food better than ours, and used to go and eat *nshima* [cornmeal] with them in their thatched huts on the edge of our compound. *Nshima* came with a musty chili gravy that burned my lips; best of all, I could eat with my hands.

Not everyone seemed to share my opinion of Africans. I remember an incident at the Zomba Gymkhana Club, the center of colonial social life. I was sitting out on the far edge of the cricket ground, watching the King's African Rifles marching band at practice. One of the trombonists couldn't get his notes right. A white officer stalked over to him, yelling something about shoving his instrument down his throat. The man was dismissed; he came and sat on the grass next to me. He worked the slide and emptied the spit valve without looking at me.

"That's the kid-shifter," I said, pointing at the saliva dribbling onto the ground.

"No," he replied. "The kid-shifter is the slide."

"Oh, is it?" I said. And then "Why was he horrid to you?"

I could see now that he had tears in his eyes, though he was smiling at me. "It is nothing. I was off tune."

"You just have to practice a little bit more," I said, by way of comfort.

I remember how wrong it felt, though, how shocked I was by the violence of the officer's words. Why would you ever talk to someone like that? It wasn't that he was black and the officer white; white people were always in charge. But why be so cruel?

I was too young, and too complicit, to grasp the fuller contours of my childhood world.

August 1, 2016—Harleston, Norfolk, England.

Went to the Imperial War Museum at Duxford to see their Mark X Lancaster. I pre-purchased an online ticket for a special tour of the plane, but this turned out to be limited to the rear end of the fuselage; to my frustration, I wasn't allowed anywhere near the pilot's seat. My small group included a middle-aged father and two bored teenagers. I can't conceive of being bored by a Lancaster, but to them it was clearly lifeless: as mute as the ammonites in my school lab once were to me.

I tapped the side of the fuselage as the docent flushed us out of the rear door; it was as thin as a biscuit-tin. The thought of night combat has always thrilled me—but the cold feel of this plane tempered such excitement. How could anyone have faced such terror, night after night, among storms of incandescent German metal?

Today the Second World War is passing from living memory, but it filled my imagination as a young boy in Nyasaland—and for me, still defines what it means to be a man. The War was everywhere; my parents and all their friends had been part of it. When I was in bed with measles, Henry Astell, a vast, red and fat "uncle," came to visit me, and the wicker chair he sat in collapsed in a welter of dust, hairy legs and spilled gin. I didn't laugh, though: I was in awe. Henry's brother Bill had died on the Dambusters raid on May 17, 1943, flying his Lancaster B III into a 110,000 volt transmission line near Marbeck. I knew all the details, and I'd seen the movie. Most of my early movies were about that war—*The Cruel Sea*, *The Battle of the River Plate*, *Reach for the Sky*.

I yearned to be a war hero. I would spend hours playing alone, fighting implacable enemies. These fantasies could block everything else out, and led at times to episodes of blank mindlessness. I blew things up; I chopped things down. Like the culvert next to our house with its tiny, mud replica of Germany's Möhne Dam, both of which I destroyed by igniting a half dozen of those CO2 soda siphon cartridges my parents used to fizz up their nasty drinks. Or my father's prized banana trees, which I slew with a *panga* (I was a Spartan at Thermopylae, they were Persian Immortals). Or the low brick wall edging the garage, through which I drove my parents' Ford Consul (transformed into a Vickers Wellington night bomber).

There were some real fights too, and I welcomed them. One evening a great battle developed at school, three or four of us trapped in a wooden hut as a crowd of screaming children swirled around us, a living storm of Red Indians. There was deep satisfaction in knowing how outnumbered we were as we ran out to attack them. Things got out of hand; there was dust, blood, teacher intervention. I remember a warm flush in my stomach, much as I would get sitting and watching lightning through my bedroom window: the sensation of being fully present.

I once read how the Buddha was asked by a passerby, perceiving some difference in him, whether he was a god. No, he replied, not a god. A magician, then? No, not a magician. An angel, perhaps? No again. The man would not let him alone, and finally the Buddha said to him "I am awake." Being enlightened is being awake.

Such moments were as close as I have come to being awake, and present; in my case, though, this quiet ecstasy could not be shared. It rose out of contemplating some great act of violence which enlivened without truly threatening me. Present, yet simultaneously absent.

Like many ex-soldiers, Dad didn't speak unprompted about the war—but nor did he duck my many questions. He had been commissioned into the Royal Artillery in 1943, and landed in Normandy on June 6, 1944, D-Day, fighting on into Germany until the surrender in May 1945. Late into my middle age, I continued to ask him about the outlandish melodrama he had lived through. I wondered, and I still do, if I would have measured up. Would I have been able to function, or would I have disgraced myself? We're told that you never know until you're tested—but I feared I might fall short, and I once told my father this.

"No," he said, "I think you'd have done what I did. You'd be scared, and you'd keep your head down. But sometimes you'd find yourself doing things that seem mad when you look back on them. Like crossing a lane under heavy fire, or pulling a wounded man to safety. You couldn't stand the lads thinking you were a coward, you see. It seemed worse than getting shot. And they'd die to help you too, if they had to—most of them. Even though you'd never see one another again after the war. You lived in different worlds, really. But you had to look out for them. It's all quite irrational."

I still have a drawing from those African days. Like countless such school projects, it shows little artistic promise. Here we are on a family outing, driving across low hills towards a big blue lake. Mummy has curly yellow hair in pigtails, a triangular dress, stick arms and legs, and red crosses for eyes. Daddy is fat and shirtless, with a pork-pie hat and dark stubble. Neither portrait resembles their subject in the least. On the back seat is my tiny sister Mandy, bright red, just as I first saw her in the hospital, with my dog Monty. The sun is shining, the sky is filled with white clouds (these are quite well-drawn). Beside the road, as you might expect, a couple of crocodiles and a zebra are out for a stroll. Mummy is waving to some stick-like Africans, who stand outside their straw huts, waving back. Another normal weekend in colonial Nyasaland? But wait—there is me, on the car roof, manning a machine-gun. From one corner, a couple of Stukas are diving at us! One is trailing smoke and flame. The other is firing his wing cannon. A bomb is sailing through the air.

August 6, 2016—Harleston, Norfolk, England.

This evening I walk over to my father's grave. He died three years ago and lies in the churchyard of Pulham St. Mary the Virgin, where Sarah and I were married last July. Although tucked into a wooded corner of the graveyard, you can't miss the large slab of polished black marble. It's quite a flash grave, befitting a knight of the realm. The ledger is inscribed with all fourteen lines of Christina Rosetti's *Remember*:

> *"Remember me when I am gone,*
> *Gone far away into the silent land . . . "*

This gentle poem acknowledges the reality of forgetfulness: how, despite your best intentions, your loved one will eventually slip from your mind. Don't berate yourself, she says: it's inevitable.

> *". . . if you should forget me for a while*
> *And afterwards remember, do not grieve . . . "*[1]

Max Sebald, whose *The Rings of Saturn* brought him to these parts in 1992, wrote this about the seventeenth-century English physician Thomas Browne:

> *"To him it seems a miracle that we should last so much as a single*
> *day. There is no antidote, he writes, against the opium of time . . .*
> *Not even those who have found a place amidst the heavenly con-*

stellations have perpetuated their names: Nimrod is lost in Orion, and Osiris in the Dog Star. Indeed, old families last not three oaks. To set one's name to a work gives no-one a title to be remembered, for who knows how many of the best men have gone without a trace?"[2]

My father's view of remembrance wasn't too dissimilar. Dad loved cemeteries, and he loved walking, two hobbies that can be combined quite easily in England. As a boy I would often find myself picking through an old churchyard with him when he was home on leave. "Look," he might say. "See this one? You can *just* see the date: look, 1795. No name though, it's gone. No one left to get it re-carved." He would then have me search among the crumbling headstones for the oldest legible name. When I found a plausibly old one—let's say George Abbott, died August 1866— he would say it was possible that someone living nearby was related to him; that the name still meant something. It was fading, though, and it wouldn't be visible for much longer. In those first years, remembering the dead matters so much, he would say: and then it doesn't. As if the gravestones mark the transition from natural life, to life remembered, to oblivion.

My father and mother are more present to me when I'm in England, and my stay in Harleston is deliberate. Possessing them, and then losing them; the memories are faint now, yet still reverberant.

———·———

When I was eight, Alex's age, my mother, my baby sister Mandy and I sailed home from Nyasaland. It was July 1959, and it was time for me to go to boarding school.

We arrived in Southampton to a cool summer and an unfamiliar country. I knew I had to pay attention; I would soon be on my own, like a spy behind enemy lines. The people here, I noted, wore shoes everywhere, and disliked the outdoors. They cleaned their own houses and cooked food crushed into tins. My grandmother drank gin in the morning, farted a lot, and had a bitter tongue. The grass in the back garden was soft and cool, unlike the crabgrass back home in Commissioner Road. Across the street was a petrol station, run by a man with the name of a fish (Mr. Salmon). For several days I wiped windshields and filled peoples' cars. They smiled and quacked at me. How pale and ugly they were!

The weeks passed, and I began to feel I had the measure of this cramped, fussy place. The food was a lot better than in Africa, and the shops were outrageous—there was more in one small Lymington store than in the whole of Nyasaland. We spent several hours at a school uniform shop, followed by a sumptuous tea at The Angel. I'd never had a uniform before, nor a tuck box. This was shaping up to be a whole lot of fun.

And then, suddenly, there I was in my stiff new shorts, watching my parents walk away through the huge oak doors of Walhampton School. Leaving me with odd-looking strangers.

I wasn't crying then, but I cried every night that term, and for years afterwards. I hadn't for a moment thought I'd miss my parents like this.

The pain of this separation permeated the rest of my childhood, and it changed me. This isn't a complaint: it is simple fact. I was never angry with my parents for sending me away. It was the only sensible thing to do; there were no decent schools in Nyasaland. I understood that. I knew they missed me, that they wished it could be otherwise. I presumed they loved me. And yet, of course, I did blame them. After seven or eight years, without understanding why, I found I had grown cold towards them. I saw them often through the remaining years of their lives, and I tried to be a good son. When eventually they died, my mother at eighty-eight and my father at ninety, I felt little. My passion for them had long since burned out.

The greatest love affairs, it seems to me, are those between a parent and a child. At first the intensity is matched, but gradually the child's adoration scatters. What once illuminated everything can become habit, often burdensome as parents grow old, weak and ugly. For many mothers and fathers, love for their children gathers and completes their life's experience of loving, and lasts throughout their lives. This constancy is not matched by their children, who drift away and become less attentive. The wiser parents understand that they have also trodden this path, and accept it as part of life's serial inequity. I was such a child—but extremely so. Once I was devoted to my parents, but the ability to love them deserted me almost entirely.

Despite constant homesickness, I grew to like the school, and made some lifelong friends. Much of our time at Walhampton was lived outdoors, unsupervised, so different from today's protective childhood world. We fished for pike. We rode ponies. We climbed trees. We played cricket with skinned tennis balls late into the long summer evenings. Famous men would visit the school and entertain us—like Dr. Louis Leakey, the father of our Latin teacher's wife Priscilla, a gentle old codger with white hair who buried fossils in our sandpit and showed us how to dig them out with toothbrushes.

At Walhampton I met that one indispensable teacher—Justin Davies, Latin and Ancient History master, school play director, cub scout leader. Mr. Davies was a magician; listening to him, the past became present. We imagined ourselves woken by the geese on the Capitol, and rushing to repel the Gauls from the walls of Rome. We understood our ancestors' horror of the wilderness as we relived the massacre of Varus' legions in the darkness of the Teutoberger Wald. For Justin Davies, the Roman and Greek past was anything but dead. It was urgent. These great civilizations were precious, and fragile. To him, and to us, Rome's seemingly unassailable creations—citizenship, law, prosperity, infrastructure—were bought with blood, sustained by sacrifice, and undermined by the very comforts they created. In the aftermath of a war in which a settled, comparatively civilized Britain was almost extinguished by Nazi barbarism, it was important to pass on these truths.

Apart from what Mr. Davies taught me, few coherent traces stand out from the thousands of hours I spent in Walhampton's classrooms. Some things I did quite well. I acted Olivia in Mr. Davies' much-praised *Twelfth Night*. In 1963, I won the choir cup, and that year and the next, the senior reading competition. I had always talked too much; this was now conferring a certain *avantage sportif*.

Yet my term reports showed frustration with a boy who was bright enough, but disengaged, of indifferent character and at odds with his environment. Even my beloved Mr. Davies could write *"He adopts a defeatist attitude to anything new or remotely difficult."*

Among the precious memories I carry with me, one in particular stands out. It is June 1964, one of those lingering summer evenings, a marvel to me after the sudden nightfall of Africa. I was thirteen, and in charge of Eagle Dormitory up on the third floor of the pentagonal west wing of the school. At 9 p.m., the matrons would order us to stop talking. That night we waited until the great building lay silent, and I then led my dormitory out through a sash window, onto the steep south-facing roof. We squatted there on our haunches, bare feet gripping the tiles and sat, in silence, watching the light fade over the sea, eating shortbread we had stolen from the kitchen pantry.

When I was a child, children were not considered exotic, or particularly breakable. We were held responsible for what we did; neither psychiatric quirks nor bad parenting cut us much slack, harsh as that may now seem. The emotions we experienced then were as true and fully-formed as any I have felt since: the addiction of danger, the silencing power of nature, an awareness that such moments were irretrievable: that everything disappears.

August 11, 2016—Harleston, Norfolk, England.

My last day; tomorrow I drive down to Heathrow.

Today I had a haircut. I tried to explain to Janey, the stylist, why I needed it shorter than it's been for thirty years. "I'm going hiking," I said. "In the Himalayas. For about eight weeks. There aren't any salons there." I said "Himalayas" because if I said "Neporl" (let alone "Nepãrl"), she might not know what I was on about.

"Oh, right," she said cheerfully, used to clients talking nonsense.

In the evening I eat some toast, lock the front door behind me and walk north, through the housing estates that surround this Regency town. Past the old railway station, stripped of its tracks by the Beeching reforms in the 1960s, down a sunken road, out into farmland. I follow a narrow lane lined by broken hawthorns and fields emptied of barley. I turn off and cross the edge of one particular field, heading for a sessile oak in the corner. There's a ladder there, attached by cables to the trunk; you can climb about fifteen feet into a metal shooting chair just below the canopy.

It's half past eight, and the sun has gone down. The air glows. A couple of pheasants are picking at the stubble. An old iron fence borders the field under the skirts of oaks and ashes; a couple of sheep poke their noses through it, looking at me with those alien eyes of theirs.

The fields are giving up the last heat. It's quiet; just the tapping of the pheasants and something rustling beneath me. A distant clock chimes. No people. No traffic.

I'm thinking of the excitement the great travel writers felt as they prepared for their famous journeys, journeys far more testing than mine will be. Bruce Chatwin, Robert Byron, Patrick Leigh-Fermor . . . not me, though. I feel more like Frodo Baggins, loath to leave the comforts of Bag End. I'd just as soon sit out the summer here, watching cricket and drifting between friends' houses.

Even the familiar pull of Nepal isn't working. As I wonder at my reticence, I'm recalling the words of a song I've been listening to—*River Towns*, by Mark Knopfler.

"So I get the bottle open
But something's hit a nerve
And I'm looking in the mirror
At the face that I deserve."[3]

Reluctant as I am this evening, my mood doesn't match the sense of doom afflicting Max Sebald as he undertook his own more modest pilgrimage through Suffolk: a walk that brought him one evening to Harleston (he hated what he saw of it; he stayed in the Saracen's Head, in reality the Cardinal's Hat, *"an inn several centuries old whose guest rooms, as it transpired, were filled with the most fearful pieces imaginable."*)[4] He had been visiting a place he calls Chestnut Tree Farm where a farmer then in his sixties, Thomas Abrams, had been building a 1:100 scale replica of Herod's Temple for the previous twenty or more years. This was in fact Moat Farm near Eye, and the modeler was David Garrard. Why Sebald felt compelled to disguise the identity and whereabouts of someone already so famous for his obsession eludes me. But this is an elusive book; its meanings dissolve as you read, the pages soaked through with melancholy and darkened by Sebald's frightened imagination.

"But the fact is that writing is the only way in which I am able to cope with the memories which overwhelm me so frequently and so unexpectedly. If they remained locked away, they would become heavier and heavier as time went on, so that in the end I would succumb under their mounting weight. Memories lie slumbering within us for months and years, quietly proliferating, until they are woken by some trifle and in some strange way blind us to life."[5]

For many years, memories of Sherborne, my secondary school, lay just as heavily on me.

At thirteen, I left Walhampton. My father "put me down" for Sherborne when I was tiny, as you did if you wanted your son to go to one of England's better-known public schools.

I was sent to Harper House: my father had played cricket with the housemaster, and presumed he was a reliable sort. As, I might say, did many of his peers: Derek Bridge was also a Rugby Blue, and such prowess guaranteed admiration. His 2012 obituary in *The Independent* describes him as a *"giant of Minor Counties cricket,"* remembered for *"the breadth of his intellect and the warmth of his personality,"* which, we are told, *"made him an inspirational guide for countless generations of students."* Those countless students did not include me or my peers in Harper. As the presiding autocrat, he was much disliked. I, for one, was terrified of him; *in loco parentis*, he was sarcastic, insightful and, I believed, saw right through me.

The first thing I remember about Harper House was looking for a playground, and finding nothing but a derelict tennis court with an air-raid shelter built into one corner; I knew then that the days of sand-pits, fishing ponds and gypsy caravans were over.

In any case, new boys were given little time to reflect, let alone play: each morning the fire alarm ejected you into a torrent of haste and noise, where raw, fearsome louts shouted you down to the changing room, into a freezing cold bath (grip the sides, swing yourself in, head under water, up and out), back up the splintery stairs to your dormitory to make your bed, and then dress—your shirt, underpants and socks folded on your chair, beneath and parallel to your trouser creases. On with the detached collar and house tie, the suit, the polished black shoes, and, for transiting through the town, the straw boater.

For the newest of us, any small interstices of time were filled with chores: fagging (sweeping, tidying and dusting your prefect's study, making him toast, washing his tea mugs), cleaning your Corps kit (spit-polishing your boots, blanco-ing your belt), looking after your Dayroom window (shine the brass catch, ensure the top sash is one-third down before breakfast, closed to a finger-width before school, shut and latched before dinner, opened a finger-width before Hall, shut and latched at bedtime).

I can see some perverse logic to this now, but at the time it seemed unhinged. Nothing was explained; there were no adults around to serve as breakwaters. A world of children, the elders bored and spiteful, showing little quarter to those who came after them, the younger ones bewildered and harried. There was discipline at Walhampton, but this was different: here the rules were obsessive, and you were beaten for transgressing them. They were enforced by boys only a year or two older than you, at times unjustly, more often without thinking. Back in those days kids expected the odd beating; here you encountered ritualized violence.

Beatings were scheduled for the evening. The victim would wait in the Dayroom with the rest of us, the house quiet around him. The doors would be opened throughout the building, so everybody could hear what happened next. The tramp of an approaching prefect. "Calcutt? Come with me."

It wasn't random, and it fell far short of real brutality—but it was chilling for all that. We all submitted; no one refused to follow the prefect downstairs. Most of the world's citizens adapt to autocracy, and in time most boys adjusted to Sherborne. The bizarre became familiar. You shared your life with people you hadn't chosen, like the crew of a ship in wartime, and some you came to care deeply for.

But the traditions, norms and rules in this place made no sense; even I, so lightly acquainted with England, could see how outdated the school was, how unmoored from modern Britain. Whatever Edwardian or Imperial duties the school once prepared you for had long since evaporated; yet the methods remained, shorn of all mindfulness. Sherborne's anachronisms were, of course, deliberate. They helped preserve class privilege, and parents sent their sons there with this in mind. We may not have been born Brahmins, but the school aimed to inculcate a similar sense of birthright.

It takes more quality than I possessed to see around such a system as well as through it, and to understand how even the most hateful of your companions are trapped into patterns of involuntary response. I was unable to step back that far; I let fear overcome me. At first it was the simple fear of all new boys. That wore off, to be replaced by something more pernicious. By my fourth and final year I had developed a pathology centering on my housemaster. I worried lest things I said or did would come to his attention and displease him. It might be a missed tackle in a rugby game, a sarcastic remark to my friends at lunch, or arriving late for chapel. I wrote coded lists of these misdemeanors; sometimes there were five or six entries for a single day. By writing them down, I established some control over a paranoia I knew was foolish, but which I could not dismiss. The fear did not disappear, but it was flattened. This was the first time I understood how writing can cage raw feelings.

Fear which you fail to confront breeds anger, and over time my anger at this school grew. I prospered in the classroom—we had fine teachers, strict timetables and few distractions. An anti-intellectual ambience hung over the school, though, and those drawn too visibly to ideas were looked on with suspicion by boys who aspired to be noticed at Sherborne. This gave me something I could fight against: I wasn't the brightest one there, but I would outwork everyone else. Work became both a private refuge, and a way to get shot of the place in four years, not the customary five. Particularly in my final A-level year, I worked without mercy. I would sneak a torch into the dormitory and read for hours beneath my bedcovers, or creep down to the study I shared with my best friend, Roger Crowley, drawing the curtains tight and working until the morning bell—a practice that bred a permanent distaste for any desk work after dark. I did well in my A-levels. The school claimed the credit; to me it felt like revenge.

My fear of displeasing those in authority kept me from the small and silly acts of defiance available to us—talking back to prefects, smoking in the yard, sneaking out to the pub. At first it seemed that I was embracing the school ethos, but by my third year I began to voice my disdain more openly, and this was noticed. Roger and I would come to share a singular distinction: we were the only boys in living memory who had been made Head of the Dayroom (or junior house)—a harbinger of future seniority—and who then left school without any further position of responsibility. We had started well, but had lost ourselves, like John Bunyan's weak pilgrims Mistrust and Timorous, faltering on the Hill of Difficulty at the sight of two great sleeping lions. We were a suspect, bolshy pair, wholly lacking in School Spirit.

Back in Nyasaland I had imagined myself as a Spitfire pilot, sneaking up on Heinkel 111 bombers over Kent, and destroying them with a single burst of cannon fire. At Sherborne I changed sides. I created a pencil and paper game in which a squadron of Lancasters, crewed by fellow schoolboys, flew missions into the heart of the Reich, running the gauntlet of flak and night fighters. Random stabs of the pencil point sprayed shells and bullets across the page, damaging or destroying different aircraft. The average life expectancy for a crew was twelve missions, and only my friend Christopher Williams completed his full tour of twenty-five. There was no Nigel Roberts among these pilots; in a game I shared with no one, played under my bedcovers or in the silence of my study, I directed the German defense.

In late December 1968 I boarded the London train for the last time. As we clattered away through snowy fields, I felt that nothing in my life would be quite so distasteful again, and that the world after school would feel like a continuous reprieve. This has proved to be true; it may be the most important of Sherborne's imprints. But there was more in the experience of those four years than I was prepared to acknowledge. In *The Loom of Youth*, Alec Waugh's lightly disguised 1917 book about the school, his hero Gordon was closer to the mark than me as he traveled that same train, never to return. Sherborne, he reflected, had taught him something after all—how to rely on himself.

Sherborne conferred other ambiguous gifts: a persistent sense of unease, a sharpened instinct for boundaries, an emotional distance from myself and from others, a mistrust of human institutions—in T. S. Eliot's sense of a *"fear of possession, of belonging to another, or to others, or to God."* [6] In time, these gifts proved valuable in the neo-colonial bureaucracy where I spent much of my working life. In my troubled future family, though, such currency was largely worthless.

—·—

I climb off the shooting platform and return home, feeling flat.

Before I sleep, I turn to my MacBook and bring up the BBC iPlayer; I want to watch a recording of Meg Rosoff's BBC2 *ArtsNight* program. Meg is married to my old mate Paul; Paul and I worked for the Britain-Nepal Medical Trust over forty years ago, running a pharmaceutical scheme with outlets in a dozen hill villages in eastern Nepal. Paul's a painter now, and Meg is a writer. Their place is an hour away, in Shingle Street on the Suffolk coast.

I met Mandana through Paul. They had been pharmacy students at Cardiff University. Mandana came out to Nepal to visit Paul, but I was in Hong Kong raising money, and I missed her. Four years later we were all back in England; I was writing up my master's research on Nepal, Paul was an art student, and Mandana was looking after her father's house in Hampstead while he clung to his pharmacy business in Tehran during the early years of Iran's Islamic revolution. Paul told me Mandana was looking for tenants, and suggested I contact her.

She was a lovely, troubled young woman. Perhaps because her internal life was so painful, the physical dangers that you or I fear meant little to her. In the following year, 1980, she decided to return to Iran to help her father start a new business after he'd been blacklisted and his factory nationalized. She drove fast, she rode horses that broke her bones, and she argued with abandon. She wasn't as taken by me as I was by her, but she was looking for a husband. Early in our relationship, though, she warned me off. We were having dinner at an Italian restaurant, Mama Rosa's, in Notting Hill—long closed now (and with good reason).

"Nigel-*joon*," she was saying. "You have no idea what you are talking about."

"What do you mean?" I replied; I no longer remember exactly what I'd just suggested, but I think I was asking her to move in with me.

"I am depressed, and I'm an addict. And you know nothing about these things. Look"—and she fished in her purse for a blister pack of pills. "These are duffies. Do you know what they are?"

"No."

"Codeine. I take ten of these a day. Nothing else works. You don't want to be with me."

She was trying, but she didn't mean it: I could see that. Thinking back, I am touched by her gallantry. At the time, though, I dismissed what she said. I would help her get better. I would be able to give her hope, and with that she would overcome whatever it was that was going on inside her. I felt certain of that.

— · —

"*Where does a unique artistic voice come from?*" Meg asks. "*Why do some books, performances and paintings move us when others don't? For me, it begins with a powerful connection to the unconscious.*"[7]

It's this ability to draw on the unconscious mind, in her view, that underlies true art.

> "*An artist might not be aware of the connection, but when it's there, you see it straight away. It's a certain stillness or resonance. And what does it take to forge, and maintain this connection? Courage. Surrender. Persistence. Practice. Releasing your inhibitions. Listening to your dreams. Connecting to the part of ourselves we've learned to tuck neatly away. I passionately believe that anybody can do it.*"

Anybody? I wonder. I don't believe everyone has the guts, the stamina and the skill to find that essential stillness.

3

THE GARDEN

August 19, 2016—Day 0, Darbang, Myagdi District—3,504 feet above mean sea level.

We arrived here by Land Cruiser from Pokhara, a three-hour drive through rain and red mud. Tomorrow, we walk. When Peter Matthiessen and George Schaller began their journey to Dolpo in 1973, no motorable roads ran west from Pokhara, and it took them five days to reach Darbang. We have done well to omit that part of their itinerary; today the route is criss-crossed with jeep tracks and all the detritus they draw in after them.

We are six weather weeks in front of Matthiessen and Schaller, who left here on October 3, 1973; the monsoon should have finished by the time they set out, but it lingered that year.

Back then, Darbang was *"this region's main village…where the slate-roofed houses are strongly built of red and white clay bricks, with carved wood windows."*[1] No longer; today it's a typical reached-by-road modern mess, of jerry-built brick and concrete cubes, flat roofs and rebar posts, dogs, trash, shit, building materials and small general stores selling rice, cigarettes, batteries and cheap cloth; it straggles for a mile along the Myagdi Khola (*kholā* = river).

From Darbang we go north for twelve days, through the hunting reserve of Dhorpatan and around the western flanks of the Dhaulagiri massif, up into the rain shadow. We'll pause for a day in the village of Tarakot to buy food and wash our clothes before heading north again, through the steep-sided Dho Tarap Valley into Dolpo.

Matthiessen and Schaller stayed in a school on the edge of Darbang, as are we. I have organized my trip through a trekking agency I've used before—Basant Travels and Tours Pvt. Ltd. My guide Palden, his son Sagar and nephew Ngima unload the Land Cruiser, pitch my tent, stuff my bags inside it, and unfold my writing table and camp stool near the edge of the compound. Behind me tumbles the Myagdi, gray, violent, screened by oily green vegetation—rhododendron, silk cotton and *sãl* trees, frangipani. My job is to drink tea, eat biscuits and look the part. My half-hearted efforts to help set up camp are met with alarm; if passers-by saw me, this would lower the tone of our enterprise. After a few feeble objections, I begin typing my diary on a Bluetooth keyboard.

In time, as is the way in Nepal, the curious come to watch me. At first one small boy, then three girls holding hands. I smile, and after a while get up and walk about with my mug of tea. Very gently, one of two teen-age girls eases onto my camp stool and starts to finger type.

Her wary nonchalance reminds me of the Kathmandu street kids who sometimes followed Tess into our garden when Suresh, our driver, brought her back from school. For them we were *bideshi*, outlanders: so pale, so strange, so much brilliant stuff, hospitable too—but no more due the deference owed Nepali adults than the snow leopard in Banham Zoo owed me.

"Do you know these children?" I asked once, as three of them, ignoring me, walked into the hall.

"Oh yes," said Tess. "They are my precious playthings."

"Playmates."

"No Papa, they are very thing-ey. They live in tiny rooms."

As if I, the one who chose a house and lifestyle so starkly different from theirs, should have known better. . . such unsettling logic.

An older man in shorts is watching the tap-typing from a distance. He inclines his chin at me. "*Amerikāmā lanu porchha,*" he says, pointing at the teenagers. "You should take them to America. *Hajurle bihā garnu porchha.* You should marry them." I remember this kind of banter: teasing, salacious, a suggestion he would never make to a Nepali. The girls giggle, and one tries to catch my eye. To my embarrassment, I am slightly aroused.

"No discipline," the man chides the girls, and in English, batting away his own hypocrisy. He points at the school gate. Painted on a semicircular plywood board above the entrance is a motto, also in English: "*Discipline is the ornament of the students—Thanks for your visit.*"

A few large raindrops splash onto the table; I gather my electronics and take them to my tent. I've not been inside it yet. It's clean and dry, a delightful blue refuge. The children scatter, the rain begins to hammer at the corrugated iron roofs of the school, and I sit cross-legged and leaf through *The Snow Leopard* until I find the equivalent day in 1973.

> *"From the river above Darbang comes evil thunder. The cliffs are falling, and three wet dogs that scavenge in the schoolyard turn to listen. Rocks tremble and bound into the river, which after two days of heavy rain is rushing, roaring, lunging through the canyon.*
>
> *The daily rain is nagging at our nerves and mine especially, since my cramped and ratty tent leaks very badly. Hunched in a cold and soggy sleeping bag amongst the puddles, I have envied the owner of the crisp blue tent next door, and perhaps these base feelings fired our first argument, this dark morning, when GS tossed used cans and papers into the schoolyard.*"[2]

We are better organized than they were, I tell myself; I have not cut corners: their journey was replete with kit failure and underpaid porters.

The rain roars unceasingly, battering the ground around my tent, bringing back memories of other rainstorms long ago; memories of my childhood bedroom in Africa and the sudden downpours of the wet season. I would lie there, safe and dry, willing the rain to fall even harder. A sense of timelessness; of contentment.

I return to the book. I am trying to understand what Peter Matthiessen does—how he transforms mundane, uncomfortable experience into a journey both luminous and charged with emotion. This paragraph from the walk into Darbang:

"The path follows the northern bank of a tributary river, the Magyandi, where the valley sides are too steep for farming, and the few poor hamlets lack even a tea stall. It is October now; the orchids disappear. Across the river, ghostly waterfalls—sometimes six or seven may be seen at once—flow down out of the clouds. A stone millhouse spans the white water of a stream where a ravine strikes into the river; there is no bridge, no sign of life, and the hermit, if he has not died, shares his solitudes with the macaques that perch like sentinels about the silent dwelling."[3]

A world emptied of color, in which nature alone is dynamic. Orchids disappear, waterfalls flow from the clouds, a ravine splits the river, monkeys gather. Human life, in contrast, is loss and dispossession: hillsides impossible to farm; incomes that can't support a tea stall; a hint of ghosts, no bridge, just solitude and an absence of speech. This is nature as a reflection of the writer's own emotions—the feelings of a man lonely, yet enlivened by the natural world.

The storm passes, and I walk out past the cooking tent, through the gate of the school and down towards the river bank. Come to think of it, this world of gray water, dark clouds and subdued vegetation does seem ominous. Earlier I saw annoying clutter and imposed schedules; now there is shape.

Darbang has had other famous visitors. On March 19, 2004, more than five thousand soldiers and porters of the Maoist People's Liberation Army camped in and around this town, commandeering houses and this school. The rebels moved out the next day, high on idealism. In *The Bullet and the Ballot Box*, Aditya Adhikari quotes a Maoist soldier who compared that procession of guerrillas to Mao's glorious Long March. The townsfolk had a more nuanced view of this invasion, according to Japanese journalist Kiyoko Ogura: those with money were forced to give the Maoists cash; those with food, rice; those with neither, a child.

The Maoists went on to attack the district capital, Beni, where they encountered a substantial force of police and soldiers. Despite achieving total surprise, the Maoists failed to overrun the army barracks or hold the town, and retired to their base area in Rolpa District. Here about forty captives were handed over to the Red Cross in a much-hyped victory ceremony. In reality, the operation had failed: outnumbering their enemies five to one, they lost over a hundred dead and four hundred injured while killing only thirty-three. The Maoists never managed to hold any district capital for more than a few hours.

Until the Maoist interlude, the middle hills of Nepal were seen by its many hiking tourists as a Happy Place—a land populated by cheerful, tough and generous-hearted people who welcomed outsiders to their world. There is some truth in this projection of The Shire onto an eastern landscape, but it glosses over the daily injustices and hardships that all of our tour guides and porters have suffered, yet make so little of with their foreign charges.

August 20, 2016—Day 1, Darapani, Baglung District—5,089 feet.

Rain is hissing in the pines. A sound like a foghorn, distant and forlorn—a buffalo, somewhere up in the mist. It's muggy, but there's a cold breeze. Sweat, red mud and a clinging T-shirt as we reach the ridgeline. The first climb, no more than a thousand feet, and my chest feels stripped.

Walking up and down Bull Run Mountain in Virginia was like practicing for a knife fight with chopsticks.

"Very lucky, suh," says Palden. "No big rain today." I grunt. The drizzle intensifies. We have sixty days of walking ahead of us; I am not going to use what little energy I have in conversation. The trail runs along a ridge and then curves steeply into a cloud; we have some way to go today. It's ugly country—eroded earth, thin pines. Crofton weed bushes everywhere, limp leaves on dull purple stalks.

The first of our mules tramps up the trail behind us. His name is Bukhé. Last night I misheard this as Bouquet, thinking it strangely fey for such a workmanlike creature. Turns out that Bukhé, the strong one, is the name given to many lead mules around here. There are six of them—tall, tan, handsome creatures from India. They have two minders: Hem Bahadur Khadka Chetri, or KC, a bit of a gentleman rambler with his belly and fly-switch, and Ram Somebody, definitely his subordinate, dark-faced, reticent, trekking in Wellington boots.

We've been climbing for over an hour, and we rest a few minutes below a stand of ancient pine trees. We then move on up through the conifers into clear air, ascending a narrow stone path through rice fields. I leave Palden behind, and before long reach two large square ponds, dug into a terrace below a *chautarā* (a rock platform where travelers can rest). A buffalo is paddling around one of them, snorting occasionally, only her sweeping horns and snout visible above the brown surface. Water spills into the ponds through the mouths of two *dhunge dharā*—stone beams carved as open-mouthed serpents. These dragon-like creatures, these *nāgā*, are mythical water guardians, the original inhabitants of the lake once covering the Kathmandu Valley.

On the terrace above the *chautarā*, two huge, gnarly trees, one a banyan and the other a peepul—both figs, often planted together in such places. You can tell them apart by their leaves: those of the peepul are heart-shaped and move continuously, even in still air, as if trembling with gossip. Villagers may tell you that these two trees represent man and woman, but their associations are far more variable. Even to botanists, the peepul is *ficus religiosa*; to wandering sadhus, it is *vriksha rājya*, the King of Trees. The peepul is the tree in which Krishna once hid from demons. Vishnu, Brahma and Shiva choose to hold their councils in its shade. The peepul is also the *bodhi*, the great tree that protected Siddhartha Gautama, the future Buddha, as he wrestled with his obsessive discontent on the way to enlightenment.

The banyan carries similar meanings, but in the plural world of Hinduism it also symbolizes the interplay of change, death and illusion. A banyan will live many years, but allows nothing to grow beneath its canopy: a malign impact that conjures up death. The tree is sacred to Yama, lord of the underworld, the god who gave man the power of choice, or—as in the Garden of Eden—the power to awaken; the power which the Buddha chose to exercise, undisturbed by any Abrahamic God's jealousy.

Shiva, manifesting as Dakshinamurti (the South-facing One) is said to sit beneath the banyan, calmly staring out through the constant storm of change and death. Like the peepul, the banyan throws out aerial roots, and when these catch and thicken, the tree can look as if it were planted upside-down. Thus Krishna, in the *Bhagavad Gita*: "*It is said that there is an imperishable banyan tree that has its roots upward and its branches down and whose leaves are the Vedic hymns*"[4]; upside-down, like the baobab in Africa—that one the Devil's Tree, this one a tree whose cock-eyed appearance, they say, can mess with our sense of reality, reminding us that the material world is the imaginary one, and that the real one lives within us.

As I sit sweating on the edge of the terrace, thoughts of the Garden of Eden rekindle old memories.

It's a warm day in 1957. I am standing by a large fishpond in our garden in Nyasaland. I'm wearing clean shorts held up by a snake belt, and a white shirt ironed by my nanny with one of those old contraptions you filled with hot charcoal. I've just been to Sunday School, and my mother has gone inside to find out about lunch. My dog Monty is sitting next to me. Monty likes to lick his balls in front of guests. He doesn't usually bother when it's just the two of us, but today he's hard at it; his brother was taken by a leopard a couple of nights ago.

I'm six years old. I'm inspired by what I've learned this morning—filled with elation. I have a new sticker for my Sunday School album showing Jesus, saturated in light, walking across a stormy sea. Mrs. Phillips gave it to me and said, in her deep, sinful voice, "Have faith, Nigel."

"I do, Mrs. Phillips," I answered. Faith and Mrs. Phillips have some relationship I can't yet work out. She told us about Peter's feeble attempt to cross the waves towards his Savior. She also explained that Peter's reluctance had nothing to do with hippos or crocodiles. "The Holy Land," she said, to underline his faint-heartedness, "is just like Hampshire."

Mrs. Phillips has dark bobbed hair, and an open, amused face which she covers with orange make-up. I can hear the squeak of her skirt against her nylon stockings as she bends down, and I can smell warm bread and fresh sweat. I had no idea my Sunday School teacher was Jewish. Not that it would have mattered; the Jews on my stickers, despite their long hair, are clearly Englishmen—from their facial features to the striped dressing gowns they wear in the middle of the day.

Lunch isn't ready yet, so I have a bit of time for my first water walk. The pond is strewn with water lilies. I don't want to damage them, so I choose a clear corner. The surface is still. I am thinking of the turbulent sea that messed with Peter's mind, and made him cry out like a girl. "*Oh ye of little faith!*" Jesus had said. That *was* a bit mean; but then again, I am no Peter. I have Big Faith.

I am planning to teach faith-walking to my parents. I'm thinking we can drive out to Lake Nyasa and faith-walk as a family.

Jesus always wore sandals; and as it happens, I have the right kit today. I place one foot firmly on the water. My sandal seems to bounce slightly, as if Jesus' hands are already beneath me. I walk on, leaving the shore behind.

And then, just like that, I drop to the bottom of the pond, collapsing like a soldier shot through the heart. There's a moment of blank astonishment, then I'm tangling with dark water and fibrous roots. My mouth must be wide open; I taste mud. Eventually I thrash my way up the side of the pond.

"Blessed are the pure in heart," Jesus said, *"for they shall see God."*[5] My heart is sour, my hair full of slime, and I have seen a God I wasn't expecting. I sit for a while, angry, hurt, betrayed. Monty senses something is up. He leaves his balls alone for a moment, and licks me instead.

After a while I gather up my anger, and splosh into the house. I tell my mother I've fallen into the pond by accident. I keep my shame to myself.

I doubt I reflected on the experience much, but it left a deep impression; the humiliation worked its way into me like a tiny flake of burning phosphorous. If I think of Eden now, I see that garden in Nyasaland. I see the Serpent, the truth-teller, cast on his belly, condemned to eat dust for daring to offer Eve the gift of sight. In my own childish way, I experienced the great paradox of Christianity: that an all-powerful, supposedly perfect God saw fit to create a universe filled with deceit, cynicism and suffering.

Many years later, reading the *Four Quartets* for the first time, I came upon this:

> *"In order to arrive at what you do not know*
> *You must go by a way which is the way of ignorance.*
> *In order to possess what you do not possess*
> *You must go by the way of dispossession".*[6]

And the buried memories flooded back: the African garden, image of a brilliant childhood; the false promise; the pain of betrayal; the compassion of my frightened dog.

—·—

I'm glad the climb is done, but I divine, with some annoyance, that this is the end of today's walking. "Darapani?" I ask Palden; this is Nepali for "tap, water." I'm figuring that we've reached our destination: the village where we plan to spend the night goes by this name.

We get up and carry on, passing houses beside the path. The short day frustrates me, even though I know it makes sense to start the walk gradually. I have to be smart about this; I'm not confident I'll be able to complete such a long trek. We've walked our first five miles and there are hundreds more to go, along with five passes of over 5,000 meters (>16,400 feet), before we reach Jumla.

And I notice that my ears are zinging; tinnitus, a continuous nuisance exacerbated by jet lag or lack of sleep, neither of which apply today. Plus my left hip is hurting slightly. Palden and I follow the mules to another schoolyard. This one is spectacular, set into the side of a steep hill and overlooking fields, forests and a small river a couple of thousand feet below us. Konzok, our cook, has lit two kerosene stoves; he's boiling water. My desk is already set up beneath a shade tree. It's early afternoon; there is nothing left to do today but eat, read or write. Yet I am restless; I have no desire to begin the diary I promised myself I would keep.

Instead I decide to arrange my kit. It is packed into two stiff blue canvas hold-alls and an orange Longchamp shoulder bag, all then stuffed into polyester fiber sacks and lashed over the mules' backs.

First I get at the green plastic dry-bag filled with my medicines; I need to put a couple of weeks' of pills into seven-day organizers. This part I'm not so keen on others witnessing; I do it in the tent. Once finished, I go over my electronics to make sure they are packed properly and protected from the damp with desiccant gel envelopes. There's the Nikon binoculars, a 21 watt three-panel solar charger and over a dozen other devices (tablets, power packs, cameras, the satellite phone, three smart phones, a voice recorder, an ultraviolet water purifier, etc.). When I first hiked in Nepal, I had a battery-powered torch and a watch: that was all.

As for my six Nepali companions, most of them have a flip-phone, one has a radio and two have head torches.

In the US, the measure of class is the stuff you possess—both quantity and quality. Here people don't have much stuff at all, but the system of differentiation isn't wholly dissimilar. In place of race, they have caste, which to some extent aligns both with ethnicity and with economic class. Out here in the country, the upper-class Aryan higher castes, by and large, have more of what meager stuff there is—irrigated land, live-stock, dairy products, corrugated iron roofs, nice saris. I may feel awkward about the amount of kit I have, but my companions seem to think nothing of such a disparity; if they do, they aren't letting on.

It's lunch time. Sagar and Ngima cover my desk with an array of plastic serving dishes. They contain some startling things I haven't seen since childhood: tinned pilchards and pink cocktail sausages, along with some puffy white rotis and a bowl of fried spinach. I eat alone while the others sit cross-legged on the ground in the cooking tent: for them it's rice, lentils and the same fried spinach—by preference. What they are eating is *kãnã*, or food (otherwise known as *dãlbhãt*, which translates as "lentils-rice"); what I am eating is *lonch*, their idea of what I will find delicious, nice enough in its own way—but certainly not *kãnã*. It's not that I don't like *dãlbhãt*: indeed, I ate it all the time when I worked here in my twenties. Now, though, I am clearly expected to eat more exotic fare, and I don't presume to disappoint.

A few students gather. It's Saturday and there's no school, so the numbers of strays is modest. They watch me eat, then they watch me read my Kindle. They are talking to one another.

"*Tyo ke ho*? What's that thing?"

"It's a book."

"Where are the pages?"

"Inside, you idiot."

After a while I relent, and ask them over by inclining my head. I show them the Kindle. A couple of them appropriate it, and in no time they are playing *Minion Rush*, which Alex loaded a few weeks ago. They show no further interest in me.

I sit back and watch the sun and cloud-shadow shift across this vast landscape. Tourists can be forgiven for associating such insouciant grandeur with human contentment: but Nepal is no peasant paradise, and its history is as bloody as that of any other patch of contested land. At the heart of Nepal's story is the ascendancy of Indo-Aryan families and religions over the earlier settlers (today's Janajati, or tribes), and their belief systems—in most cases animist. The army that the Hindu prince Prithivi Narayan Shah used to unify the country in the 1770s was led by high-caste Hindus, but consisted largely of Janajati troops. These foot soldiers and their descendants received little from the state they created, and eighty years later found themselves baked into an exclusionary caste system in Nepal's first civil code, the 1854 *Muluki Ain*. It is still in force today, albeit in amended form.

A core tenet of Hinduism is the maintenance of ritual purity; this can be sullied in various types of contact with those of lower caste, including mere touch, or the injudicious sharing of food and water. While the *Muluki Ain*'s thousand-plus pages codified all Nepalese law, setting out the rules governing land tenure, crime, trade and finance, its driving impulse was the management of inter-caste relations—and in particular, the subversive anarchy of sexual desire. More than a third of the document focuses on this.[7]

Caste is exclusionary, and self-reinforcing: someone of high caste deserves privilege, since his current incarnation rewards his virtue in preceding lives. Because non-Aryan ethnicities occupy lower positions on the caste ladder than Aryans do, Nepal's caste system formalizes racial exclusion in a more subtle, less contestable way than the Jim Crow laws in the pre-civil rights southern states of the US once did. In the 1970s, as now, Brahmins dominated government, and Chetris the officer corps. Brahmins still lead all of today's political parties, from the right-wing

Rastriya Prajatantra to the centrist Nepali Congress, to the Unified Marxist-Leninists (*Umalé*) and the Maoists.

August 24, 2016—Day 5, Dhorpatan, Baglung District—9,367 feet.

No walking today; we arrived yesterday afternoon and are resting up. From here we must cross several passes en route to Tarakot and the southern edges of Dolpo.

Our tents are pitched on bumpy turf next to a government guest house, a dingy set of stone buildings with bare rooms, bare beds and small wooden windows. I prefer my tent, though it's raining and the ground is wet; we have set up camp in a water meadow, next to Dhorpatan's defunct grass airstrip. An open plain like this is a rarity in the hills of Nepal. It's too high up for rice or maize, though; the land serves as horse and cattle pasture, with a few potatoes and some thin barley.

The settlement of Dhorpatan is best known as a refugee center, established in 1961 by the International Committee of the Red Cross for Tibetans fleeing from the Chinese. What was once a tented camp is now a village of brick, concrete and tin-roofed houses. Up to five hundred people once lived here, but fewer than two hundred remain, most of them elderly: the youngsters leave for Pokhara and Kathmandu, where the bulk of Nepal's twenty-thousand-plus Tibetans now live. These refugees bring grim stories with them, as do all who are forced into exile; who among us would leave our homeland without possessions or prospects if we thought we had other choices?

I sit idly in my tent after breakfast, bored and out of sorts. Unlike my Nepali companions, I have been bad-tempered and prone to negativity for the past couple of days; that same reluctance I felt back in Harleston is still dragging at me.

—·—

After we left Darapani three days ago, a short walk brought us to Muna, and another schoolyard of curious, bored school children who followed me to and from my tent. Once again, it was a very short day, only two hours of walking. When Palden told me "We are here, suh," I took out my annoyance on a bothersome child.

"*Namaste*" came from behind me.

"*Namaste*," I replied, without enthusiasm.

"Give me dot pen," said the child. I turned to see an imp of about ten with a snotty, morose face.

"*Neh.*"

"Give me *paisā*. Twenty rupees."

"Bugger off."

The next day, Day 3, put paid to my concerns about insufficient walking: we were on the trail for almost eight hours. I discarded my Teva rubber sandals for trainers. In the 1970s I had trekked in flip-flops, so much cleaner than socks and shoes when there's mud—but my feet are soft now, and the Velcro straps soon left blisters.

From Muna we dropped down through maize fields to a turbulent river, charged with cloudy soil. For the rest of the day we climbed the flanks of a forest ridge. We began with a traverse of an unstable scar left by a recent landslide—gray, schistic mud full of glittery fragments, slick between your fingers. Smashed trees. Running water. Palden said that five houses and twenty-four people had been swept away; "cows also, suh." Their bodies lie buried deep beneath this chaos.

We cleared the scar; I fell. My hip hurt, but once on firmer ground I found a walking rhythm and the pain disappeared. For the first time, I plugged in my earbuds, shut out the sentient world and focused on the climb. Spotify. The Boxer Rebellion. *Safe House*. Music is an accelerant for me, fueled further by the satisfaction of the climb.

> "*One eye open I look away,*
> *I was searching but can't take any more . . .*

One eye closed to indifference,
To the things I did nothing about..."[8]

Nathan Nicholson's falsetto wrapped itself around the forest, around the houses with their slate roofs, ocher-washed walls and gardens of red canna lilies, around the distant double helix of stratus clouds up over the ridgeline. Entranced, detached, I climbed through the insubstantial backdrop. Up, through the maize fields, through the millet and the buckwheat, into the tangled trees and aerial lichens of a cloud-forest. I left the others behind, and for some time my only companions were a small man wrapped in a pink plastic sheet and a tasseled kids' owl hat, driving his cows and followed by a black dog with a feathery tail.

For me, the Walkman, and now my smartphone, are the greatest hiking aids invented. Messrs. Matthiessen and Schaller would not have approved; at this point they were looking for signs of the Asiatic Black Bear, admiring the viburnum, barberry and rhododendron, listening to woodpeckers and the chickadee-like calls of the tits. Not me; I am steaming on up, measuring myself against this bastard of a hill, both here and absent, both focused and distracted, in control.

What Peter Matthiessen doesn't mention are the leeches, which we encountered in abundance—*Haemadipsa sylvestris*, the Indian Leech, purposeful evolution at its very best. Years of past walking taught me to expect them here: the air was cool; mist and drizzle, long spears of grass draped over the path. And here they were—tiny black filaments, standing upright on their posterior suckers, waving sinuously. Leeches are almost blind, but they have an acute sense of movement. They feel you coming, and they jump. Their simple genius is contained in a mouth filled with tiny teeth that cut you without pain, and inject you with hirudin, an anticoagulant enzyme. They can drink ten times their body weight in blood in half an hour: as if a bulldog could puff itself up to the size of a dolphin, or a human could eat 1,500 pounds of rice at one sitting.

I intercepted thirty-three of these creatures on my legs, my shoes and my arms, picking them off and flicking them back into the undergrowth without rancor—but two got through my defenses, working their way beneath my shorts onto my hip, and into the top of my butt crack. I only noticed a couple of hours later, when Konzok caught up with me in a high clearing and pointed to my shorts, by now soaked with blood. The leeches had long gone, falling off asleep and sated.

It was evening when we crested the Jaljala ridge; the pass is just over 11,000 feet, and we had climbed almost 5,000 of them since the river. I was pleased. It hadn't been easy, but I could still walk.

We wound down around a hillside to a flat meadow and a single timber teahouse. Through bands of clotted clouds, glimpses of the bright ice shelves of Dhaulagiri, the seventh tallest of all mountains at 26,795 feet. Dhaulagiri falls away southwest into the Kali Gandaki River, from which Annapurna (26,545 feet) rises on the far bank—making this the deepest river gorge in the world. We will work our way around Dhaulagiri, leaving both rain and verdant woods behind on our way to the high country.

My companions pitched my tent in a field of yellow oxeye daisies. That evening, Konzok cooked in a nearby teahouse, and I joined the owner's family in the warmth of their single room. The fire burned in a grate in the middle of the house; above, on chains, hung a square iron frame from which two haunches of goat meat were suspended. With no chimney, the smoke had blackened the mats nailed to the underside of the rafters, covering them in shining tar. A rat scuttled above the fireplace; I drank hot water as the man and his wife spoke of life in this lonely place.

They were Tamang, like Palden and the two boys. Palden translated for me.

"Son is going in army. In Hend. India. Daughter, she is here—there, you see her. Nice girl, you think so? Little bit dirty, maybe."

This was apparently hilarious; the old man, his once-beautiful wife and their alluring daughter were all laughing.

"How many other children do they have?" I asked.

A complicated conversation ensued, the woman using her fingers and continuing to laugh.

"Two more, suh. And two died."

"Oh... A long time ago?"

More discussion.

"One when baby. One last year, young man. Very bad. Very bad." He grimaced and shook his head. "Accidented in bus, down in the river, you understand suh?"

"Yes." I felt awful. The woman looked at me, laughing still. Some would say this was an odd cultural habit. Others might think it was the momentum of the previous conversation. But I knew, looking at her, that it was neither. This was the kindness of the bereaved, of someone who does not wish you to be discomfited. Because she knows that you think, in your naïveté, that you have reminded her of something you shouldn't have; something, of course, that needs no reminders.

Affected by this, alone again in my tent, I found myself thinking of a conversation with Mandana from many years before. It would have been 1995, after we'd returned to the US from Kathmandu and were living in McLean, Virginia. Mandana had encouraged me to visit a past-life regression therapist. I couldn't recall much: a middle-aged lady with a lacquered blond bob; a sickly smell of lavender. A white living room, and a large porcelain Siamese cat on the dresser. She had tried to hypnotize me. I went along with this, though it didn't seem to work. But I let my mind wander, and at some point I saw myself clinging to a huge fishing net as it moved across bright fields, high in the sky. I saw Mandana, falling, and reached down to catch her wrist, twisting her up so she could fasten herself onto the net beside me.

"That's what I remember," I told Mandana.

We were sitting in the back garden, a wedge-shaped piece of real estate that ended in a sound wall overlooking the Dulles Airport access road. In those days, Washington summer evenings were still filled with mosquitoes, and I was slapping at them (they had no interest in

Mandana). She smiled at me, and she had tears in her eyes. The last two years had been difficult for her, for all of us; away from Nepal, depression had often overwhelmed her. Her life of great promise had been betrayed by a simple chemical flaw, like the errant stitch left by a Persian carpet weaver to avoid blasphemous perfection. She was born beautiful, kind-hearted, intelligent and wealthy—with an invisible susceptibility that came to unravel it all.

"My forever friend. You'll always come and find me. That's what you saw. Wherever I am."

Where are you, though? I now thought. Where? And when you were here, I let you go. I watched you fall, and I turned away.

"How strange everything seems," writes Matthiessen. *"How strange everything is. One 'I' feels like an observer of this man who lies here in this sleeping bag in Asian mountains; another 'I' is thinking about Alex; a third is the tired man who tries to sleep."*[9]

—·—

The following day we descended through swampy meadows and forests of conifers towards Dhorpatan. After yesterday's exertions, my body ached, with a persistent pain above my heart.

The grasses were filled with tiny flowers—purples and yellows and blues. In one field, a cloud of butterflies drinking, pestered by hungry birds. An iridescent green flash, a butterfly I recognized—an Indian Peacock. I waded into the ooze, shaking my walking stick; the birds flicked away, tiny balls of rufous fluff; these must be the redstarts Matthiessen keeps mentioning. I know little of birds, a deficit that constantly astonished my mother. Or of butterflies; my mother collected them, and several cases hang on the walls in Harleston, left to my sister Mandy, but too delicate to transport to her home in the US. Mum caught some with me in Nepal in 1976, north of Pokhara—including this character. I never shared this enthusiasm, but I am glad to have them still; each time I look at them, I can see her firm hands piercing their fusty bodies.

The forest was open, needles on the floor and gnarled old *chir* pines leaning over us, their bark layered and peeling. On the western side of this valley, patches of dead trees coursed up the hillside, some a translucent white, others varying shades of yellow—but not from any visible act of man; the area is uninhabited. Matthiessen wrote of a vanishing landscape here, but his forebodings, in this place at least, were misplaced. He believed that this particular wilderness would be gone by the end of the twentieth century, and such views were widely shared at the time. Nepal's rapid population increase, stagnant technologies and moribund political system presaged a continuous stripping away of forests, and a disastrous loss of biomass. Although the country is now disfigured by hundreds of ugly jeep tracks that did not exist in 1973, forest shrinkage has in fact been reversed. This is largely due to far-sighted community forestry programs that turned state land over to village management—such that a NASA remote-sensing project shows trees now covering 45 percent of Nepal, as opposed to only 26 percent in 1992.[10] Good things can happen when you let ordinary people run their own affairs.

— · —

In Dhorpatan, Peter Matthiessen asked George Schaller to shave his head. Matthiessen cut off an old bracelet, and put away his watch; the real pilgrimage would now begin. Beset again by porter trouble and by incessant rain, they spent three frustrating days here. A passing traveler told them the trail to Tarakot was tough—"*very hard, very steep and slippery, too many ups and downs.*"[11] The place annoyed them no end.

As he ended this preparatory section of the book, 'Westward,' and turned 'Northward' from Dhorpatan, Matthiessen set up the spiritual premise of the journey. Restless myself, I struggle with this in my tent, willing myself to concentrate: but his long meditation on the similarities between Eastern and Native American pre-religious thought defeats me, bores me—my mind slipping like a worn clutch plate. When I return to what he wrote about his young son and his own duplicity, though, the book comes back to life.

> *"In his first summers, forsaking all his toys, my son would stand rapt for near an hour in his sandbox in the orchard, as doves and redwings came and went on the warm wind, the leaves dancing, the clouds flying, birdsong and sweet smell of privet and rose. The child was not observing; he was at rest in the very center of the universe, a part of things, unaware of endings and beginnings, still in unison with the primordial nature of creation, letting all light and phenomena pour through."*[12]

He recounts a dream of Alex, *"my beautiful eight-year-old boy, whose mother died of cancer just last year."*[13] He wakes up stricken by guilt, knowing he will not be home for Thanksgiving, as he had promised. But he has no intention of giving up this journey.

There is something so wrong with this. If the search for liberation is a search for one's origins, why this flamboyant trip to Asia? Is crossing the Himalaya to Crystal Mountain the *"true pilgrimage, a journey of the heart,"*[14] or is it something much more self-indulgent? *"The courage-to-be, right here and now and nowhere else, is precisely what Zen, at least, demands: eat when you eat, sleep when you sleep!"*[15] he wrote; yet he allowed himself to be drawn away. Drawn into an act of romanticism and vanity, you might say: for he knew he would write a book about the experience. He should have stayed home, with his motherless children.

He left, selfishly, as have I. I am thinking about leaving my particular Alex, who is also now eight years old. Reading about Matthiessen's forty-three-year-old dream in this dingy kitchen brought tears to my eyes, tears of both pity and shame. We have this in common, then: we both left people when they needed us.

4

KALI YUGA

August 26, 2016—Day 7, Tatopani, Baglung District—7,908 feet.

We are camped in drizzle, in a nasty grassless paddock; just mud and the green leaves of the *banmãrã*, or "forest killer", a.k.a. *eupatorium*: a red-stemmed shrub whose leaves blot out any other seedlings.

It's cold. One of our mules fell into the river while crossing the bridge to the campsite, shoving past the pack in a futile stampede for pasture. He flipped as he tumbled, landing unhurt on his back, courtesy of my sleeping bag, which is soaked, and drying now over a smoky fire. I have retreated to my tent and am lancing a large blister on my left foot. My scalp is itchy. My clothes are damp, my legs covered in tiny insect bites. I have had my dal and paratha delivered to me here, like some sulky Greek at the siege of Troy.

Yesterday we left Dhorpatan for Thakur. For Peter Matthiessen,

> *"Tomorrow begins the trek into the north. By the Jang Pass, we cross the Dhaulagiris to the Bheri River; we ascend the Suli Gad and the Phoksumdo River, and by the Kang Pass cross the Kanjiroba Range to Crystal Mountain."*[1]

More prosaically, Lonely Planet's *Trekking in Nepal* says that this is the beginning of *"the second phase of your trek, north into largely uninhabited wilderness,"*[2] and that it takes seven to eight hours to reach Thakur.

Which it did. Throughout the morning we climbed almost 4,000 feet, gently at first through meadows filled with tiny, unimpressive alpine flowers—blue gentians, yellow marsh marigolds, white chickweed—and then through cedar woods, where the trail wound sharply up through deep beds of brown needles that muffled the sound of footfall. Despite the rest day, I had no energy; my attempts to put distance between myself and the others came to nothing. We paused where the forest opens onto a wide, stony river basin, at the base of a treeless gray hill. More school food for *lonch*: this time, fried Spam with my rotis. I sat wordless, watching the others set up, cook, chat, eat quickly and repack. All done with a lightness and good humor that quite eluded me.

Clouds had set in, with a chilly wind. Small knots of sheep and goats passed us in both directions, buffeted slightly, the odd wooden bell clocking, shepherds whistling. After an hour I got up, feeling better, and quickly climbed the nose of the ridge. The path was damp white gravel, so steep that my face was sometimes only inches from the ground in front of me; I grasped at rocks and grass for balance. This was no place to slip. After about 150 feet, the slope flattened and the path meandered more reasonably through wet rocks, into a low line of mist. Palden was soon on my tail again.

We crested the Phagune Duri at 13,315 feet. You have to smile when you reach a pass, even a modest one like this. Loud, unnecessary congratulations to all from Palden, who used up one of our five rolls of prayer flags, stringing them across the pile of stones that marks the top of any serious climb; I presume he was relieved I'd made it this far. We took photos. There's one that captures us well. In the background is a wide treeless meadow, our mules grazing near a flock of sheep. Ngima is covered in a coarse, brown woolen blanket he's borrowed from a shepherd; his hair is wild from the tumpline on his basket, and he's grinning as if he's just woken up. The mule wranglers, Hem Bahadur and Ram Somebody, look composed and bored, as if they've just strolled out into the street. Sagar too. Palden is in front, hands to his sides, shades up, trying to look cool. Konzok, the self-effacing one, is taking the photo. Behind this scruffy outfit is me, legs crossed, one arm on Ngima's shoulder, the other one pointing my walking pole to the sky, the impresario of this ragtag band.

For the next couple of hours, we dropped down towards Thakur, a small settlement on a stream that feeds the Ghustan River. From somewhere around here, Matthiessen and Schaller saw unparalleled views of Dhaulagiri and other peaks—according to Schaller, a prospect unmatched by anything he'd seen even near Everest.

> *"Just at darkness, the clouds lift: at 12,500 feet, the campsite is surrounded by bright glaciers. The five peaks of Dhaulagiri shine in the black firmament, and over all this whiteness rings a silver moon, the full moon of October, when the lotus blooms."*[3]

We saw clouds.

That evening I ate with my team in the cooking tent. Palden was talking about Dubai, where he'd worked as a crane operator in Jebel Ali Port. Good money, he was saying, but hard. What about the Emiratis? Never much met them; his whole crew was Nepali. Tamang mostly, a few Rai. Some Terai-*wallahs* too: strange people, Indians almost. Some even *bāhun* [Brahmin]—"but not like real hillside *bāhun*. He never go hillside!"

"How do you get a job like that?"

"Agency, suh. In Kathmandu. Many Nepali there. I have good connection!"

As the days passed, I would learn more. Palden's family owns an acre or so of cultivable land near Salleri, south of Mount Everest. This is about average for a middling poor family. The government's ten-year Living Standards Survey says that a quarter of Nepal's rural households own 1.2 acres or less—a fifth of our empty garden in Virginia.[4] Palden's land, moreover, is located at about 6,500 feet, and is steep and rocky, yielding only enough maize and millet to feed the family for three months in a good year.

Palden quit school when he was twelve. He worked as a day-laborer on the farms of local landlords, and as a porter in the winter, carrying loads up to 40 kg from local roadheads to the more remote towns and villages. Being personable and hard-working, he persuaded a Tamang-run trekking agency in Namche Bazaar to give him a chance to carry for them, and in time he became a high-altitude climbing Sherpa, and eventually an expedition guide. By the age of thirty he was getting too old for this work—"also little bit scared, suh!"

But he knew people, and they helped him get work in the Gulf. Now he could save, despite the swingeing finder fees the hiring agency took. It meant accepting a bonding process that committed him to five years away with no leave, and surrendering his passport to his employers. A life of crowded dormitories, enforced celibacy, exposed worksites and sapping heat.

The money meant his family could move to Kathmandu, where the kids went to half-decent "private English boarding schools" (the second and third adjectives are merely decorative). It meant city life, away from the dirty grind of an unproductive farm, and the boredom and invasive gossip of the village. Palden found them all rooms in an unfinished concrete house in one of the new suburbs of northern Kathmandu. He owns several beds, a sofa, plenty of clothes and a 48-inch LG TV, and they eat well. But the savings are depleting, and there is no work in Kathmandu. This trip is something of a godsend—two months in all, with three family members on the payroll.

"After this, don't know, perhaps back to Dubai. Guide work only one time, two times each year."

Palden's is a typical modern Nepalese story—and a relatively successful one.

Nepal's population grew slowly in the nineteenth century, from about four to about five million. Even by 1900, though, land in the more crowded eastern parts of Nepal was becoming scarce, and Nepalis began wintering on Indian construction sites to earn vital cash. By 1951, the population had increased to 8.6 million inhabitants; this doubled to 19 million by 1990.[5] With the vast majority of the population still living in the countryside, family landholdings shrank from an already paltry average of 1.11 hectares in 1962 to 0.96 hectares by 1992.[6]

This land scarcity, along with the violent displacements of the ten-year Maoist civil war, combined to create a torrent of mobile labor: labor that Nepal's moribund industrial and service economy was unable to absorb. Once again, the poor escaped destitution by finding temporary work abroad—and by now, there was much more of this available. In 1993, incomes earned abroad ("remittances") contributed just 1.5 percent of Nepal's GDP; by 2015 they constituted 27.6 percent of GDP, $6.7 billion in all—the largest share of remittances in any economy of comparable size in the world. Nepal has become one of the great beneficiaries of globalization, seeing itself transformed from a predominantly rural economy into one now based on services (albeit with those services provided abroad).[7]

In *Emigration of the Nepalese People and Its Impact*, published in 2016, Laxman Singh Kunwar tells us that as many as six million Nepalis are working outside the country: more than one in five. Much of this work is classified by the Nepalese government as 3D: Dirty, Dangerous, Demanding—or in some versions, Demeaning. Yet this forced migration, and the high reputation Nepali workers have earned themselves in India, Malaysia and the Gulf, has done far more to reduce poverty than sixty years of development aid. Nepal's absolute poverty rate fell from 42 percent in the mid-'90s to 12.5 percent by 2010, the direct consequence of those remittances.[8]

Palden's journey is a remarkable one—an inverted, Nepali version of the American dream. Like today's American dream, though, families like Palden's are one serious hospitalization away from penury. Much as remittances have pulled the country up by its bootstraps, global trends change, and the wealth of nations can stagnate. When that happens, temporary immigrants are the first to lose their jobs.

These are long nights, up to ten hours on your back, but the hard ground allows only shallow sleep, and each time I wake I am deluged with dream fragments. Most of these vanish at once, leaving only a dim sense of disturbance: but occasional sequences linger. I see myself driving Tess on a blistering summer's day in Falls Church; we are off to Safeway, to buy groceries for her new family. The passenger side window is down, and Tess, in white shorts, has thrust a bare right leg out into the airstream. Her left hand lingers over the CD player; she has just pressed home a Goo Goo Dolls CD. Her fingers are long, even, olive-colored; her mother's fingers. Seeing them again, every aspect is at once familiar: the way they taper slightly towards the nail, the faint pink shadows along her knuckle-lines. If I glance sideways, the memory is sharp; as I turn my eyes towards her hand, the details dissolve. Like finding distant stars in the darkness.

Today has been easier. I took my medications last night, instead of this morning, allowing them to work through me while I slept: I'd figured that Bystolic, the beta-blocker that restricts your heart rate, wasn't letting me walk properly. Driving with the hand brake on, so to speak.

From late morning, rain sets in and the path becomes slippery. Mostly it traces the top of a ridge, in and out of cloud-forest. Palden insists on holding my hand at times to prevent me from sliding down the steep hillside. The mules have trouble; Palden says they aren't used to such cut-up paths. Few people live here, and no one seems to maintain the trails. We're all bitching about them; it's as if someone deliberately seeded them with stones and tree roots.

Matthiessen and Schaller saw pheasants and droppings of fox and yellow-throated marten, and enjoyed *"lithe wild olives that dance in the silver breeze of afternoon;"*[9] for us, above the north bank of the river, no pheasants, no silver or golden light, and certainly no illumination—just hard bloody work. Perhaps, I am thinking uncharitably, a subtle glaze has been added to Peter Matthiessen's fine book. Or perhaps it's just me, a much less present creature than either of them: my mind prefers to riff away from this place. I walk insulated by music, imagining myself on a ridgeline in Rohan, shield over my shoulder, hunting for orcs in the woods below.

At this altitude, rain means cold, and Nepal is a pale mess. In late afternoon, just before we drop down to Tatopani, we pass through a small Kami village near Kayam, a settlement of untouchable blacksmiths—in Matthiessen's evocative words, *"soot-faced familiars of the smelting fire and the iron stolen from the rock, feared and despised as black magicians by primitive people throughout Eurasia and Africa since the beginning of this Dark Age of Iron."*[10] He is referring to the *Kali Yuga*, the Age of Kali, Earth's fourth, degenerative cycle, in which only a quarter of the initial Golden Age's morality remains, and the Great Bull of Dharma has only one leg left to stand on.

According to the *Mahabharata*, the Sanskrit epic of ancient India, this is the time when rulers levy unfair taxes and shun their religious duties; a time of great migrations, of men saturated with greed who cannot tell lies from truth, who pollute the earth's waters and their own bodies, who murder without compunction—and for whom sexual pleasure is the main purpose of life. The *Mahabharata* also assures us that this age of iniquity will end in ruin, that God will chastise the degenerate, and that the cycle will begin again, working its way towards a new Golden Age— the *Krita Yuga*.

When should we anticipate ruin and chastisement? This seems a non-trivial question, and much thought has gone into answering it. You can, for example, find a closely reasoned explanation of why the Kali Yuga will end in 2025 in Bibhu Dev Misra's article on Graham Hancock's website. If we think our prospects already look grim, Mr. Misra says, then just wait for 2026: "*According to the Yuga Cycle doctrine, the transitional periods between Yugas are always associated with a worldwide collapse of civilizations and severe environmental catastrophes, which wipe out virtually every trace of any human civilization.*"[11]

The Kami settlement boasts a water point built by an NGO—the pipe enclosed in a neat concrete column, its tap missing. Water cascades into the concrete basin beneath, flooding over the brim and saturating the path for the next quarter of a mile.

"These people are stupid," says Palden. "Like cows."

"Cows are holy" I say.

"I am Buddhist, suh!" he protests. "We may eat them sometimes. When they fall off a mountain," he adds, laughing.

The Kami, who know a thing or two about our age of iniquity, eye us balefully from their porches. One of them is the spitting image of my long-dead grandmother Nea, whom I now remember mostly as a foul-mouthed, abusive drunkard.

—·—

Both Mandana and Tess were alcoholics; like Nea, they drank in part from despair. I have come to hate drunkenness in anyone close to me, even though I understand depression better than I once did.

The seeds of this distaste were first sown in the spring of 1962; I was staying with my grandparents during the Walhampton Easter holidays. My grandfather Louis was away for the night, doing the rounds of West Country sports shops with his patented fishing flies and bamboo rods. Nea, as I would discover, fell apart without him.

Late that afternoon I ran into the kitchen in search of something to eat. Nea was sitting at the kitchen table with a glass and a bottle of Harveys Cream Sherry. She looked up at me with fishy eyes.

Children immediately sense any trace of abnormality in the adults who patrol their world. My breathing slowed; I tried to walk soundlessly into the larder.

"Just getting a biscuit, Nea," I said cheerfully, snatching up a couple and making to leave the room.

"You stupid little boy," she muttered. "Singing in your room like that. What a racket. You don't think, do you? You are selfish."

"What do you mean?" I said, despite knowing I should be quiet and get out of there.

"Why must I do everything around here? Hmm?"

"Do you want me to help with something?"

She poured herself another, spilling sherry down the side of the glass, then drank some more. She looked at me again, as if she'd forgotten I was there. I stared at this old, ugly woman, with her wattles, her sour mouth and her rheumy eyes.

"What are you doing here?" she asked. "Go on, go upstairs and play with your silly little aeroplanes."

An evening of creeping back down the stairs and listening for noises behind the closed kitchen door: her pacing the creaky floor, her breathing. Wishing it would stop. The sound of glass on glass, a sliding chill in my stomach, as if *I* had been caught doing something abominable.

Late that night I heard snoring, and carefully opened the kitchen door. Nea was sprawled over the table. I felt I should cover her with a blanket; I fetched one from the airing cupboard and laid it over her, terrified lest she wake up.

I went up to bed, and lay wide awake in the cold moonlight, hoping she wouldn't come upstairs. Eventually I slept. In the morning I tiptoed downstairs, smelling bacon. The radio was on.

"There you are," she said, smiling. "Breakfast time." As if nothing had happened. And I knew that I was bound to silence too, in a British version of *omertà*, the honor code of the bandits of Sicily and their Mafia descendants.

Later that morning Louis came back, and I was in big trouble. Before he left, he had put up his old army-issue pup tent for me in the garden. At some point during that endless evening, I had taken my bow and arrows outside and shot the tent full of holes. He couldn't understand how I could do such a thing, and I couldn't explain. This was my first experience of enabling an alcoholic, and of the damage they can do to everyone around them.

Knowing nothing of mental illness, and like all children, lacking much sense that grown-ups were almost as powerless as we were, I found my increasingly erratic grandmother frightening and repellent, and I came to detest her. It never occurred to me to wonder what it was that made her drink, and nor could I understand Louis' endless patience. He seemed, well, pathetic—under her thumb. I would not be so quick to judge him now.

My mother grew up amid the ruins of Nea's alcoholism. On one occasion she had to fetch her from the police station. On another she had to get a neighbor to help Nea climb out of a ditch. She never brought friends home in case she found Nea drunk.

August 29, 2016—Day 10, A ruined village somewhere short of Sahartara, Dolpo District—12,850 feet.

We are camped in a valley below the main trail; imperfect, but it has the two attributes essential to any campsite: running water, and land flat enough to pitch a couple of tents. Both today and yesterday we've been caught short of our destination: we tried to compress three days walking into two, and we're still several hours short of Tarakot, today's destination.

We left Tatopani three days ago, seeking early sunlight above the cold, dark Pelma Khola gorge. We threaded up through a pine forest; I had read ahead and was prepared for a small treasure—a bridge with carved female deities opening their vulvas wide in welcome. For us, no bridge and no wooden vulvas: we were on a different path. Climbing through Pelma, though, we came upon the hamlet that so intrigued Matthiessen on that October day almost half a century ago: a village from a different age, its houses stepped up the hillside like a pueblo, the roof of one the floor of the next, the inhabitants ignoring him.

We found the same flat-roofed stone houses, wooden ladders and bee-hives made of hollowed logs perched on extruding beams; we, though, arrived to laughter, waving and the smiles of three young women in jeans and T-shirts, oiling their hair in the sun. Our two handsome young por-ters, Ngima and Sagar, hammed up the loads in their baskets (less than 20 kg each, in reality), staggering past the houses and groaning.

"*Kosto baliyo, dhãi,*" said one of the girls slowly, feigning indifference and pulling a comb through her hair. "How strong you are, my brother."

"*Eh bahini, timile yesto bãri bokhnã sokchau-ni?*" Sagar replied. "Well, my sister, can you carry *this* load?" implying himself, a well-known line in Nepali flirtation. None of the grandeur or mystery of the Matthiessen description here; this was modern, light, prosaic, the surfaces of two worlds washing into one another.

Soon after this we arrived at a terrifying landslide—much worse than that river of shale near Muna. Seeing it, I took off my earbuds: this was no time for distraction. The scar was only a couple of hundred yards wide, but it must have taken me twenty minutes to cross. I soon hes-itated. Palden and Konzok took over, Palden carrying my day-pack in one hand and holding my left hand with his other, and Konzok pushing at my backside from below. They were laughing at my awkwardness, yet they knew that if I fell, they would go with me, and nothing would stop any of us until we hit the river several hundred feet below. As I shuf-fled forward, averting my eyes from the near-vertical scree below, I was thinking of a passage in *The Snow Leopard* where Matthiessen uses his own terror of heights to practice a form of tantric contemplation, "*forc-ing myself to look over the precipice whenever I can manage it*" [12] as a way to confront the horror of death. No such masochism for me; I concentrated instead on the placement of my feet, observing the texture of the ground beneath each footfall, and how my trainers gripped the wet soil. Palden's warm, relaxed hand helped me balance.

Once across, I was ashamed. As there was no point feigning nonchalance, I asked if they were ever as scared as I'd just been.

"No, suh," said Palden, laughing. Which is what I expected.

Konzok, a more sensitive man, said "This is *dor lãgne* [frightening] for foreigners, and also for Nepalis who are not used to it."

The mules took a longer jungle road, high above the landslide, and would arrive sometime later. We waited; it was hot. I was suddenly tired. I laid my head on my day pack, and my arm over my eyes. I fell asleep, something I rarely do in the daytime. I dreamed, skimming in and out of consciousness. It was dark, noisy. I was copiloting an aircraft—a big old Bristol Beaufighter from the 1940s. The weather was terrible, wind and rain, the grass below us whipped flat under low clouds. This was a training flight; the instructor was next to me, cursing. He was slipping the heavy plane, the control column all the way to the right, the rudder full left, his spare foot jammed under his seat to brace him as he fought the wind down towards the runway, and I was thinking, no, there's no way I can fly this, what am I doing here?

"Lunch is ready, *saheb*," said Sagar, smiling. The storm receded. Time for orange sausages and a glass of warm powdered lemon juice.

We reached Dhule at dusk, after a long final climb. The village sits in a bowl at almost 11,000 feet. Several rough-hewn wooden houses with courtyards, guarded by large, gentle dogs—mastiffs these, but nothing like the frightening beasts Matthiessen and Schaller encountered on the outskirts of Dhorpatan. We set up our tents on flat roofs that also serve as threshing floors.

The air was clear, the stars unlike anything I could remember since my African childhood. Clouds of them, filling the pitch-dark sky. High above us, a bright satellite passed over the face of the universe. Around me, silent people smoking.

—·—

"Just like the Oily Man," I found myself saying the next morning, as I lay in my sleeping bag listening to the others get up. It's a phrase my father used if he suspected me or Mandy of wriggling out of something. Dad was referring to the time he discovered a burglar in his room in Bombay. After Germany's defeat in 1945, he'd been transferred from Hamburg to join Operation Coronet, the second stage of the proposed allied invasion of Japan. He was in transit in Bombay when the Pacific war ended, and while waiting for transport home spent several delightful months overseeing military rail traffic up and down the Malabar Coast ("best job I ever had," he would say). One night in February 1946 he awoke to the crash of breaking china; there was a burglar in his room; the man had knocked a water jug off the chest of drawers he was rifling through. Driven more by instinct than good sense, Dad jumped out of bed and tried to tackle the intruder, naked but for a loincloth—and found himself unable to lay a hand on him: the thief was covered in oil, and was impossibly slippery. He ducked back out of the open window, and disappeared into the night *binā kisi loot ke*—without any swag.

We left Dhule through oak and maple, emerging on high grasslands. To the east gleamed the ice flutes of Putha Hiunchuli, marking the western end of the Dhaulagiri massif: we were skirting the edge of the high Himalaya, moving northwards into the rain-shadow.

This path was also unpleasant. The *Trekking Guide to Upper and Lower Dolpo* talks about *"exposed"* trails in this area, and I am beginning to learn the meaning of this innocuous word. Of this section, Peter Matthiessen wrote:

> *"… we climb quickly to 12,000 feet. The paths around these mountainsides are narrow, there is no room for a misstep, and at this altitude one is quickly out of breath … these mountainsides of shining grass are so precipitous, so devoid of trees, that a stumbler*

might tumble and roll thousands of feet, then drop into the dark where the sun ends, for want of anything to catch hold of.[13]

I walked clumsily, shunning the edges. One false step is one too many, and concentration was vital: twice that day I started listening to music, but stopped after a couple of minutes. Matthiessen here mentions *The Tibetan Book of the Dead,*

> *"a guide for the living, actually, since it teaches that a man's last thoughts will determine the quality of his reincarnation. Therefore, every moment of life is to be lived calmly, mindfully, as if it were the last, to insure that the most is made of the precious human state—the only one in which enlightenment is possible."*[14]

My last thoughts sliding down a mountainside would be the antithesis of calm mindfulness, but at least I remained polite to my team, whose concern both comforted and irritated me.

Our bodies are in some ways quite unsophisticated: differing varieties of peril can evoke much the same physical reaction. The iciness in the pit of my stomach as I negotiate these precarious trails ... it's the same dread feeling I experienced whenever Mandana, and later Tess, would plead with me to buy them alcohol. I would protest, reason with them, all the time knowing I would, in the end, give in: both to head off some despairing flight from the house, and to calm my own rattled mind.

—·—

We stopped too long for lunch, lost the good weather, fell short of our destination and made a makeshift camp on steep grasslands at Phuphal Phedi, at just under 14,000 feet.

This morning, though, we awake with few ill-effects: all but Ngima have slept (he has a pulsing headache and needs Tylenol). The morning cold is intense. For the first time, I put on my boots; my trainers are soaked. Today we will climb the Jang La (*La* = pass, or *"more properly, the deity or keeper of the pass who may or may not let the traveler cross over.*")[15] This is the gateway to Lower Dolpo. The Schaller expedition faced deep October snowfields, the absence of a clear trail and snow-blind porters who ignored instructions to shield their eyes from the fierce glare. In August, though, this pass is much less daunting. We start up one of those steep knife-like ridges, pivoting every few steps from zig to zag, but most of the day lacks drama—just the usual broken paths, slippery pebbles and water spilling across the trail.

We find the notch of the pass at 14,950 feet, crossing over into the southern part of Dolpo District. No views; just chilly mist and clouds. We have crossed a natural frontier. The north-facing hillsides are still green, but with more undergrowth than trees, and more moss than grass. Large screeds of rock.

Naturally, Peter Matthiessen saw a print near here that could have been that of a snow leopard, and George Schaller another that might be from a yeti. Quite apart from said unseen spectators, a whole menagerie of animals and birds seems to have accompanied the intrepid pair over this part of their journey: foxes, blue sheep, pheasants, skinks, lammergeiers, snow cocks, accipitrine hawks. Our wild mammal sightings have been limited to one *pikā* (an engaging gray cousin of the rabbit that resembles a hamster with big ears), a dead rat outside the Kami settlement, and a lammergeier.

I note with satisfaction that Messrs. Matthiessen and Schaller got lost on the Jang La; perhaps they were distracted by the abundance of wildlife. I realize that I am often tired, or watching my feet to make sure I don't fall, and I appreciate that they were more observant and knew where to look—but even so, it's as if a boatload of Potemkin animals had been tipped out for them as they traveled, like the cut cabbages that civil servants planted along the Pokhara road whenever the late King Birendra took his annual drive to his summer palace.

It is forty-three years since they came this way, and wildlife apart, the world we are walking through today looks substantially the same as it did then—but that is no longer true of most of the middle hills.

I arrived in Nepal in June 1974, six months after Peter Matthiessen and George Schaller returned to Kathmandu from Dolpo. In those days, only three motorable roads connected the Terai with the hills, and only one went north to Tibet. As they had for hundreds of years, everyone walked, and almost everything was carried: on the backs of people, mules, yaks, and even (in Humla, in the far west) sheep and goats.

By the mid-'70s, as I have mentioned, the average hill family owned insufficient land to feed themselves, their effective yields often reduced by obligations to local moneylenders. In the fallow winter season, whole families would travel the footpaths to find temporary work on construction sites down in the Terai, or across the border in Bihar or Uttar Pradesh. Along the way the poorest would sleep on the trailside, sometimes in small open-sided shelters [*pāti*] built by the philanthropic, others in village houses.

In every hill settlement I visited, at least one house would take in travelers; you would ask *"Bhās kahā paincha?"*—where is the night available? And you would eat with the family in their dark kitchen, and sleep on a straw mat on their porch. Among my sparse belongings I would carry a plastic container of DDT, which I would sprinkle liberally into my sleeping bag liner; in the morning I would tip out a host of insects—fleas, bedbugs, tiny scarlet cockroaches, all dead. When I tell people this, they flinch, since DDT is now largely banned as carcinogenic—but I am comforted by the work of the Centers for Disease Control and Prevention, which informed us in 2016 of a bizarre experiment whereby adults given 35-mg doses of DDT daily for eighteen months suffered no ill effects.[16]

Walking through a landscape bears no relation to driving it, and this was part of the uniqueness of those days. Instead of remote road-rage, polite greetings and questions about the route. No reliable maps existed, nor did you think to carry one.

"*Phidim pugnalai kati lāgchha*?" you would ask; how far is it to Phidim?

Answers varied wildly, and often came in *kos*—a measure that has no equivalent in English, as it combines both distance and time.[17] In principle, a *kos* is 2.25 miles, about an hour's walk in hilly country for the moderately fit: but your respondent would assess your walking potential before answering. If he thought you would take two hours to walk that far, he would say "*dui kos, hajur*"—two *kos*.

When you walk, you can never shut the world out—not even with today's noise-canceling earbuds. Nature predominates; you cannot suppress its inflections, its interactions with the things we carry, or the things we build. Once in the early 1990s I walked up the Karnali River near Chisopani to inspect a bridge the World Bank was financing—the second-longest suspension bridge on earth at that time. As I wound around the riverbank, suddenly, there in the distance stood a steel tower in the shape of an H, soaring almost 500 feet above the jungle gorge, a sharp shock against the dull green jungle. I remember thinking how it must have been to walk on pilgrimage across the Salisbury Downs in medieval England: cresting a hill, you would catch sight of the extreme, disproportionate spire of Salisbury cathedral, so different in scale and texture from the insistent natural world.

But that Nepal is disappearing, and we are walking the last of it. In the better-off, more populated central and eastern regions, jeep tracks scrawl across the hillsides, connecting almost every village. These makeshift roads cut across the old footpaths; the stone-platformed *chautarā* with their peepul and banyan trees languish, neglected, beneath thick ribbons of red dust. The fine veins of a walking society have been severed. Nepalis drive now, like the rest of us.

5

THE HOOPOE

August 31, 2016—Day 12, Tarakot, Dolpo District—7,950 feet.

A day of rest. It's warm here; we are camped on a flat roof above the Thulo [big] Beri River. I've washed several pairs of socks. I'm recharging my Kindle and my iPad, and leaning back against a wall among strings of pink hemp. It's overcast; the sun is reluctant. We are in a valley, steep sided, with the comforting roar of a river below us. Arriving yesterday afternoon, we passed down through the modern village of Sahartara, stopping in a hot, fly-infested pasture for lunch, then moving on until we found this place.

Tarakot lies behind us, across ripe maize and open-panicle rice fields, a mile or so west of this house. Clustered up the side of a promontory.

Tarakot translates as "distant fortress," a name deriving from the eighteenth century and its days as one of the new Gorkha state's armed frontier camps. It was built over the ruins of the former *dzong*, or castle, of the Tibetan mini-kingdom of Tichurong, a local power that rose and then receded on the back of the musk trade. Musk is used as a base oil by perfume makers and as an additive in Tibetan magical pharmacy; it is extracted from the scent gland of the musk deer, a creature the size of a beagle with canines like the tusks of a warthog. This elegant creature has been hunted out of existence, and the political frontier has moved north; what remains is a poor and purposeless village—one of the filthiest places I've seen. Dark, decrepit stone hovels are built on platforms of ancient rubbish; a town foundering in trash. You can smell Tarakot from here when the wind gusts in over the valley floor—a sweet, fetid aroma of shit and vegetables.

As we came through the village yesterday, we met a teenage boy in a tight shirt and torn jeans, the fringes of his long brown hair dyed a disastrous peroxide. By then I was angry; we had failed for the past hour to find a decent campsite. I was about to mutter something unpleasant to Palden when I heard the boy stutter as he pointed us onto the right path.

I kept silent. A few minutes earlier I'd been asked by a little girl for a pen and I'd said *"paisā deu* [give me money]," countering her demand with an irritable one of my own. The girl looked at me thoughtfully. *"Kun paisā*? [what money?]" she said. "We don't have money. But *kuhiré* always have pens."

Kuhiré means "misty"—i.e. a white man. It's mildly offensive.

The house we are staying on is owned by a Magar woman in her fifties. We are by no means the first trekking group to come here—the door has a small sign in English telling us this is a "Lodg." There are daughters, but no husband; and as I sit with this landlady, drinking tea, she tells me he was a policeman, and that he died seven years ago in a fall.

"Kahā?" I ask without thinking, "Where?"

"Up there," she says, pointing to a steep hill behind the house. "I found him," she continues, tipping her chin towards the back of the house. "His body was broken." She smiles at me, as if to tell me that such things can just happen. My mood dims, and my throat thickens.

Just before he reached Tarakot, Peter Matthiessen wrote

"In the clearness of this Himalayan air, mountains draw near, and in such splendor, tears come quietly to my eyes and cool on my sunburned cheeks... all this feeling is astonishing: not so long ago I could say truthfully that I had not shed a tear in twenty years."[1]

I have shed quite a few tears in recent years, but this trip has done little to clear my heart of a lifetime of incrustation. Boarding school taught me to swallow my feelings, but the unexpected will sometimes prise me open. The poignancy of this woman's experience unlocks something, and a few minutes later I find myself talking to Palden, of all people, about Tess.

I was asking about his family, and he then said "Where is your daughter?"

I often invent something innocuous when asked about her, but today I tell him that she is dead, that she died almost six years ago. And I begin to cry, which I don't often do any more. I also tell him her mother died too, two years ago, and that my trip to Dolpo is in memory of them. He is saddened, kindly, and embarrassed—as people almost always are.

In the evening the wind dies back, and the grasses on the canyon walls glow in the fading light. We eat before darkness, and I sit out on the lip of the roof, my legs dangling. The air is cool, thick. At some great distance, thunder reverberates.

—·—

Perhaps it was that glimpse of the Caspian from the airplane two weeks ago, and now the thunder: there was thunder over the sea that day in 1991. We were visiting Mandana's parents in Iran. Mandana and Tess had preceded me, from Tehran to Nur, on the southern shore of the Caspian; we would all stay with Mandana's uncle, Dr. Fotouhi, the local country doctor. I was being taken there by Afshar, my father-in-law's driver.

At Babolsar, Afshar turned off the main road and ran the car up to the beach to show me the shoreline. The waves were gray-green and forbidding. Nearby, unfinished concrete beach houses with rusted steel rods poking from flat roofs, awaiting the next floor. No women or children here, just a few unshaven men in black trousers and creased white shirts. We carried on and soon reached Dr. Fotouhi's house, past a tall iron gate and into a walled orange orchard. Tess ran to the car, a blur in a bathing suit. From below the window, she passed up a plastic bucket and spade. "Let's go to the beach, Papa."

And so we did, Tess pulling me past my host, his wife Shahin and my wife, me opening my hands in a gesture of helplessness, them laughing.

"You must make sandcastles," Tess said. And then, "I have a new cat."

"You do?"

"Yes, and he eats tadpoles. Shahin-*joon* and I found him in the garden. His paw was hurt, and I cried so much she let me keep him."

I sat on the sand, splashing in a tidal pool and messing about with my plastic spade. As always, I felt a certain powerlessness in the presence of this beautiful child.

"It might be hard to take him home with us, darling," I tried.

"I know that, Papa," she said, to my relief. "Shahin-*joon* will look after him. And if he gets run over or someting, he will have had some *very* nice days." She had thought it all through.

I treasured these moments, but they also frustrated me. I spent a lot of time with my daughter, reading to her, playing—but I would often feel detached and uneasy, and I never felt fully engaged. Why? What was the matter with me? Why this restlessness? She adored me. She often said what was in my mind. When the world intruded and we had to go and get things done, I felt bereft—but also unburdened. And this made me feel a fraud, some replicant copying the gestures of a real person.

That day the wind blew and we persisted, and in an hour we'd built a big wall of sand with many towers. We raced the tide and watched in glee as it demolished our fortress: the thrill of destruction. The sea was bottle-green, the waves loud and trashy.

"I'm too old to marry you, Papa," she said. I was both sad, and thankful; this had been a sore subject between Mandana and me.

"Who will you marry, then, my darling?"

"Someone who will love me and potect me," she said. "Like you, but more hamsom."

"Just remember, he must also be your best friend too. Someone you can have lots of fun with. Like your Mama and me."

She turned her enormous deep brown eyes on me, flecked with the foam of the sea behind me.

"Well, all I know is you squirts fight a lot," she said.

I was shocked. Was that what she saw?

"And *you* are my bestest friend anyway so I don't need another one."

**September 1, 2016—Day 13, Laina Odar,
Dolpo District—10,795 feet.**

We are camped behind a low stone wall next to the Tarap River, and a hoopoe has been scampering on the ground among the thorn brush. Matthiessen saw this bird several times, and I find a reference to its *"harlequin feathers"*[2] as he was crossing the Jaljala Pass. He had smiled, recalling a sighting in Umbria, and I smile too, more for the hoopoe's comedic appearance than for any place it might have in Sufi mythology (as the *"messenger of the world invisible,"* per Sufi poet Farad ud-Din Attar's *The Conference of the Birds*).[3] This hoopoe is salmon-pink and very tame, cocking his head and looking at me with button eyes, his extravagant fanned crest tipped black and white. I am recalling the cold-eyed hoopoe in Hieronymus Bosch's *Garden of Earthly Delights*, sitting among *that* conference of birds, next to the mallard and the kingfisher, watching hordes of naked humans circling a shallow pool like pale, intoxicated minnows. Some think Bosch was a Cathar, a Christian heretic who believed that the devil created this world of flesh, trapping the souls of angels in endless cycles of frantic reincarnation: his painting is crazed, manic, devoid of peace and privacy.

This morning we paid off Hem Bahadur and Ram Somebody and said goodbye to our tired Indian mules, replacing them with some motley local creatures and a single young wrangler, Kedar Roka. The new mules didn't match and were buzzing with flies; they did not look promising. And yet they have surprised me by leaving us far behind. We had all become impatient of Hem Bahadur's handsome show ponies, their heroic looks belying a flatlander's distaste for climbing.

This morning we also part ways with Peter Matthiessen and George Schaller for the next several days, much to my annoyance. Annoyance with myself, I should say—I didn't scrutinize the itinerary carefully enough before agreeing to it. Matthiessen went west from Tarakot to the district center at Dunai, then north up the Suli Gat River to Phoksundo Lake, and from there on up to Shey Gompa, the Crystal Monastery. We are doing a reverse version of his route, looping out to the east. We will reconnect with his route at Saldang, tracking it backwards from there to Shey.

At first, I have no energy at all. The trail is easy enough, a gentle uphill climb along the eastern bank of the Tarap to the bazaar town of Khanigaun. My legs are tired, though, and my lassitude is such that I think for a moment of calling the whole journey off and going back to Kathmandu.

Khanigaun is split by a suspension bridge that crosses the Tarap Khola. Today is market day, and the narrow cliff-side streets of this wooden settlement are stuffed with women in their best clothes, bright lungis and plaid turbans, gold pendants in their noses and ears. We stop at a check post, where my permit to enter Upper Dolpo is examined by two young policemen. A permit isn't needed until we reach Saldang, still far from here, but they are curious. No wonder—these permits cost a fortune: $500 for an initial ten days, and $50 per day thereafter; police constables are paid the equivalent of $130 per month. The cost of the permit, I am happy to say, is designed to control tourist numbers. Fewer than 150 visitors get into Upper Dolpo each year, according to Palden.

The police are dark-skinned and Aryan-featured, with neat mustaches; they are from the Terai, far to our south. I speak to them in Nepali and their surliness disappears.

"*Khatarā chha,*" says one of them. "It's dangerous. Be careful up there. A person died."

"Two," says the other.

"How?" I ask.

"Fell. A woman. French."

Konzok is beside me and he is shaking his head in distaste, tut-tutting. As we cross the bridge, I ask him what happened.

"*Ekdam narāmro,*" he says. "It was awful. From my family—*kakako srimatiko kanchha bhai* [my uncle's wife's youngest brother]."

It happened about a month ago. There was a group of French trekkers (many of those who visit Dolpo seem to be French). They were coming back down the valley from Doh Tarap, the village we'll reach in three days. A young woman in her twenties had developed debilitating dysentery, and could no longer walk. She rode a mule on the easier parts of the trail, but some sections are too perilous for this, so Konzok's relative Pemba said he would carry her. It's easy to lose your footing when you are carrying 120 pounds of deadweight low on your back. They were crossing an old landslide when he slipped. There was nothing to grab onto—just a steep slope of loose pebbles and dry soil that pitched them over a cliff into the river, some 300 feet below.

"Pemba's body, it was white like a fish, they said. They burned him down by the river. They never found the girl."

We eat lunch on the other side of the river. I am extremely thirsty, and drink a whole tea kettle of warm orange juice. As we stand up to leave, I realize I was dehydrated, and this is why I feel so weak—not because of my age or my heart. Idiot.

The path climbs, steep and broken, up the western side of the Tarap canyon, and yes, I am indeed feeling better. This trail has some alarming moments, though my *Trekking Guide to Upper and Lower Dolpo* gives no inkling of what we are encountering. "*This unexplored valley hardly sees any trekkers but its mysteries must be well worth the effort,*" it says.[4]

Must be? Didn't the writer come here? What fucking mysteries? In some places the trail is no more than a couple of feet wide, with a mighty drop to the right; there are recent landslides, also steep, saturated and mobile; there are pitches cut through the rock of cliff-faces where you have to bend low to avoid snagging your backpack (these are described as "*well-engineered steps*" by my bloodless guidebook).[5]

There is more hand-holding, more bum-pushing by my companions, and much cursing by me—at the road builders, at the authors of this deceitful tract, at the Dolpo-pa for choosing to live in such an absurd, inaccessible place. My anger helps channel my fear, though, and I can even laugh at myself as we cross some of the more enervating sections.

Here at our campsite, decompressing now, I spy two langurs across the river. They are lolling among dwarf cedars, on an eroded hillside riddled with natural caves. I retrieve my binoculars, and watch them watching me. They have magnificent white ruffs around mean black faces, ruffs that blend into soft gray body hair so smooth and even that it looks synthetic. Still watching them, I wash my face and feet in the river—violent, cold, milky. Red bark chips litter the shoreline. The monkeys stare on, inscrutable.

We have set up camp near a Sherpa tea tent, dirty white canvas pitched around a tall metal chimney and wood stove. Tonight Konzok will share their hearth and will cook for us inside. I think of joining them, but I am enjoying the solitude of my own tent. I'm far away from here, reading Constantine Pleshakov's book, *The Tsar's Last Armada*, about the Battle of Tsushima—where in 1905 Admiral Heihachiro Togo's fleet annihilated Tsar Alexander's Pacific Squadron. It was one of those episodes that military historians call "tectonic": unexpected, and consequential. Many such upheavals involve the overturning of smug racist assumptions—like the conquests of Constantinople in 1453 and Singapore in 1942, or the battle of Dien Bien Phu in 1954.

"Another gigantic ironclad, the Oslyabya, was sinking. The bat-
tleship was listing to port more and more. Several hundred sail-
ors crowded on her starboard side, hesitating between diving or
staying for a few more minutes. Some of them were completely
naked. Suddenly, the Oslyabya started capsizing. Her glossy bot-
tom emerged from the sea like the skin "of an enormous sea mon-
ster". Knowing that if they waited longer, the terrifying maelstrom
would suck them under, the Oslyabya crew were ready to jump
into the sea. But they could not dive, for the keel was barring the
way. So they slid downward, some on their stomachs, others bal-
ancing on their feet, others head over heels. Many of them were
hitting the keel and breaking their bones. Those who were already
in the water were crushed by frantic, yelling peers. The Japanese
kept firing on the drowning mob."[6]

The images of shocked nakedness—the men, the rolling ship—stay
with me as the aura of light fades around my tent. I am thinking, too, of
Konzok's dead cousin in the river, of the naked humans in Hieronymus
Bosch's garden, of the precarious trail ahead.

I'm also thinking of the last time I saw Mandana, in her casket in
the funeral home. Her fine oval face, now blackened and pinched. She
had lain dead in her bathroom for a week. Although long separated, we
would speak every few days—but then she wasn't picking up, which was
so unlike her. After a few days I called Paul; he'd also been unable to
reach her. I was in Lebanon, so it was Paul who went round to her flat in
London, then had the police break the door down.

I stood in that windowless room with its yellow chintz curtains and
faint smell of formaldehyde, trying to see in this dead face my wife of
over thirty years. I touched her forehead. A deep, utter coldness. Then
I heard my sister opening the door, and I turned and hurried out with
her—I didn't want her to remember Mandana this way.

There is a passage in *The Snow Leopard* that always brings that day
back. Matthiessen is writing about the great eleventh-century teacher

and ascetic Milarepa, who lived in the Tibetan border regions north of Kathmandu. One day Milarepa returned to his home village to find it destroyed by earthquake. He came upon his mother's desiccated corpse in the ruins of her house. Instead of shrinking from the horror he felt, he remembered how his guru, Lama Marpa, had taught him *"to embrace all that he most fears or finds repugnant, the better to realize that everything in the Universe, being inseparably related, is therefore holy."*[7] Milarepa created a headrest from his mother's bones and lay on this for seven days *"in a deep, clear state of samadhi,"*[8] making his peace with decay, dissolution, and death. This extreme form of tantric meditation, *"often performed while sitting on a corpse or in the graveyard in the dark of night, is known as chöd."*[9]

The lives of Himalayan saints and mediums abound with this kind of savage purpose.

September 6, 2016—Day 18, Dho Tarap, Dolpo District—13,395 feet.

Five days have passed. It's evening. I'm still weak, but I am recovering.

Diarrhea crept up on me as we approached this settlement on September 3, requiring two sudden asides in the brush. Fortunately we had planned to rest here, as on the following day I peppered the toilet at least a dozen times—and twice didn't make it that far. Yesterday morning I abandoned the gut-friendly herbal remedies Sarah's German doctor friend in Mali gave her, and went for the hard stuff—500 mg of azithromycin each day for three days, along with Imodium (which does to your intestines exactly what it suggests).

This is our third day here, and my companions are clearly relieved that their income source will be able to walk again tomorrow.

Dho Tarap is a village of perhaps thirty flat-roofed houses, hunched over a confluence of shallow streams. Together they have no more than fifteen acres of irrigated arable, the only such land we have seen since

Tarakot. The fields are yellow with barley, but a cold, high harvest can only provide a few weeks of grain for the village. It has always been thus, and since their earliest settlement these people have made their living mainly from their livestock, and from participating in the great trans-Himalayan salt-for-grain trade (salt from frigid Tibet, once the floor of the Tethys Ocean; grain from the temperate hills and lowlands of the Ganges Basin).

The people here are all Tibetan; only Konzok can make himself understood. Most seem well-off, but their lives remain uncertain. Until the Red Army arrived in Tibet in 1950, the Tarapis eked out a living mainly through livestock sales, grazing their yaks, sheep and goats on either side of the border and basing their movements on the prevailing winds, temperatures and conditions of different pastures.

As the border hardened and then closed in the 1960s, they found themselves shut out of the best winter grazing land. Yaks now had to be taken south, where the much lower elevations didn't agree with them. These creatures are marvelous at altitude, with their thick coats, huge lungs, oxygen-guzzling blood, generous subcutaneous fat deposits and absence of sweat glands—but all these attributes conspire to overheat them when daytime temperatures exceed 60°F. Fortunately for the Tarapis, the collapse of their livestock economy was offset by a slice of geopolitical good fortune: if they lived within thirty kilometers of the border, China still allowed them to cross for trading purposes, and there they could buy cheap rice. This was in fact recycled Nepali rice, complete with a hefty socialist subsidy. Thus the Tarapis became ambassadors of a diplomatic strategy that reverse-engineered the grain exchanges of the past. Over time, border trade diversified, and we have seen several yak and mule trains carrying beer, instant noodles and plastic shoes along with the rice sacks.

A couple of motorcycles roam the streets and the dikes bordering the fields. The Tarapis, like all Nepalis I have ever met, look forward to the advent of a motorable road. The newer pitches of the trail we have just come over foreshadow this with widened platforms cut into the rock.

A road from Upper Dolpo to Dunai: the prospect would have horrified Peter Matthiessen and George Schaller. Me too; I find myself filled with possessive regret, even though I doubt I will ever come here again. There is more than a hint of condescension in such feelings. Here are we, avatars of global overconsumption, wishing these villagers would moderate their material ambitions so this *"last enclave of pure Tibetan culture"*[10] can be preserved for our leisure moments.

—·—

It took us two days to reach Doh Tarap from Laina Odar, most of it through the same nasty Tarap canyon. The first of these, from Laina to Nawarpani, was short but brutish, with half of the six hours spent on treacherous trails—Palden took pleasure in pointing out the old footpath, which looked even worse. Once again, he and Konzok took my pack, and then my hand, showing their customary patience and good humor. I focused on my boots and on the ground I was stepping on, emptying my mind of all thought and blurring out the precipices. I could hear the river far below, a sound that stayed with me long after we passed through the canyon.

Matthiessen writes *"Tibetans say that obstacles in a hard journey, such as hailstones, wind, and unrelenting rains, are the work of demons, anxious to test the sincerity of the pilgrims and eliminate the fainthearted among them."*[11] A sincerity test presumes that the pilgrim can turn back. For me, the prospect of retracing those pathways is unthinkable; far better to continue into unknown territory, protected by my lack of imagination. I find myself wishing this was over—but that doesn't mean I'm prepared to go back. Just too frightening, and too embarrassing, after all those texts to my friends and family.

Nawarpani is a weedy stone-walled corral and a couple of tents, where the trail ducks down to the river and flattens out at 11,680 feet. Here we saw Blue Sheep, the *bharal*, for the first time—fourteen of them, balanced for a while on the near-vertical inclines above us, then picking their way after a ram with enormous scimitar-like horns. I drank a cup of smoky Tibetan tea in one of the tents (the probable cause of my intestinal anarchy) and watched a young mother caring for her three children, cooking, serving *chhyãng* and chatting with a couple of flirtatious traders. All so capably, and in such squalor. One of her children was about three, and his goofy gestures reminded me of Alex. I thought of my grandson with sadness, of all the time I spent with him when he was tiny, and of how that intimate bond is now fraying.

And I thought, too, of the day my own child was born, in Georgetown Hospital in Washington, DC, and of the reluctance with which she entered the world.

Due to placental insufficiency, Mandana had needed a C-section; I was allowed to sit beside her during the procedure. A screen was set up so she couldn't see what was happening, but I was positioned so I could watch the operation in an overhead mirror. I had doubted I could look, but the indirect, flattened screen image provided sufficient separation. I remember Mandana's distended belly, painted yellow with iodine, the sudden angry cut, the speed at which deep red blood spilled from the wound, and the invasive gloves—and there was Tess, bloody and creased, drawn out into the bright room. As the nurse held her towards Mandana, she opened one eye and gave a piercing scream—furious at this unseemly invasion of her quiet, watery home.

Later that day I went for dinner to Chit and Oey's house in Capitol Hill; they would become Tess' godparents. I brought with me a surreptitious audio recording I had made on a hidden dictaphone, a recording subsequently lost in one of our many moves. I played it to them. Hearing her first shrill, incandescent cry, their old English mastiff—the calmest of creatures—sat suddenly upright, and began a siren-like wail that continued for several minutes.

He had never done anything like this, nor would he ever again. He had recognized the trauma of her birth far more clearly than any of us.

6

BURNING BUSH

**September 7, 2016–Day 19, Camp by Solun
Khola, Dolpo District–15,345 feet.**

Tired, but content. Today something welcome and unexpected happened, against the emotional grain of this journey.

For the first time, we took a packed lunch: today's walk would be too long for a cooking stop. I was still feeble from three days of illness. After some time we left the barley and the motorcycles behind, and began a long, slow climb to the northeast, towards the first of our five 5,000-meter passes. My boots felt heavy, my thighs stiff.

We halted after a couple of hours. I sat apart from the others, depressed by my weakness. My satnav read 14,300 feet; still 2,000 to go, and steep. May as well eat. I explored the various twists of foil that Konzok had given me. Salt. A boiled egg. What else? A tangerine. What's this? A twisted, yellow roti and some tinned tuna. Very dry.

In a moment of anger I stood up and decided to walk ahead of everyone else: Palden was fighting with his food, so I could escape him. Up then. Count the steps. One, two, three, four. One, two, three, four. One, two, three, four. Keep going. I noticed a gradual easing. I shifted a gear. This was better. Finally some energy.

Above me, singing and banging and bells. A herder and two yaks, clumsy, dusty black creatures—like woolly rhinos. They gurgled angrily, at me it seemed. They were slightly intimidating. The herdsman had gray pigtails and a bright red, filthy dress shirt. And green felt boots with pointed toes. He smelled sweet, of sweat and unwashed everything. He was grinning, his face brown and cracked, his Nepali atrocious. Not far, he said, pointing up, although I could see it still was. Had I eaten? I had. He offered me some *chhurpi*. If I didn't know what this was, I'd have mistaken it for second-hand chewing gum—but that was just the dirt on it. I knew this stuff. It's dried cheese made from buttermilk, hard as a stone, no taste. I gnawed at it and smiled back; I was still full of antibiotics. He slithered on down, accompanied by clouds of dust. Like Charlie Brown's friend Pig-Pen.

I watched him go. The others were far below me. I was standing on a sloping meadow, looking back south to a broad range of mountains. My map told me the big ones were Putha Hiunchuli (7,246 meters, or 23,770 feet) and Churen Himal (7,286 meters, or 23,905 feet). As far as I could tell, that was. To my left, to the west, numberless brown sugar-colored hills flecked with snow drifts. The wind dropped; a sudden silence. I folded my map away and sat. For once, I stopped doing anything. The constant chatter in my mind ceased.

The beauty of this rough place overwhelmed me. Nothing comfortable about it; nothing familiar—but here it was. Here I was; really here. Something shifted, and out of nowhere this whole trip seemed worthwhile. I'd done little other than walk badly and grumble for three weeks, but now it felt right. It was good; it was very good. I did the right thing in coming here after all.

But it was bitterly cold, so I got up and pressed on; I wanted to see the view from the top. I remembered how I always walk much better from the front, with no one on my heels. I kicked on, determined not to let anyone catch me.

What if I *had* given up, though? In a small way, I can see, I am carrying the hopes of others—of at least some of those I am texting my progress to. On a much grander scale, this is what athletes do, footballers and cricketers and Olympians. There's an obligation to continue.

The Choila La came after several false crests; you could tell by the cutting wind and the mess of prayer flag strips and stones. I was at 5,050 meters, or 16,570 feet. It was truly desolate. I wasn't sure which way I was facing or what I was looking at, but I was transported.

Now I understood why great religious revelations arrive in such places: mountain, desert, wilderness. The private intoxication you get from physical hardship and isolation; the illusion of possessing a landscape empty of all others. I could imagine God speaking to me here. Telling me—me personally—that I was special, that I had only to exercise that power we all possess. A few stunted juniper bushes edged the pathway; if I looked at them long enough they might burst into flames. I could almost hear the rustle of a dark angel's wings, up there behind my shoulder in the twisting wind.

Brief moments of ecstasy are all that are granted to the sane, the normal, the conventional among us; and this one duly passed. It left a warm hand on me, though, making today exceptional.

By this pass, we have entered the eastern marches of Inner Dolpo. Tomorrow we will reach Tinje. We've a long way to go, but I am finally up for it.

—·—

"(Inner) Dolpo lies at the same latitude as Cairo, but there the similarity ends. It may well appear as inhospitable a land as any human beings could choose to settle in. It lies across no route from anywhere to anywhere else," writes David Snellgrove, in *Four Lamas of Dolpo.*[1]

The region we will traverse contains some of the highest villages in the world—all of the main settlements are above 11,000 feet—and is cut off from the rest of Nepal by snow-bound passes from December to May. Snellgrove likens the geography to a horseshoe pointing southeast, edged by mountains, and with three main valleys scored northwest to southeast across it. Shey, the most westerly, which is barren, then Namkhong and Bantshang, in which most of the Dolpo-pa live, in settlements clustered along the rivers or on hills above them. The headwaters of the Karnali River drain westwards, out of the open heel of the horseshoe and down towards the former Kingdom of Jumla. The whole area measures some seventy miles heel to toe, and up to forty miles across.

I haven't found any confident estimates of the population of Inner Dolpo, but a guesstimate of around five thousand in the summers seems reasonable. With the exception of those small irrigated parcels adjacent to the rivers, the land is largely uncultivable: too cold, too dry. Dolpo lies north of the Great Himalayan ranges of Dhaulagiri and Kanjiroba, in the monsoon shadow, and receives well under twenty inches of rain each year; in Darbang, where we started our walk, you would expect five times that amount. The mountains dividing Inner Dolpo from Tibet are less formidable, and can be crossed throughout a normal winter; thus, until recently, the Dolpo-pa enjoyed easier access to their Tibetan cousins than to their Hindu countrymen immediately south of them. The Tibet-side north-facing Himalayan slopes, moreover, offered superior winter pasture for the Dolpo-pa's yaks. As Kenneth Bauer explains in *High Frontiers: Dolpo and the Changing World of Himalayan Pastoralists*, north-facing slopes are less exposed to the sun, and hold more snow during the winter. This protects both soil and plants, and results in better vegetation.

The Dolpo-pa are Tibetan in origin, and are believed to have settled here well over a thousand years ago. As we saw in Doh Tarap, they grow some of their food in the short summer seasons—barley, buckwheat, millet, mustard, radishes—but they rely heavily on trading, and rather less on their livestock. Dolpo may once have been on *"no route from anywhere to anywhere,"* but the Dolpo-pa changed that: for hundreds of years they have catered adroitly to the food cravings of both Tibetans and Nepalis. In the book on Dolpo that she and her husband Éric Valli published in 1986, *Dolpo: Hidden Land of the Himalayas*, Diane Summers describes how the Dolpo-pa used to perform feats of food multiplication that Jesus himself would have admired: "*By first trading one measure of barley for two of salt in Tibet, the Dolpo-pa profit in the Rong-pa [lowlander] villages by receiving eight measures of maize, wheat or barley for two measures of salt, a net gain of seven measures.*"[2]

Peter Matthiessen might have come to Inner Dolpo to find a pristine, unaltered society—but timelessness is something quite absent from the lives of the Dolpo-pa. For them, the past seventy years has been a period of wrenching change. When China invaded Tibet, the nomadic *drokpa* [herders] who once pastured Dolpo's livestock for them in winter were resettled, and by the early 1960s the border was closed to transborder pasturing. China then took over the salt trade, reducing the Dolpo-pa's margins; and in time, new Indian sources of cheap, iodized salt destroyed this business altogether.

The Dolpo-pa have ridden an economic roller coaster. In the turbulent 1950s, animals starved, herds were culled, and many family incomes collapsed: those living close enough to the border to benefit from China's subsidized Nepali rice exports were the exception. Many were impoverished. Some found work as laborers on construction projects, a common default for the displaced and the destitute in Nepal; some resettled in India and were lost to their communities; others began to sell wool and woven garments to the Hindus. Those with access to nearby rangelands could pasture their animals locally in winter, but others had to take their herds south, competing with local livestock on land enclosed by the national community forestry program in the 1980s.

Globalization has brought "development" to Dolpo: the first government land cadastre, the establishment of primary schools, various halfhearted efforts to deliver health and veterinary services. The 1990s also brought post-*Snow Leopard* tourist groups, abuzz with urbanized guides, cool gear and cash—and the first of the NGOs that sought to develop Dolpo, or preserve its cultural and natural heritage, or both, or something. Now, in 2016, mobile phones and TVs are common, motorable roads are spreading and many families decamp to Kathmandu each winter. Dolpo may still lie at some distant periphery, but a competing consumerist religion has arrived. Even a decade ago, Kenneth Bauer wrote of the *"deep lacuna between those who once traveled with the herds to Tibet and a younger generation that aspires to different opportunities, work, and lifestyles."*[3]

September 9, 2016—Day 21, between the Panjyang and Polte Rivers near Tinje, or Tingkhyu, Dolpo District—13,607 feet.

A vivid dream of Tess. A long ramble through an old house, similar to my father's home in Norfolk. At one point we are running through rooms strewn with Christmas wrapping paper. Then we are in another house, staying with friends, and I wake up to find her missing from her bed. I get up and look for her; she's asleep in a bath, naked, and I put a towel over her and wonder how I can best pick her up. But then we are sitting across a wooden kitchen table, and I'm asking her what it's like where she is now. Are you alright, I say? I tell her, this is what parents always need to know, wherever their child is; we never stop worrying. Her expression is sad, and it's hard for me to hear, but it seems that being her is still difficult. She wants to stay with me, but she has to go back that evening; I say I'll come with her, but we both know this is forbidden.

Today we are relaxing on a flattish pasture between two streams that meet just south of the village. This is how we have planned the journey: three or four days of walking, and then a day of rest so bodies can heal.

To my annoyance, two white trekkers have arrived, and are also resting here—out of sight, fortunately. I am told they are Swiss. I fear they are on the same trail as us, up through Shimen and Saldang to Shey Gompa.

—·—

The walk here yesterday was easy, about six hours of relatively flat paths along a wide, stony watercourse, the Panjyang Khola, with much crossing and re-crossing of its braided streams. Some tents, the odd yak, a few herds of goats. Palden and I stopped in one of these; he drank tea, I declined it. A raw, drying hock of sheep was hung on the wall of the tent; the owner—a lama—shaved pieces from it and added them to the Chinese pot noodles that Palden had bought from him.

"*Shyaw*," said the lama, pointing over his shoulder with his paring knife.

"*Chituwa*," said Palden, translating for me. A leopard. Really? Surely a fox, or a jackal perhaps? This didn't look like snow leopard country to me—too open, too many people. No; the sheep was killed several miles away—"*U māthi* [up there]." Several sheep and goats had been slaughtered, he said—you see, the leopard goes mad when it finds livestock inside a corral. It kills them all, it can't stop. Then it eats to bursting and staggers away. Like a drunkard. That's when the villagers catch them and beat them to death. Though not these days, he quickly added.

As we walked on, the sun flickered behind dirty clouds. A stiff wind blew into our faces. Across the river, some ancient stone walls, hard to differentiate from the rocky hillside and thornbush. If you looked carefully, though, you could trace a long curtain wall interspersed with broken watchtowers. Set on higher ground above these outer fortifications stood a ruined keep, one massive wall and two corner columns still standing—like the last teeth in a dead jawbone. Those outer walls measure a mile or more in circumference, but there was no sign of the town they once enclosed: just a shambles of rocks scattered across the brush and the dust. As if to emphasize the dissolution of a once-thriving settlement, these ruins lie beneath a range of sharply eroded hills, gray rock serrated like the spines of sea dragons—hills as extreme as the mountains of Mordor.

I've been looking for some word on this place, but my map shows nothing, nor is it mentioned in the *Trekking Guide to Upper and Lower*

Dolpo, or *Trekking in the Nepal Himalaya.* No one we have spoken to in Tinje knows anything about it; it must have been abandoned a very long time ago. I am guessing that this once extensive armed town pre-dated Tinje, which has displaced it at the head of the valley; in more belligerent days it would have been easier to defend, or better placed to extort taxes from caravans passing by on their way to Tibet, Mustang or Nepal. Now it is wholly forgotten.

As we entered Tinje, we crossed a flattish area with marker stones along its edges. "Airport, suh," said Palden. Apparently so: in *High Frontiers*, Kenneth Bauer tells how a Swiss engineer was sent to the Panzang Valley to build an airstrip for the Khampa resistance fighters—an airstrip that was never used.

— · —

We've been washing clothes and catching some of this narrow valley's brief sun. I've been lying in my tent, reading Ian Rankin's *Even Dogs in the Wild*, rubbing shoulders with Detective Inspector John Rebus again. Cigarette smoke, the dark and damp of Edinburgh, India Pale Ale and chicken curry, '60s rock and roll. I seem to have tweaked my left hamstring, and my right knee feels slightly unstable.

On a steep hillside to our west is a herd of Blue Sheep. They are several miles away, and even my excellent Nikon binoculars are unable to capture much detail. After an hour or so they move around the mountain, and are lost from sight.

I have also been watching Kedar deal with his mules. They were, as usual, staked out in a line last night, a rope around their left foreleg, shitting and farting prodigiously through the hours of darkness. This morning Kedar gave them a nosebag of maize kernels (huge anticipatory snuffling). On a travel day, Kedar will then dance around them, putting on their saddles while dodging the back legs of Bukhé (No. 1 mule) and Kancha (No. 2 deputy mule), who try to kick the living daylights out of him—much to his amusement (*kãncha* is Nepali for youngest son, while *kãnchi* is youngest daughter: children are commonly referred to in order of birth, and confusion reigns whenever different families congregate). No saddles today, though—Kedar walks off with the mules to look for pasture, Bukhé leading, Kancha at the back, nipping at the other four ragamuffins strung out between them.

By evening I'm persuaded out of my tent by Palden, and we walk between tall, rammed earth houses towards the village boarding school. It's several hundred feet up the side of something the map calls the Baikher Danda. We encounter the wretched Swiss, who are coming back down—apparently the school is where you take the tourists. I pass them with a curt "*Namaste*", avoiding eye contact. They remind me once again that I am just another trekker, with my guide, my faux-European food, my silly electronics and my toilet tent.

The school itself lies above the willows and poplars of the village on a windswept slope, a three-sided array of bare classrooms overlooking the plain we walked across yesterday. The kids have finished for the day and are in dormitory huts behind the school, but the principal is still around. He greets us. His name is Tenzin, which marks him as a Sherpa or a Tibetan.

"*Hajur kahãko?*" asks Palden. "Where does mister come from?" Tenzin is from Kalimpong, in the eastern hills of India, near Darjeeling.

If he is fed up with casual visitors, he disguises it well and offers us tea and some Chinese glucose biscuits. It's late afternoon, and the temperature is falling; we sit inside his office, leaving the door open to catch the light. Behind him in a locked glass case are several hardback books in English; through the amber blaze of the sun's reflection I can see *Harry Potter and the Goblet of Fire* and Neil Gaiman's *American Gods*. There is a box marked "Donations for Indigent Students" in English, no doubt aimed at the likes of me. The courtyard is dust, bare of all grass; a tattered Nepali flag cracks above us on a steel pole. The tea is black, but sweet; sugar, I am thinking, must be scarce here.

Tenzin has been in Tinje for ten years. His wife and kids are home in India; he sees them each winter—the school, along with most other government services, shuts down for six months in mid-November, and the teachers and many of the students leave the area before the passes become blocked. They return with the spring, in mid-May.

"It must be difficult, being away from your family for so long," I say. Tenzin's English is excellent, so I forgo Nepali.

"I am a teacher," he says, looking at me with apparent amusement. "This is a common thing in my country. In Nepal too." And it is; I remember how most government health workers in the eastern hills lived far from home.

"I was working in Dubai seven years, suh," says Palden, keen to better this. "I did not come home during contract."

"Not once?"

"Too expensive!" he laughed.

"Your wife?" I ask. "And Sagar and Ngima?"

"Babies then, big boys now," he says. "You see them. Strong boys. Wife strong then too. But sick now," he adds.

"She is sick?" I am conscious that I haven't asked after her at all.

"Yes, suh. Too much sick. *Pet dukhne.* Stomach ache. And pressure."

"Blood pressure?"

"Maybe," he says vaguely; he's repeating something he doesn't understand. "Doctor not making her better." He looks down, his face suddenly tired and disconsolate.

A couple of youngsters in brown shorts and ragged pullovers have been squatting outside the dark office; the light is all but lost as Tenzin offers to guide us back to the campsite. I leave the expected donation in the box and we follow him. The boys come too; my torch beam picks out their delicate bare feet. I stumble after them like an old ox.

"Next month, everyone gone," says Palden. "Kathmandu, Dunai, some go India. Tenzin suh's home is Kalimpong, many Tibetan refugees there.

You know Khampa? Finish now, but once this very good place for them. No government. No one can see them."

He's right. Apart from a few police, the state has almost no footprint up here for half of each year.

"Also good for Maoists," says Tenzin. "Back in the day."

"They came up here?" I ask.

"Sometimes. Not such bad people. If," he adds, "If you gave them food and said nothing. Have you met any?"

"No," I say. "I wasn't in Nepal then. I did meet some Naxalites. In eastern Nepal, in the 1970s. Back in the day." He is nodding. The Naxalites were Maoists too; they foreshadowed Nepal's modern variety.[4]

He stays for some tea; we have milk. Palden presses him on the Khampas, as if he must know something about them.

"General Wangdu was here," says Tenzin. "On his flight to India, I believe. Forty, maybe fifty years ago."

The Khampas are a people of eastern Tibet, but "Khampa" is now used as a generic for the armed Tibetan resistance that fought the Chinese, first in Tibet and later from Nepal. Kenneth Bauer and Mikel Dunham (*Buddha's Warriors*) describe how the CIA trained and supplied the Khampas. Although the recruits believed they would one day liberate their country, the US held no such illusions: for them, the guerrillas' purpose was to provide useful intelligence on a Cold War enemy. During the 1960s, up to 4,000 Khampas operated from bases in Mustang District, carrying out cross-border raids, destroying bridges and trucks, shooting Chinese soldiers and gathering odds and ends of information for the CIA.

In time, US and Indian strategic priorities shifted, and their interest in the Khampas waned. In the build-up to President Richard Nixon's 1972 visit to China, one of Beijing's two preconditions for reestablishing diplomatic relations was that the US cut off all assistance to the Tibetan resistance (the more important one was that the US no longer recognize Taiwan as an independent country). The Khampas were then abandoned, to the considerable anguish of the CIA officers who had trained, supported and come to love them—a repetitive theme in recent American small-war history.

The new King Birendra of Nepal was also keen to build bridges with China, and at the end of 1973 demanded that the rebels lay down their arms. In the spring of 1974, a large contingent of Royal Nepalese Army soldiers marched up the Kali Gandaki Valley to Jomosom, at the southern end of Mustang District, while the Chinese sent a force across the northern border. Most Khampas were disarmed; Khampa leader Gyatso Wangdu fled west towards India, with thirty companions and a stack of confidential documents; he planned to carry on fighting. He reached the Tinkar pass on the western Nepali border, where the Nepalese army ambushed and killed him.

It is a story that ended poorly, in betrayal, defeat, and disillusion. The majority of the survivors of this movement have died; a few live on with their families around Pokhara, or in Kathmandu.

"Most people have forgotten the Khampas, but not in these parts," says Tenzin. "Here they are remembered." Smiling, he adds "For some time still, at least."

7

YOUTH

**September 10, 2016—Day 22, Shimen,
Dolpo District—13,025 feet.**

An easy four-hour walk up the Panjyang Khola, arriving here in the early afternoon. From afar, this is a bucolic village of several dozen flat-roofed houses set among terraces of potato greens and ripening barley. In an otherwise treeless landscape the settlement is framed by an abundance of tulip-shaped willows. We find an enclosed courtyard on the edge of the settlement, which we share with a herd of goats; at this time of year all animals are shut away from the ripening crops. The village is dusty but otherwise clean; there is no trash here, although a couple of motorbikes are prowling on the rough path, anticipating the arrival of the motor road from Tinje—and with it, the consumption, rubbish, and diesel that roads will always bring.

Our planned route had us walking north up the Panjyang Khola before circling over the Muri La, our second five-thousand-meter pass, and rejoining the Panjyang on the way to Yangser Gompa. From there, the trail goes south down the Nagaon Khola to Saldang—in all, a three-day trip. From the villagers in Tinje we learn that the initial stretch has been seriously damaged by landslides.

"Quite dangerous, suh," says Palden, looking at me hopefully.

"Ah," I say. And "Is there another way?"

There is: due west to Saldang, a two-day walk with two smaller four-thousand-meter passes. I have wanted to see Yangser Gompa, reputedly the oldest monastery in Dolpo, and I have wanted to cross all five of those five-thousand-meter passes.

But perhaps not *that* much, I decide, thinking about precipices and sliding mud.

My crew are good sports, but they are clearly relieved. Thus we pass up the opportunity of visiting the most spectacular monastery in Dolpo, a collection of temples set three hundred feet above the Panjyang behind a long rock wall—founded by a lama with the self-effacing name of Religious Protector Glorious and Good, at the turn of the seventeenth century.

After that, my day feels light and free. Now I can envision the end of the trip: this decision means we are halfway, and I am still standing.

I take a quick walk around the village in celebration. Shimen's houses have a comical look to them: each with a Beatle-like fringe of dry, stacked brushwood around the roof-line, and carved wooden windows set into its walls like tiny eyes.

I sit out in the cool sun on a camp chair; Konzok has made some tea. I must be getting old, I tell him, you see how happy I am we aren't going up that valley? He laughs politely, demurring, insisting I am a very strong walker.

I lean back and close my eyes, letting the weak afternoon sun play over my face, and I'm remembering one of my favorite conversations with Tess. We were in an Olive Garden restaurant in Manassas; I was visiting from Sydney, where I'd been stationed by the World Bank—I'd chosen to go Australia (as opposed to Pakistan, which was also on offer) so she could join me: there was an excellent acting school near the house I'd rented. But then she'd become pregnant with Alex.

"Listen, Dad," she said, "You know we don't talk about feelings and all that stuff. That's because I know you understand me, right? I just want to say—I, well, I'll always take care of you. When you're old, I mean.

You've taken care of me all of my life. You'll come and live with me. Don't laugh. I'm serious."

I see the Swiss coming, so I keep my head down; they pass further up into the village, but my dreamy mood is broken. I sit on the wall and try to read, but I am too curious an object to be wholly ignored. Dogs pace below, growling vaguely up at me. A goat eats part of my tent's flysheet. Urchins come and ask for dot-pens.

In the early evening, a sharp smell of resin, accompanied by the dull thock of wooden clappers and by low, energetic grumbling. I look up; a caravan of a dozen yaks is passing through the village, ten-foot sawn timbers lashed to their saddles.

"Who are they?" I ask Palden. "Where did they get all that wood?"

"I no know, suh—I will ask them."

The exchange is brief; a quick round of pleasantries, then a palm in the air, telling Palden to mind his own business.

"Not legal, suh," he says, looking upset. "They taking to Terai, I think. Bad people."

"I see."

We eat early. Konzok asks me why I first came to Nepal. He knows it was a long time ago. Was there no work in my country?

"I had a job here," I said, sensing where this conversation might go.

"With medical trust," said Palden. "Big man."

"Not so big," I said, and left it there.

I graduated in 1973, the year before I first went to Nepal. I flew out to Hong Kong to visit my father over the Christmas holidays, and stayed with him for a while. By mid-year I felt I should go back to England, though I had little idea of what I would do when I got there. Before university I'd worked in Thailand for Voluntary Service Overseas, teaching English in a Thai high school. There I'd met Mary, a Peace Corps volunteer in a nearby town. Come and visit me here in Kathmandu, she now wrote. Why not, I thought? I knew nothing of Nepal. I'd stop off briefly in Thailand and Nepal, and head on from there.

June 1974. My Thai Airways flight landed over brilliant rice fields and burnt brick houses. The air was fresh, cool after the humidity of Bangkok. This was my first time in the Indian subcontinent, and as my rickshaw pedaled through the streets, the difference was palpable; the harmonious colors and relative tranquility of Thailand were replaced by something more basic: dark wood, mud, filth, pluperfect reds and yellows, cacophony, bulls wandering through the traffic, shrines everywhere. I had crossed an invisible border, like the Wallace Line that runs between Bali and Lombok and separates the ecozones of Asia and Australasia. After a few hours I felt more at home than ever I had in Thailand—or, indeed, England.

A couple of weeks turned into a couple of years, most of it working for the Britain-Nepal Medical Trust in the eastern hills.

Kathmandu in the early 1970s was a city with few cars, more bicycles and many pedestrians. Most men wore traditional cotton trousers and tunics, the women saris. Kathmandu and the nearby cities of Patan and Bhaktapur still resembled medieval towns in Tuscany, built in this case of timber and brick, their old royal centers crammed with tenements and temples, at ease with the fertile world surrounding them: crops left to dry on rush mats spread out on the roads, vegetable gardens lacing the cities, goats wandering into government office compounds, monkeys and fruit bats in the trees, Hindu pilgrims sleeping in open-sided wayside shelters, coils of steaming human shit dotting the street in the misty autumn mornings. That extraordinary harmony is long gone, overwhelmed by concrete, asphalt, a flood-tide of immigrants from the countryside; by vehicles, by smoke, by dust, by diesel fumes. In 1974, once the monsoon clouds cleared in September, the great ice-peaks of the Langtang range tracked you as you rode around the city; now they are veiled, occluded, almost invisible.

Mary told me of a British anti-tuberculosis medical trust in the east of the country that sometimes took on volunteers. I wrote to them. Dr. Nick Maurice, the director, replied, trying to put me off in a kindly English way. The trust might be able to fit me in as a junior vaccinator, he said, but only if I could speak Nepali: and I should understand that the trust couldn't finance my language training, nor indeed could it pay me, insure me, or fly me down to its headquarters in Biratnagar. This all sounded perfectly reasonable to me, so I taught English each morning to pay for Nepali classes each evening, and four months later showed up in Biratnagar—to Dr. Maurice's evident annoyance.

That same evening I was given an hour's training: I checked out the contents of my portable vaccination kit, learned how to light the kerosene burner and sterilize needles, and practiced intradermal vaccinations on a tangerine. Thus skilled, I boarded a plane the next morning for Tumlingtar, a small island of red earth far up the Arun River, one of the few places in the eastern hills flat enough for an airstrip.

After an hour of climbing out of the Tumlingtar Valley in the midday sun, trying to keep pace with my new boss, Frank Guthrie, I was vomiting beside the trail. Our destination was four hard days' walk away. By the second day, my feet were blistered and my back raw from the friction of my ill-designed rucksack. The pace was relentless. Occasionally it rained, and as we passed over the Milke Danda, there was snow. I fell several times; it was a filthy, depressing journey. Frank showed no sympathy, and my anger at this sustained me. On the final day, after an hour spent binding up my feet, I took something I'd discovered in the drug cupboard in BNMT—a 5-mg tab of Dexedrine (dextroamphetamine, more conventionally used to treat ADHD and narcolepsy). The effect was electric. I flew up the last hill, a vicious climb of several thousand feet, arriving in triumph an hour before Frank. A lesson was learned, and never relinquished—though the choice of chemical accelerants has been refined over the years.

In Taplejung I joined a TB vaccination team of seven—six Nepalis and a nineteen-year-old Scot. Taplejung district slots into the top right-hand corner of Nepal, bordered on the north and east by the Kanchenjunga massif and on the west and south by the Tamur and Mewa Rivers. Most of the district's population of around 60,000 lived above the banks of these rivers in a rucked arc of foothills, their tiny fields nourished by glacial streams and by the monsoon, which drags water vapor out of the Bay of Bengal and deposits it on these south-facing mountainsides. The campaign operated in monthly cycles. In week 1, a team member would walk down to Biratnagar and return with freeze-dried BCG (Bacille Calmette-Guérin) vaccine, which only remained viable for four weeks after removal from a refrigerator. That same week, an advance party would scout the next bloc of villages, arranging vaccination times and locations. In weeks 2–4, we would fan out in four teams of two, sometimes vaccinating at several sites each day. In this way we aimed to cover the district in about six months.

It was an accidental, itinerant life, and all of us were dislocated in some way. There was Prabhu Ram (PR), tall, intense, a Brahmin from the Terai; he sometimes introduced himself as "Prabhu Ram Acharya, anti-national element," referring to the year he had served in prison for membership in a banned political party. Competitive politics had been outlawed since 1960, when King Mahendra dismissed parliament and took over the state. In place of democracy, which he characterized as a corrupt foreign implant, Mahendra introduced the party-less Panchayat system of "guided" democracy, under which loyal individuals stood for election to village, district and national councils. PR had joined the clandestine Communist Party of Nepal as a student. He'd been arrested in the aftermath of the Jhapa Naxalite Movement in 1972.

The others were all Janajati, or hill tribespeople, and all wanderers: two Rai, both ex-British Gurkhas, abroad for many years; a Tamang from a distant landless family who'd been a porter all his adult life, and two Limbu—both called Drona Bir, and labelled DB 1 and DB 2. DB 1, Drona

Bir Subba, was the son of wealthy farmers, an older, warm-hearted man. He had finished high school and left the family farm ("soft hands, *saheb*"), but had not found consistent work; he'd filled his time with gambling and evading debt-collectors: a life of sudden departures, false names, and occasional beatings.

Drona Bir 2, last name Libang [archer], was ill-favored, snub-nosed, with a bilious complexion and constant sniffle; he too was indigent, but lacked Drona Bir 1's good humor. A year or so or previously he had disappeared for three days and then returned with a wife, Radhika. It was an unhappy marriage, their dissatisfaction played out in front of all of us: she had become the team's cook. Grumbling, cursing and the occasional thrown utensil preceded most of our meals. One night, as she sat chopping vegetables, she told me part of her story. She was a Chetrini, of a higher caste than DB 2; marriage with a Limbu, particularly this sour-faced character, was out of the question in her social circle. Even he had not been keen—"but I burned for him," she said with pride. She would not give up, threatening to take poison. In the end he relented—provided she eloped with some precious gold earrings her father had given her. She took them; he pawned them. "I was mad," she told me. "Love is a disease, like *kustharog* [leprosy]. But now I am cured"—and she laughed, turning her arms over as if to prove it to me. Her situation was wretched, but her sense of irony remained strong. She was an awful cook, unused to the kitchen, and she would often draw a finger across her own throat when she served us.

Radhika added a small element of grace to this male household, moving without sound through our cluttered dormitory. Her family had forgiven her, it seemed, but they insisted she bring back the price of the stolen gold. "That husband, he wants to send me home," she said, smiling, "but he needs 1,000 rupees. Imagine! How many months of salary is that, Nigel-*saheb*? You do the accounts, correct? Three months? Eh! Drona Bir is a moron [*lãtha*], he cannot save it. So you must all suffer my food. What about your country, what happens in *Belait*?"

"It's . . . it's similar," I said, not wanting her to feel hard done by. I sometimes wonder what became of this spirited woman, in a society where an act of emotional lunacy like hers was close to irretrievable.

In Taplejung, over the winter of 1974, I learned to walk decently enough; and though I missed the company of my own people, I began to love much about that beautiful, hard place. Few Europeans had been to the more remote areas of the district, yet the people of those isolated villages treated me, for the most part, without suspicion and with many small acts of unnecessary kindness.

Typically, we would arrive at a settlement after a long day's work, often exhausted. We asked where a visitor could stay—there was always somewhere, usually those homes with the most food. After washing at a nearby water tap or stream, we would be invited into the house, where we ate cross-legged on the floor by an open hearth, the family watching. The diet was simple, but people discover variety in whatever they have: I was told there were twenty-six types of rice in southern Taplejung, and that villagers could identify most of them by taste. After eating, we would sit out on the open porch, and neighbors would come by to take a look at us. There we would smoke, drink tea (in a Brahmin household) or *rakshi* (aquavit) pretty much everywhere else, and listen to stories of wandering livestock, fallen women, money-lenders and compound interest. The evening light would disappear, the guests would flick their cigarette butts away, sniff and slope off home.

Those were days I still cherish; the light lingers on. I was often lonely, uncomfortable, dissatisfied with my restless inattention to much around me. I knew that grasping after awareness was self-defeating, but I was incapable of patience. Still in my early twenties, I was intensely conscious of time, of aging and of lost opportunities—ridiculous as that may seem. I stand now at the opposite gate of a healthy adult life, and those frustrations have largely flaked away. What remains are the lasting gifts: comradeship, purpose, great physical satisfaction, exultation even; at times I felt I could outwalk anyone. And, though I could not see it then, this was a time of emotional freedom—a time between the years I needed my parents, and those when my wife and my child would depend on me.

In *Youth*, Joseph Conrad's sometime alter ego Marlow tells a group of former sea-dogs the story of the fire on the collier *Judea*. "'*I remember my youth and the feeling that will never come back any more,*'" he is saying;

> *"'the feeling that I could last for ever, outlast the sea, the earth and all men ... and, tell me, wasn't that the best time, that time when we were young at sea; young and had nothing, on the sea that gives nothing, except hard knocks—and sometimes a chance to feel your strength—that only—what you all regret?'*
>
> *And we all nodded at him; the man of finance, the man of accounts, the man of law, we all nodded at him over the polished table that like a still sheet of brown water reflected our faces, lined, wrinkled; our faces marked by toil, by deceptions, by success, by love; our weary eyes looking still, looking always, looking anxiously for something out of life, that while it is expected is already gone—has passed unseen, in a sigh, in a flash—together with the youth, with the strength, with the romance of illusions."*[1]

Not so big a job, perhaps—but worth a lot to me.

September 12, 2016—Day 24, Saldang, Dolpo District—12,925 feet.

Yesterday was long and hard; almost eight hours. We began with a short scramble down to the Panjyang Khola (12,900 feet), followed by a steep hour and a half of unstable, slippery dust and hand-holding before the trail leveled out and climbed steadily to the first pass, the Shimen La, at 14,400 feet. From there we descended into a barren, echoing valley, tracked by vultures and a lammergeier that wheeled over us and screamed like an irritated child—suddenly it was Apache country, complete with rocky mesas hanging over the trail. Perfect for those lithe Hollywood cowboys of the 1960s, firing their Winchester repeaters with one manicured hand. Instead of mustangs and hypomanic Indians, though, flocks of sheep and goats maneuvered on the pinched trails above us.

"Suh!" Konzok was pointing up. The sheep had dislodged a shower of stones. Some settled in puffs of dust; others, the size of apples, jumped down with purpose. Years of facing fast bowling as a schoolboy now paid off. I kept still and watched each bouncing rock. If one stayed on track, I would flinch one way or the other and it would fly on past my shins, or my head.

All the way down from the Shimen La to the Koran Khola, twelve hundred feet of the most irritating trail we had yet encountered—all loose fist-sized pebbles, attesting to a millennium of clumsy goats. It was impossible to stay upright, and I fell three times, the last painfully. Perhaps because there was no real danger, the usual solicitousness of my companions disappeared in uncontrolled giggling. Despite my fury, I too dissolved into hopeless, bruised laughter.

We ate lunch; the Swiss passed us, waving. I glared at them over my rotis. But we encountered them again a short while later in Khoma, a village where they had decided to stay for the night.

"Nice place," said Palden. It was. "Perhaps suh is tired?" Suh was not.

I carried on pointedly, ahead of the others. At this end of the valley, bare rock gives way to sand hills and tufts of sage grass. I clambered through several deep gullies and reached several false summits, always a demoralizing process. At last, prayer flags up ahead—the Khoma La, 15,125 feet. Just then I noticed a number of burrows; what could this be? I took off my pack and sat down. In time a head poked up, then two, then a dozen. Groundhogs! Or, more accurately, Himalayan marmots. Several of them stepped into the open, and raised themselves on their hind legs. They appraised me in silence, their whiskers flickering. I got up; they stayed where they were. As I left them behind, they began to chatter—a trilling, bird-like whistle (which is why groundhogs are sometimes called whistlepigs, or *siffleux* by French Canadians). This sibilance was soon extinguished by the baffles of wind colliding at the pass.

From the pass, long views east and north, far into Tibet. A land, even in late summer, of dust, ice and desolation. I waited for the others in the lee of a gale. We left prayer flags on the stone cairn and worked our way down to the Nagaon Khola, some fifteen hundred feet below, as Saldang came into view on the far bank. The path was steep, treacherous, once again slick with powdery gray dust and pebbles. To slip here was unthinkable: nothing would break your fall for several hundred feet. Again, the automatic offer of hands from Palden and Konzok, despite the danger to them.

In one of her texts, Sarah had said how much she admired their courage, but felt sure they knew I would not fall. I lack such certainty, but perhaps she is right. Peter Matthiessen had also admired the dedication of his Sherpa team:

> *"As GS says, 'When the going gets rough, they take care of you first.' Yet their dignity is unassailable, for the service is rendered for its own sake—it is the task, not the employer, that is served. As Buddhists, they know that the doing matters more than the attainment or the reward, that to serve in this selfless way is to be free. Because of their belief in karma—the principle of cause and effect that permeates Buddhism and Hinduism (and Christianity, for that matter—as ye sow, so shall ye reap)—they are tolerant and unjudgmental, knowing that bad acts will receive their due without the intervention of the victim."*[2]

The grace and humor of my companions stand out too. But the karmic awareness that Matthiessen describes? All of these men are from poor backgrounds, with no comfortable choices of the kind he, I, or many of my Nepali friends have enjoyed. These are men who, in the United States, might work as linemen for a power company, as firefighters, miners, or as soldiers. Life-limiting, risky occupations that pay the bills when times are good. And yes, it is the task that is served—it isn't their attachment to me that makes them run these risks. But this is good work if you are poor, and they have accepted what comes with it; there is nothing particularly transcendental about that sort of contract. Nor are they curious about what I am doing here: the leisure and the money behind such a trip are as alien to their lives as the purchase of a Matisse is to mine.

As for me, I have been given the chance to learn from this alarming experience, though I am not yet able to turn my full face towards what frightens me so. To walk on such "exposed" trails forces you to concentrate on each footfall, each foot placement. I turn off any music when the trail feels edgy. I take off my sunglasses—even they add a dangerous scintilla of distance. I am not frozen by fear, but I carry enough foreboding to make me focus. There is a balance, between attention and forgetfulness, as I steer my mind away from images of disaster. I will never find the patience or the desire to meditate—but perhaps this is a close cousin.

Tomorrow we rejoin Peter Matthiessen's pilgrimage route at Namgung: when he left George Schaller at Shey Gompa to return home, he walked east out of Dolpo to Namgung, before heading south down the Namkhong River (what Konzok calls the Nagaon Khola). We will follow his trip in reverse until we join him again at Ringmo Gaun, on Lake Phoksundo.

We have spent today resting in Saldang. These are our eighth and ninth consecutive nights close to or above 13,000 feet.

We are camped next to Saldang Gompa. I go and sit on a buckwheat terrace above the monastery. A scatter of two- and three-story *chorten* ascend the hill, white circles on their walls like astonished eyes. The sun is evasive; the sky, a mass of oily clouds against a receding gray sea of hillsides. The red walls and gold ornaments of the *gompa* catch like flame as the sun passes, their bright, confident colors signaling human warmth across this harsh desert landscape.

By afternoon we are bored enough to go and visit the local school. Soft, distracted chanting seeps out from the classrooms; I find myself directed into the school office. I sit on a mattress in the dark, crowded by textbooks. There is a stove built into the corner and a couple of disused computer screens stacked on top of a bookshelf. Three teachers are in the room, a man and two women, all young, and all from Dolpo. Am I keeping them from class? No, no, they say, laughing—this is "tiffin recess."

The school takes children from age five, and offers eight years of instruction: Kindergarten 1 and 2, then Grades 1–6. There are seventy kids at present, many of them boarders from outlying villages. As at Tinje, the school is open only six months of the year.

I ask what problems the teachers face. The lack of heating, one says. No medicine for the children, says another. Absenteeism—kids taken out of school to plant and harvest the summer crops. Very few textbooks. Families unable to pay the boarding fees.

"*Hāmro talab pani*," mumbles the man, shy, looking down at a book he was marking. The two women shush him, but seem amused. And? Our salaries, he says, they arrive late, sometimes not at all. What then? He shrugs. You have to go and get it yourself. Where from? From Dunai, Dolpo District headquarters. Five days walk. Each way. And does the education office pay your expenses? Sometimes, yes.

Then Palden enters, and hijacks this deflating conversation. He tells them, as if I have been speaking English, that my Nepali is "delicious." That I'd been a health worker in eastern Nepal. That I understand everything about Nepal. And we are on a sixty-two-day trek—sixty-two days, look you! And how frightened suh is on the steep parts. Very funny, isn't it? Our suh is the best!

Everyone laughs, me too—Palden is so lacking in guile; he is telling them that he too, by leading this strange enterprise, is a man of quality.

On our way out of the school, one of the teachers follows us, leading a small boy by the hand. "Can I speak to you?" she asks, pointing at the boy's skull. It's misshapen, displaced over his right ear. He fell a few years ago, she says, and now he has bad headaches, and problems learning. He needs to see a brain doctor, in Nepalganj down in the Terai, or in Kathmandu, but his family is poor. Can I help? She can bring the boy's mother to see me later, perhaps? And the father? No, he is no use and he is always away.

What can I say? Yes, of course, bring them.

Later, as I sit at the portable table typing my diary on my iPad, the usual crowd of kids gathers. One of them is dressed as a novice, a young monk.

"What is your name?" he ventures.

"My name is *Kuhiré*," I answer. "White man."

"My name is Gyaltsen," says this scamp, leaning in over my shoulder. "I am good at reading English." His face gleams with ingrained dirt.

"You are? Show me then."

The kid is—he starts declaiming loudly from the diary in front of him.

"*The characters of my five companions take shape. Palden, as I had fig-ured some time ago, is a bit of a bl-ow . . . hard and not very smart.*"

"I think that's enough!" I say, gently removing the iPad.

In time, I drift up to the cooking tent to find Palden's son Sagar at the primus stove. Where is Konzok? He's sick, apparently—but he'll be fine by tomorrow, nothing to worry about.

After some dal and paratha, the teacher, the damaged boy and his mother come by. He says nothing, smiling and holding onto his mother's skirt. His name is Chimi Tsewang, the teacher says. He is naughty, but he is clever, he needs help. I am so sorry to give you trouble, but I have to try. It's alright, I say; can they go to Kathmandu? Yes, but it means walking east for a week to Kagbeni, in Mustang District. There is a bus there. OK, I say—I will give them some money to travel to Kathmandu, and to stay there for a while. But he must see a good doctor. I will ask Basant to help us find one. After that, we will see.

"Please, can you give the money direct to this lady?" asks the teacher.

"What do you mean?"

"If you give it to her husband, he will spend it on alcohol," she says.

They walk out of the light of our solar lamp, the shy mother and the dark-faced boy, into the gathering night wind. I doubt they will make the long journey to Kathmandu—it's a lot to ask of a woman who's never been out of Nepal's Tibetan hinterland. A small financial risk, and a necessary expenditure: I would be shaming my crew if I did nothing.

As I settle back in my tent I become aware of a low droning, punctuated by the occasional sniff. Somewhere inside the monastery, Gyaltsen is chanting scripture. He reads, pauses, stumbles occasionally, reads on with little emphasis or pacing. It reminds me so much of Tess; I rummage around for my voice recorder.

Here it is. A weekend afternoon in Oxford, in the autumn of 1992 (I was there on sabbatical).

Tess is nearly eight. We're doing her reading practice. Tess is squirming in the armchair, blinking her eyes furiously at me—like a driver gurning at the oncoming headlights to keep herself awake.

"Okay," I say after a while, "That'll do. Well done." Truthfully, she was struggling. "Why not tell me a story?"

"Alright." Her tone changes. She focuses. "This is the story of Alphonse."

"Alphonse?"

"Yes! And it goes like this. 'When Alphonse went to visit his Uncle Vaseline—'"

"Vaseline?"

"Don't interrupt, Papa. 'When he went to visit his Uncle Vaseline, it was for the very first time, so he wanted to make a good *impression*. But he banged his peg-leg on the doorstep and, um, he cracked his head on the door, so when his uncle opened it he fell flat on the kitchen floor. 'Jesus wept,' he said—"

"Tess, you can't say that."

"You say it all the time. 'Never mind' said his uncle, 'Have a cup of tea.' He sat Alphonse on a very rare, um, *tapestry*. Then Alphonse reached forward and the milk jug tittered on the edge of the table, and with a great crash it fell off and milk splashed all over the tortoise. Alphonse jumped to pick up the pieces, but he slipped on the milk-stain and fell on his bum. Shall I carry on Papa?"

"Of course!"

"Well then. At this point in the proceedings, his aunt arrived from town in a big brass motorcar. Aunt Makeshift—that was her name, believe it or not—Aunt Makeshift was a black magician and turned children into frogs, like they do in Africa. When she came in there was a crash, and her car collapsed like a pack of cards. Her face looked like Doom. Just then another catastrophe happened, the sink fell, fell out from the wall and smashed into *tiny* pieces. Alphonse didn't want to be a frog, so he said, he said 'Thank you for a lovely afternoon Uncle Vaseline,' and ran out of there as fast as his wooden legs could carry him. The End."

"That was brilliant. You should be a writer one day."

"I will be, Papa. Just you wait."

8

NO MOUNTAIN

**September 13, 2016–Day 25, Namgung,
Dolpo District–14,460 feet.**

A day that began very poorly has ended well.

I hardly slept, largely because of a barking dog; in the end, I had to admire the unvarying, mindless pitch of the animal. Today, as a result, has been plagued by the continuous hiss of tinnitus in my left ear—the sort of day I tend to write off in the hope of better sleep and quieter ears tomorrow.

By 7 a.m. we are packed and ready to go. I stroll up to the cooking tent and see distressed faces. Palden says "Konzok not coming."

"What do you mean? "

"Um, I don't know suh."

We switch to Nepali.

"What's going on? Can someone please explain?" I catch sight of Konzok, sitting on a wall, out of earshot, his back to us.

It becomes clear that Konzok wasn't ill last night—he'd shut himself up in his tent after a mighty argument with Palden's son Sagar. Now I remember I'd heard shouting outside my tent before dinner, but I'd paid it no mind. So what's the problem, I ask? Palden looks helpless; he says he isn't sure.

I go and sit on the wall next to Konzok. He won't look me in the eye. His expression is wretched.

"*Maphgarnos, hajur,*" he says, almost moaning, looking at his feet and pulling at the zip on his jacket. "I'm sorry, sir. I can't continue. Yesterday we were in the kitchen tent. I was asking Sagar to clean properly—everything must be clean or we'll get sick. Maybe I was a little strict with him. But he got so angry, so quickly. I told him to stop shouting at me. He said he would hit me if I didn't shut up." Never, he says, in all his years of trekking, never has anyone spoken to him this way. He can't spend another thirty-five days with this boy. He is very sorry, but he is leaving. He will speak to Basant-sir when he can find a radio link. He won't take any pay for this trip.

I believe his account, not least because he admits that he provoked Sagar. "Look," I say, after a while, "we have to deal with this. I need you. I trust you. You are the most important person here. No one else knows these paths."

At this point, Palden has begun to hover. I take him aside and tell him his son must apologize.

"Suh," he says, insisting as usual on English, "I sleeping, did not see this fighting. I don't know what happened."

"Palden, I don't care. This is your team. You must fix it." He looks helpless, caught between his belligerent son and the future of the trip. For a man who seeks to please and placate, this is the worst of leadership tests.

He shuffles off to speak to Sagar, and returns empty. Sagar has told him he has never been bullied and insulted this much in his life.

I speak to Palden and Sagar together. I am angry, and because of this my Nepali fails me; all I manage to convey is my irritation with everyone.

Then Konzok calls Kedar as a witness, and Kedar speaks to me at length. I can't grasp enough of what he is saying to get a proper purchase on his story.

Now everyone is unhappy. They mill about without conviction; I can see they are losing faith in me. Stung by this, I say to Palden, in English, "You have to make peace between them. I am not going anywhere without Konzok—we must all go together. If we have to stay here today to sort it out, fine—but no Konzok, no trip. We go home. And that will be bad for all of you—*all* of you," I emphasize, looking at each of them.

Out of words, I retreat into the building next to the *gompa*, where there is a small Tibetan dispensary. Good God, the Swiss are in there! I exit smartly, walk down below the *gompa* and sit on the edge of a field of barley. The stalks are still green at their base, yellowing at the top and fluffed with full, whiskery ears. I withdraw to my smartphone, bringing up *Plants vs. Zombies 2*. I select my plants to confront the zombies of the Far Future; one of them I pick is the redoubtable Lightning Reed, a favorite of Alex's.

——·——

After about fifteen minutes, Palden comes and tells me it's all OK now. I am surprised. Somehow, against my expectations, he has brokered a truce.

I check with Konzok, and I find he is still prevaricating. I ask him to come for *my* sake, repeating that I need him, and promising to make sure this will be dealt with properly by Basant. Again, unexpectedly, this seems to work. Alright, he says, I will come with you, at least until I can speak to Basant-sir. There is a radio in the police post at Shey Gompa.

We set off, a couple of hours late. The emotions have taken their toll, and we all struggle. This is the Mother of all steep climbs, too—almost two thousand feet of nasty scree paths, up to an unnamed 14,850-foot pass. We had planned to reach Shey today, but none of us wants to walk any further; there is yet another high pass in the way, so after only three hours we stop among the tourist tents in Namgung.

"Everything good now, suh," says Palden, "Konzok happy, Sagar happy." I doubt this, but we should at least make it to Shey together.

The Swiss have preceded us, and in tonight's crowded campsite we find ourselves obliged to set up our tents next to them. I suddenly decide I am being ludicrous, and go over to introduce myself.

"*Entschuldigen Sie, mein Herr, meine Frau,*" I begin.

"Beg pardon?" says the man. "Um—do you speak English?"

And thus begins a warm friendship with Jamie and Carolyn, a charming, inquisitive Canadian couple.

They invite me over for tea. Tea in someone else's tent today sounds preferable to hanging out with my own lugubrious bunch; what's more, their cooking tent is twice as large and has room to relax, as well as space for the cooking stoves.

I apologize for being so unfriendly—but Jamie gets it. "Well, you didn't come here to hang out with a bunch of white guys, did you?"

This campsite is infested with tourists, probably twenty of them, and most of them British. Fortunately they are going the other way. They are Northerners—a fathers-and-sons trip. The dads are younger than me, in their fifties, several carrying beer bellies. They are doubling down on this with cans of Lucky Buddha ("the enlightened beer"), crushing the empties in their large, pink hands as they cheerfully curse the huge pass they have just come over.

My new friends go down the defile to look at a more conventional representation of the faith, the ancient Namgung monastery, taking with them their copy of David Snellgrove's 1961 *Himalayan Pilgrimage.* Somewhat guiltily, I decline their invitation and remain in the warm tent with their guide, Chandra Rai, drinking their tea and eating shortbread biscuits baked by Songkhram the cook. At Namgung, Matthiessen (who of course visited the monastery) was struck at how "*a splendid bronze of Dorje-*Chang *on a platform above the centre of the room seems to vibrate in the dusty light; I keep expecting it to speak, and can hardly turn my back upon it.*"[1] Dorje Chang, a.k.a. Vajradhara in Sanskrit, is the primordial

Buddha for the Kagyupa sect, and is often depicted in deep blue—suffused with awareness.

Around me, my rowdy fellow countrymen are treading a path designed to take them in the opposite direction.

This alcoholic Buddha abuse brings to mind His Holiness Dorje Chang Buddha III, a Californian guru whose website says this of him: *"In the entire history of this world, H.H. Dorje Chang Buddha III is the one of tremendous holiness who has truly manifested the holy quality of selflessness."*[2] According to an April 2015 article in Arts and Entertainment, *"He sold one ink drawing for $16.5 million in a recent auction in NYC. The piece is called 'Ink Lotus,' and the artist's statement is: 'An utter chaos strewn with broken strokes: a peculiar sight, yet wondrously empowered with soul-soothing charm.' The buyer is someone from California who has elected to remain anonymous."*[3]

The same article contains the priceless sentence *"Buddha and his wife bought a $2 million house in Pasadena, and his family also owns homes in Long Island."*[4] To nitpickers like me, this seems a slight deviation from the post-enlightenment lifestyle of Buddha I.

Namgung has long been celebrated. It features in David Snellgrove's *Four Lamas of Dolpo,* in the autobiography of Lama Religious Protector Glorious and Good (who lived from 1536 to 1625, and who founded the great monastery at Yangser Gompa which we wimped out of visiting). To make up some lost ground, I take a look at this section of the book as I drink my tea.

> *"When I was practicing meditation in wild places, I was once at the place called Namgung of Saldang, where there are a lot of streams and places for meditation. I had passed one night there, and at dawn there protruded from under my couch what seemed to be three spear-heads. I was raised on these points and so transported to the summit of the heavens. Looking down, I saw they were three great snakes. Now this was achieved by my religious*

practice, and as these beneficent yet unreal appearances came upon me, I composed a small song beginning 'The yogin who understands appearances as hallucination.' So I awoke in a happy state of mind. Appearances floated vaguely around me, and I looked on everything in this blissful and tranquil state. The day was already breaking."[5]

Perhaps it's the translation, perhaps it's me, but this lama does seem rather too pleased with himself and his dream of tumescent serpents.

Soon I find myself chatting with Chandra Rai, whose English is fluent. Of all things, he is from Shantang, near Dhankuta Bazaar in the east of Nepal.

"Shantang? Really? So you are Atpuriya Rai?"

"How do you know that?"

Not, it turns out, because I am a scholar versed in the tribal arcana of the Rai people, but because I once worked closely with this little-known clan (Atpuriya is a borrow-word—an elision of the Nepali for "eight families"). Chandra is the first college-educated Atpuriya I've met.

—·—

In 1978, I returned to Nepal to administer a Save the Children Fund (UK) project based in Dhankuta, a Newari hill bazaar in the east—the same area I had worked in with the Britain-Nepal Medical Trust. The project's outgoing doctor was David Nabarro (the UK's candidate for the post of Director-General of the World Health Organization as I write this). Our project focused on child nutrition, and many of the malnourished children who came to the SCF clinic were from the nearby Shantang area. Shantang women were distinctive, wearing a particular broadcloth shawl marked by stylized green and red "fishes." Their clan numbered no more than two thousand people, all living in the immediate area. Most Atpuriya family settlements stretched down the southern flanks of the Dhankuta ridge, on poor desiccated maize plots of well under an acre.

In those days, orthodox thinking imputed chronic diarrhea to bad hygiene and misguided cultural practices (like denying water to a child to help "dry it out"). The relationship between poverty and undernourishment, while obvious in itself, was not understood in detail, and health practitioners tended to set economic factors aside in favor of health education—in this case, oral rehydration and feeding practices. This made little impact; the same mothers would come back a few weeks later with the same wretched child, or perhaps another, sometimes far gone, his eyes bulging and vacant, skin slack and pallid, limbs as floppy as a chicken carcass. Our kindly English nurses were driven to anger by these recalcitrant, foolish mothers, but David soon grasped why a disproportionate number of Atpuriya children were so sickly.

In the US, wealth is seen by many as a reward for hard work. The Atpuriya Rai would have laughed at this: for them, wealth was testament to cunning and ruthlessness, and came at their expense. We are the ones who work hard, they would say, not those fat shopkeepers up in the bazaar. Whatever you or I think of this, it is clear that wealth buys time. Those Nepalis who earn little for their labor must work longer hours to survive; being poor means having no leisure to speak of.

With so little land available, only a handful of households could grow enough food for themselves, so the modern Atpuriya spent most of their time cutting and selling firewood, portering, or day-laboring on nearby highway work sites. The pay for such things was pitiful, and both husbands and wives would walk long distances away from home each day to make ends meet. Tiny children were left with young siblings, decrepit grandparents, or even alone. Nepali villages are unsanitary, and intestinal diseases common—but with both parents' income essential, mothers often couldn't afford to stay home to look after sick children.

From the stand of gnarled *bodhi* trees above Shantang, you could look out over a bucolic middle hills landscape: maize terraces, thatched houses, small herds of goats, stone pathways, gullies and the occasional fodder tree. Inside those quiet houses, evil dilemmas played out each day. Shall I carry my sick child with me to the road tomorrow? Shall I stay home? Which child shall I give the milk to: the baby boy who is throwing up everywhere, or the healthy toddler? Decisions like this—decisions with deadly implications—are the true exoticism of Nepal, more alien to most visitors than the mountains and monasteries that bring us and our cameras here.

There is a cruel symmetry to the story of the Atpuriya Rai. Their origin myths tell of a man who traveled from the northern mountains, encountering a woman on her way up from the Indian plains. They met on the hilltop where the *bodhi* platform now stands. The place was pleasing to them, and they to each other. They decided to claim the ridge as their own, and they built a house. But they were harassed by two great forest demons, also a male and a female, shaggy creatures with ears so long that one served as a mattress and the other an eiderdown when they slept. These monsters were fearsome, predatory. In time, the man and woman managed to trap them both in a pit and slew them, burying their bodies where they had fallen. Trees grew over their grave, and were never felled.

Those ancient evergreen oaks, twisted and broken by time, mark out a sacred grove below the crest of the ridge, a grove which no adult male may enter and where women still perform secret ceremonies. This singular tribal memory speaks, to me at least, of how the early Atpuriya dispossessed the former inhabitants of those forests, and of their guilt at so doing; the clue is the fantastic description of the vanquished, whose monstrous appearance and threatening behavior justified their destruction—but a destruction that demands constant expiation. An exaggerated fear of the "other" and retroactive excuses feature in all genocides, from Armenia through central Europe to Rwanda.

This first couple, it is said, had eight sons, and they then created the *āht poriwār*—the eight families. The clan was blessed with abundant forests, which gave them timber, firewood, and leaf compost for their fields. The more children born to a family, the wealthier it became, for each individual could produce a surplus from the woods and the earth. The land of this ridge and several nearby hills was claimed by the clan, and redistributed as families grew or shrank—a system of communal tenure similar to the *kipat* of their Limbu neighbors.

In the late eighteenth century, Newars displaced from the Kathmandu Valley by their Gorkha conquerors came to the ridge and settled on the saddle, a short walk up from the Atpuriya. This site commanded the trading routes of the Arun, the River of Dawn, one of the great trans-Himalayan arteries: the Arun rises in Tibet, rages through the eastern Nepalese hills and dissipates into a wide, slow-flowing floodplain as it joins the Ganges.

The Newar and the Atpuriya coexisted without much friction; at first the Newar lived by trade alone and made no claims on the land. They also brought cloth, money, sesame oil, salt and pepper, and consumer goods like mirrors, pins and bangles to the same long ridge, along with their Hindu and Buddhist feast days. They built a small row of houses, brass workshops and stores. Gradually the Atpuriya began to acquire a taste for this new culture's materials. Having no cash, they sold land to the Newar at rates of exchange reflecting the value they placed on surplus land (not much) and on what they desired (a great deal). By the 1940s, this surplus land was exhausted, but the marriage, death and feasting rituals that the Atpuriya had adopted were costly, and land continued to be sold or mortgaged away beyond all possibility of repayment.

Most Atpuriya families of my generation had become low-wage laborers who farmed part-time, though they still thought of themselves as farmers. It was perhaps five hundred years since the Atpuriya replaced the former inhabitants of Shantang; now they, in their turn, were being dispossessed.

Our capacity for self-pity transcends cultures and generations, and just as the Atpuriya affected to see their ancestors as blameless, so they now saw themselves as the victims of deceit. It was easy to sympathize with these affecting people and their struggles with grasping Newar money lenders, just as it is easy in today's America to feel for the millions of working class families who have been ruined by deindustrialization, and to castigate the globalist elites for the economic policies that shifted manufacturing to Asia. Like many Americans, though, the Atpuriya had become accustomed to living beyond their means, and few were prepared to acknowledge how the desire for what they could no longer afford had hastened the demise of their society.

I ask Chandra how the village has fared in the twenty-five years since I had last been there.

"Some good, some bad. There is drinking water there now. A school. Some families did well from goats and tomatoes. SCF was responsible for that, I think. More Atpuriya are graduating high school, university even; I am not the only one. But not much land is left. Most of the *khet* [rice land] has gone. The *bāri* [dry terraces] are not fertile, and the *sāl* forests are far away now. Shantang is a village without young men—they go to India or to the Gulf. It is still beautiful, but the life is gone from it."

—·—

We are camped on the edge of a valley, overlooking ranges of mountains to the west. It's a clear, cool evening, a few clouds aflame in the setting sun. I have eaten, and I leave our kitchen tent for my own. Many of the campers sit outside in the cold dusk, looking at the mountains—as we trekkers do. As if searching for something we cannot quite define, yet know in our hearts is of great importance.

"*First there is a mountain,*" I say to myself, "*Then there is no mountain, then there is*"—the old Donovan song.[6] I could never grasp what it meant, nor could I ever force myself to work towards understanding this famous Zen Buddhist *koán* [riddle].

Tonight, quite suddenly, I think I can catch something of it.

In Zen, you wrestle with a *koán* to exhaust your intellect, and thereby unlock your intuition. The mountain *koán* has been described as a summary of the Buddhist path: at first, things are seen as solid and substantial; after time, effort and work you are able to grasp their impermanence; and then finally, hopefully, you will see them as they are—composed of mutable particles of dust, like everything else, and thus both real and connected with you, and also transitory. D. T. Suzuki's 1927 *Essays in Zen Buddhism* quotes the ninth-century Chinese master Qingyuan Weixin:

> *"Before a man studies Zen, to him mountains are mountains, and waters are waters; after he gets an insight into the truth of Zen through the instruction of a good master, mountains to him are not mountains, and waters are not waters; but after this when he really attains to the abode of rest, mountains are once more mountains, and waters are waters."*[7]

Tonight, though, I stop my half-hearted logical wrestling and let my mind wander about; perhaps it's my exhaustion after three weeks of walking. Perhaps it's the warmth of this afternoon's conversations.

At first, as a child, you look at a distant mountain and you see it without question or judgment. It is there, and you accept it as part of an emerging world. Like Peter Matthiessen's son Alex at rest in his sandbox, in unison with everything.

Later, as you grow and as the experience of living adheres to you like barnacles to a moving ship, you see such mountains as projections of your own attachments, fears and ambitions—as majestic, perhaps, or frightening; maybe they are soaked with dramatic meaning, or fill you with dread; you may wish to test yourself against them, or ignore them altogether. They are mountains no longer: you have imposed yourself on them, obscuring the simpler understandings of your childhood.

Later still, if you can achieve some degree of distance from the turmoil of your life, you might see them as mountains again; not as the simple facts of a child's accepted world, but as alien, inanimate objects coated in personal meaning, and because they *are* now understood as such, precious to you. You see the mountain and you see yourself, distinct but connected. This is the journey T. S. Eliot is describing in *Little Gidding*:

> *"We shall not cease from exploration*
> *And the end of all our exploring*
> *Will be to arrive where we started*
> *And know the place for the first time."*[8]

But why I am thinking about such stuff, here in a tented camp on a cold hillside in Nepal? And why (apart from the obvious presence of monasteries and reincarnate lamas) did Peter Matthiessen need to come here to create his pilgrimage? How does a context so hard and mundane for those born here create feelings of self-worth among the global travellati?

Kenneth Bauer's book on Dolpo tells an illuminating story about *Himalaya*, Éric Valli's 1999 film about yaks, Tibetans and the salt trade. This "factional" movie was set in Dolpo and was nominated for Best Foreign Film at the 2000 Oscars. Valli and his wife Diane Summers had spent many months traveling in, writing about and photographing Dolpo; this was their attempt to showcase the region's beauty, timelessness and authenticity. Dolpo was also a deliberate metaphor for Tibet. *"What I have tried to show,"* said Valli, *"is the traditional untouched Tibetan culture. It doesn't exist in Tibet anymore ... Dolpo is truly hidden country, guarding the inviolate heart of Tibet"*[9]—echoing Matthiessen's own view of Dolpo as *"the last enclave of pure Tibetan culture."*[10]

But achieving "timelessness", or a place outside history where modernity is held at bay, required not true authenticity, but sleight of hand: all actors had to wear Tibetan clothes given them for the purpose: no jeans, no wristwatches. And no shots of election posters, Wai Wai noodle packets or visiting tourists. The romanticized picture of a Tibetan Shangri-La touched Western audiences: this was the height of the celebrity Free Tibet period, of Tibetan Freedom rock concerts and Martin Scorsese's *Kundun,* a film about the Dalai Lama's early life. It also appealed to Nepali audiences in the capital, who were equally unfamiliar with *"the harsh life of the mountain people and their strange rituals,"* in the words of one local film critic. [11]

Bauer sees this film as *"tied to a global economy of ideas—ideas about civilization and savagery that have a long history in the West and in Western encounters with things non-Western."* [12] Alongside its nobler intentions lies a degree of exploitation, based on a formula that links authenticity to primitivism, hence naïveté, from which comes an unstated, possibly unrecognized right to manipulate. It may be no coincidence that Valli left behind controversy about promises broken—construction of a school and the renovation of various *gompa*—as well as un upsurge in what he himself refers to as the *"tourist invasion."* [13] An invasion inadvertently encouraged a generation earlier by *The Snow Leopard.*

Peter Matthiessen's account of Dolpo was also directed at the alienated readers in his own society—not to those he was writing about. Most of them could not have read, and none could have obtained his book at that time. In this sense, the impassioned nostalgia that *The Snow Leopard* evokes is ironic, a byproduct of the wealth and leisure that Americans have earned from exploiting nature; the same exploitation that so disturbed him.

9

SEVENTY-THREE MOONS

September 15, 2016—Day 27, Shey Gompa, Dolpo District—14,150 feet.

We got here yesterday after a six-hour hike. I had little energy, particularly as I watched Jamie out ahead of me, walking with such ease. We climbed the two thousand or so feet to the Sela La (our second five-thousand-meter pass—5,095 meters, 16,715 feet). A brief pause at the summit cairn; the wind was too fierce to linger. A wide panorama, all dust, smashed slate and bare gray hills—a magnificent, broken world.

On the way down I found Kedar lying on the ground with his arms crossed over his eyes, his mules far ahead of him.

He peered at me between his fingers. "Headache; it's nothing." I gave him some Tylenol, but the remedy for altitude sickness is always to descend. Two hours later he was shaking his head ruefully, as if he'd just woken up.

We arrived off the shoulder of Shey Valley in the early afternoon. Peter Matthiessen and George Schaller reached here from the south, from Lake Phoksundo, on November 1, 1973, crossing the formidable, snow-bound Kang La (or Nagdalo La, 17,550 feet). *Though battered by winds,* writes Schaller, *"I am filled with savage joy. Shey is ours."*[1]

Matthiessen stayed almost three weeks, Schaller five, before heading eastwards to Saldang along the trail we've just come in by, then circling back south and west to Phoksundo and crossing the Kagmara La west towards Jumla.

Below me, some hints of rough pasture in an otherwise barren valley. A huddle of stone and mud buildings—the *gompa*, a half dozen outbuildings, perimeter walls, a field of scattered prayer stones, and a number of square stupas. This is Shey Gompa, the Crystal Monastery, described by David Snellgrove when he first saw it in 1956 as "*quite an impressive collection of red-washed buildings ringed with prayer walls and chötens.*"[2]

The settlement has changed little since then; if anything, it is smaller, as the outlines of several ruined houses attest. The *gompa* is unremarkable: its appeal is in the warmth of its homely red buildings. Unlike the more renowned Dolpo monastery of Samling, further up the Tartang Khola, or Yangser Gompa on the Panjyang, the age of this *gompa* is indeterminate—though it is generally assumed that some sort of lamasery has stood here for more than a thousand years.

Tibetan legend tells of how the famed teacher Guru Rinpoche traveled north from India in the eighth century AD and brought Buddhist *dharma* to the savage sky-and-wind worshippers of the land of *Bhōt* [Tibet], vanquishing their demons and discrediting their sorcerers; yet when the yogi Drutob Senge Yeshe visited the Shey Valley some two hundred years later, he found a people who seemed to have lapsed a bit. To his dismay, they were still revering the spirit of one particular mountain.

That same peak rises above the valley to our west as we descend—a peak I would not have noticed without my books. This is Crystal Mountain, described by Peter Matthiessen as a white pyramid sailing on the sky. George Schaller, like me, saw a different mountain; Crystal Mountain, he wrote, is not impressive; its name is derived from the crystal veins in its flanks, not from its shape.

Schaller tells of how Drutob Senge Yeshe first meditated in a nearby cave, then came out to fight the mountain spirit. This was a heroic age, so he whistled up a flying snow lion. The mountain countered with a horde of flying snakes. The snow lion promptly replicated itself 108 times, the number of beads on a Buddhist rosary, and the number of earthly temptations we must overcome to achieve nirvana. With these reinforcements, Drutob overcame the spirit and encased it in a *"thundering mountain of purest crystal."*[3] Thus was its caged energy put to the service of the *dharma,* harnessing ancient power in the service of a new religion.

After his victory, Drutob enjoined the population to do *kora* around this re-sacralized mountain, somewhat incredibly suggesting that none of his celestial feats could equal in merit one pilgrim's circuit. Each July, on the full moon before the barley harvest, people still gather and walk the ten miles around the mountain. *"By a glacial lake,"* writes George Schaller, *"where the snow lions gamboled in victory, they join hands and dance in a circle to the music of a lute."*[4] Which brings to my mind a more farcical image: Edward Lear's owl and pussycat, dining on mince and slices of quince, dancing by the light of the moon.

In an alternative version of history, the Dolpo-pa seem to have arrived here between the sixth and eighth centuries, perhaps fleeing from the conquering people of Yarlung who established Tibet's first dynasty. That dynasty collapsed in 842 AD, with Dolpo remaining under the authority of the breakaway Purang Kingdom. For the next nine hundred years it was part of Tibet, first under the Purang to the north and then under the Principality of Lo to its west. In the 1600s Lo, the modern-day Mustang, controlled the main north–south trade routes along the Kali Gandaki River.

As something of a backwater, Dolpo never acquired the wealth that accrued to its suzerains. It came to be known more as a *beyul,* one of the hidden Himalayan valleys consecrated by Guru Rinpoche on his eighth-century travels. The image of a hidden paradise, a living Eden, is known to most of us from James Hilton's 1933 novel *Lost Horizon* and Frank Capra's 1937 film of the same name, in which a plane carrying Hugh Conway, a British diplomat, crashes in a valley in the Kunlun Mountains of Tibet. There Conway finds a society in perfect balance, presided over by a beatific lama from the monastery of Shangri-La.

As well as collecting grain and wool taxes from Dolpo, Lo's rulers would come on pilgrimage to Dolpo every year. By the 1700s, Dolpo was also paying tax to a power to its west, the Kingdom of Jumla. In 1789, as the Bastille was stormed in Paris, Lo and Jumla were both conquered by the expanding Gorkha state. Dolpo was politically severed from Tibet, but "Nepal" remained a distant reality. The region was left to its own devices, the inhabitants affected much more by developments in Tibet than by a nominal border cutting across natural geographic and social links with their northern neighbors.

The first Westerners to visit the area arrived in the 1950s—Giuseppe Tucci, a Tibetologist, and Toni Hagen, the Swiss geologist and development specialist. A clip of Hagen's porters skirting Lake Phoksundo can be found today on YouTube.[5] Others like Christoph von Fürer-Haimendorf[6] and David Snellgrove followed in the next decade, as the state made cautious nation-building inroads. The first Nepali-medium primary school was built in southern Dolpo in 1963, and elected Panchayat councils were inaugurated the following year. Matthiessen and Schaller were not that far behind.

—·—

Shey was Matthiessen and Schaller's destination. They write extensively of the weeks spent there, and the two accounts should be read together.

Winter has come, and many villagers have left; the few who remain huddle inside. The landscape is frozen, the passes all but sealed. "*The nights at Shey are rigid, under rigid stars*," writes Matthiessen.[7] "*The blinding snow peaks and the clarion air, the sound of earth and heaven in the silence ....*[8] *There is so much that enchants me in this spare, silent place that I move softly so as not to break a spell."*[9]

They go about their days speaking little, walking with care. Both of these intense, somewhat difficult men work easily around each other, the inevitable frictions of their arduous journey largely dispelled. They spend most of their time in the field, Peter Matthiessen either meditating or helping George Schaller observe the Blue Sheep for signs of the impending rut. There are foxes in the snow, lammergeiers turning slowly overhead, and there are wolves.

In country of breathtaking cold, of wild sheep and quiet predators, a crippled reincarnate lama meditates in a mountain eyrie. There is distant ice thunder, and impossibly hardy birds. *"Storms of Hodgson's mountain finches hurl up the canyon ... I marvel at the energy, at the intense fires that fuel these wisps of feather and bone in an environment where man breathes so laboriously,"* says Schaller.[10] And over everything, the gaze of an invisible snow leopard. *"Of the many mountain spirits at Shey,"* Schaller continues, *"I seek to meet only one ..."*[11]

The Buddhist practitioner is Peter Matthiessen, and he rejoices in their isolation and in the immediacy of their world and, at times, feels truly awake. *"I am returned into myself,"* he continues, in a *"kind of homecoming, to a place of the Sun, West of the Moon—the homegoing that needs no home."*[12]

Yet there is a constant shadow, a foreboding and an unease in him. He will not read letters from America lest they contain bad news. The full moon troubles him. George Schaller remarks on how Matthiessen frets almost daily, fearing he may not be able to leave if the snows intensify. His temporal and spiritual homes remain in conflict: *"In the longing that starts one on the path is a kind of homesickness, and some way, on this journey, I have started home. Homegoing is the purpose of my practice, of my mountain meditation and my daybreak chanting, of my koán: 'All the peaks are covered with snow—why is this one bare?'"*[13]

Schaller had a practical reason and a professional obligation in coming to Shey—to observe the *bharal* in mating season, and thereby shed light on whether this mysterious, little-studied creature was sheep or goat. His "purpose," I think, focused him in ways less available to his friend, and allowed him an unselfconscious escape from the incessant yammering that Matthiessen was so beset by.

> *"In spite of our disparate reasons for being here, Peter on an inner search, I on a scientific quest, we are nevertheless travelers on similar paths. The aims of Buddhism and science are in some aspects alike ... science still remains a dream, for it takes us no more than a few faltering steps towards understanding; graphs and charts create little more than an illusion of knowledge. There is no ultimate knowing."[14]*

Perhaps because he was not directly seeking it, he found the immanence, the wakefulness that Buddhist practitioners so desire. Leaving Shey for Jumla in early December 1973, George Schaller ends *Stones of Silence*, his account of several years of mountain travel in Pakistan and Nepal, with this:

> *"Already within me Shey remains only a strange combination of memory, dream, and desire. I know that all things in nature are transient, that species vanish and mountains dissolve, yet I hope that nothing will change at Shey, that from reincarnation to reincarnation the lama will still occupy his ochre-colored eyrie, that the medieval silence will continue to be broken by the clashing horns of fighting bharal, and that Drutob Senge Yeshe will fly forever on his magic snow lion around the Crystal Mountain."[15]*

And it was he, not Peter Matthiessen, that sighted a snow leopard near Lake Phoksundo—the irony implicit in the title of Matthiessen's book.

Both men, in their different ways, achieved a few rare, hard-won, impermanent moments of transcendence in this *"bitter white waste, at the edge of darkness."*[16] They have left them, alive and vital, for you and I to find and to reimagine.

Ironically, and perhaps only half-truthfully, Peter Matthiessen disparaged his attempts to capture what he experienced here. *"Frustration at the paltriness of words drives me to write, but there is more of Shey in a single sheep hair, in one withered sprig of everlasting, than in all these notes; to strive for permanence in what I think I have perceived is to miss the point."*[17]

Perhaps; but without these words, there is no lasting journey, no mountain—and no secret spark in the mind of the reader, separated by acres of space and time.

Peter Matthiessen and George Schaller left the Shey Valley, cradle of some of their greatest writing, late in 1973. Matthiessen never returned; Schaller, though I didn't yet know it, was on his way back for the first time.

—·—

Other trekkers had claimed the high ground behind the *gompa*. We camped on a rocky floodplain beneath the monastery, at the confluence of the Sephu and the Tartang Rivers. This has turned out to be a mistake—it is damp here, and the damp magnifies the cold. We are lower down than at Namgung; it is only mid-September, but the nights are already bitter.

As we set up camp, a policeman arrived. Did we have a satphone? Not exactly, but I can send texts; why? A German tourist, he said. *"Thaukomā chot lãgeko chha"* [his head is damaged]. Inside a small *gompa* overhanging the Tartang gorge a couple of hours north of here. He'd slipped on a steep ladder connecting the rooms of the building. He needed to get to a hospital.

We used my InReach to text the tourist's insurance company in the US. After a while came a reply—helicopter evacuation not covered. So I said, why not use my policy? But no, everyone replied: the pilots would check, they could only take the policyholder; there'd been too many helicopter scams, they were checking carefully now. The German would have to get out by mule. It would take time. It was too bad, but *ke garne*? What could be done?

Matthiessen and Schaller had relished the absence of such fallback options, of being fully accountable for their mistakes. Which is fine—until you actually make one. I'm glad to have the helicopter option should I need it, and I'm glad Basant has made sure my team is also covered.

The sun disappeared by 5 p.m.; we retreated to the cooking tent and the kerosene stove. Konzok and Sagar were talking without rancor; Konzok was teaching Sagar to cook. I said nothing—the impossibilities of two days ago had been set aside, for now at least.

Sleep was hard to come by; the bag I'd hired from Basant was failing to keep me warm, and I realized it was stuffed with nylon, not feathers. How could I have not checked this back in Kathmandu? And how could he have given me this piece of junk? I put on my down jacket and wrapped my feet in a pullover. Still cold; the trick, I remembered, is to get into the bag while you are warm, and I had stood around outside watching the moon on the mountains. So I gave up, propped myself against my day pack and read Helen Dunmore's *The Betrayal*, a grim tale of Soviet spite in post-war Leningrad.

Outside, the air was dead still, and the cold magnified all sound. The rustling of the shallow river. Voices, and the snort of a horse in a stone building across the stream.

I opened the tent flap, looking north at the gray mountain over the Tartang Valley, a pillar of vertical stone with crenellated summits like an old molar tooth. Alien, slightly foreboding, a projection of a state of mind from which I cannot detach myself.

September 16, 2016—Day 28, Shey Gompa, Dolpo District—14,150 feet.

A strange and painful day, transformed somewhat in recollection.

I slept little, and I have risen early. Konzok brings tea to my tent, and mentions in a matter-of-fact way that the lady in the house across the stream died last night. What, just like that? No, she'd been ill for some time. She was, it seems, the grandmother of the little boy in Saldang—the one with the fractured skull. Her son, the little boy's father, is on his way here. The Saldang lama will come too; there is no lama in Shey; these days there are few monks in Dolpo: most of them live in Pokhara. Or Kathmandu. Yes, really.

The Saldang lama will decide if the corpse should be burned or given "sky burial." Konzok points at a bluff far above the *gompa*. Tibetans, like Zoroastrians, often dismember their dead and leave the pieces as a gift for vultures, crows, and wild dogs. In a land where there is no firewood and where the ground is frozen hard for most of the year, neither crema- tion nor burial is easy.

He sits with me; we watch as heavily-wrapped people bustle in and out of the small house.

"*Purnima*," he says. "Today is the full moon. This is a good time for her to die."

"Is it?" I ask. I am thinking of another death, on a full American moon six years before.

Konzok tells me her family has placed a white cloth over the dead woman's face; no one should touch her now. When the lama comes, he will do divination with *mo* dice to help determine when her spirit has left her body and traveled into the *bardo*—the intermediate state between death and rebirth. At that point, the body can be disposed of. This could be several days from now.

In the *bardo*, the consciousness is thought to replay our recent expe- riences, often in terrifying form. For those trained to recognize what is happening, the *bardo* can be used to navigate the way to a favorable rebirth; for the rest of us, guilt and confusion cause panic and can lead us to disaster. While there is no escaping the consequences of an evil life, even the relatively innocent are in danger in the *bardo*. Only the prayers of lamas, family, and friends can guide us through this daunting maze.

The sun comes out, and it's warm enough to wash clothes. Palden suggests we hike out to Tsakang, a monastery a couple of hours up the west bank of the Tartang where the German fell yesterday. We set off; the trail is narrow, the hillside below steep and grassy, and I become frightened. I decide not to continue. You go on, I say, but Palden won't do so alone. We walk back to the camp, searching the mountains for *bharal*—we have seen none in Shey so far. As we arrive, we are told that the German has left on horseback; he will travel to Do and thence to the airstrip down at Jufal, at least six days from here. This is no way to deal with a serious concussion, but the choices he made before coming to Nepal leave no alternative.

"He will die, suh," says Palden, clearly affected by this man's ill fortune.

In part I have begged off Tsakang because I have business of my own today, in my tent. It is early afternoon; with great reluctance I close the flap and pull out a document folder I have brought with me and have so far left unopened.

—·—

My daughter died on September 23, 2010, on the night of a full moon, and today is the seventy-third moon since then. Every month I look for it, clear or obscured, wherever I am in the world. Often a faint halo surrounds the orb, its light refracting through icy cloud particles. When Tess was young, we used to look for a rabbit on the face of the moon. The ears, the tail, its head resting in the Sea of Tranquility.

Inside the folder is a little booklet that Tess brought home from school in Kathmandu when she was six, and various other drawings she gave me around that time.

My daughter was unusually bright. Parents will say this out of loyalty—but she really was. She spoke before she was one, and by two her language was fluent and complex. In the fall of 1986 we watched the leaves separating from a chestnut tree on a stormy day in our garden in McLean, Virginia. She was just short of two years old. "Look, Papa," she said. "The wind, it destroyed the tree. Will it die now?"

"No. It will sleep for the winter, and then wake up when it gets warm again."

"But will it get warm again? Are you sure? Maybe this is the last summer ever in the world."

My mother believed Tess contracted some unseen illness soon after this; what else, she asked, explains how such a brilliant child could find reading and writing so difficult? When she was eight, we took her for tests. In England they said she had a "non-specific learning difficulty" or dyslexia; in the US, shortly afterwards, the diagnosis was attention deficit disorder, ADD, and the solution was Ritalin. Perhaps it was that simple: perhaps the circuitry in her brain had developed in ways that made writing such a struggle. Whatever had happened, the cruelty of school disheartened and humiliated her.

The memory of this pain spreads through me as I shuffle among these few remaining traces of her childhood. Her pain, and my inability to make it right.

On one page, I have written 6/91, the date. There is a double border, drawn with a teacher's ruler. Inside this border, all around the page, are simple colored tulips, like three-fingered hands. At the bottom, a stick princess in yellow harem pants and a blue dress, surrounded by falling leaves. "*I am in the fields,*" Tess has written above, the effort in forming every letter apparent; "*it is windy and I am happy and I am playing and I am going home I have a stove—Amytis.*"

Next is a picture of the *"Robert family."* There's me on the left, in a pencil-gray suit, with a tie and a mustache, smiling. The focus is elsewhere, though—on her mother and on her. Mandana is wearing a pink ballet dress and dancing shoes; she's up on her points, hair streaming, red rouge dots on her cheeks, her arms crossed, her face open and happy.

Next to her is Tess, pint-sized in a blue party dress, her arms extended. She too is smiling, her hair thick and long. She's smothered with pets. A purple cat sits on her skirt; at her feet are three yellow ducks and a black-and-pink dog (Erica, her springer spaniel). Near my feet, a pond with a tiny fish, and behind us a fence, some purple slug-shaped clouds and a watery sun. It is typical of children's art projects, I suppose, but I see a yearning for a life that wasn't quite there. She missed America; her mother was often wracked with depression.

I would just as soon put these relics back into their folder, but with a heavy heart I turn to the booklet. It has a yellow card cover, inside which are eight colored pages and a spine sewn with coarse thread. The pages alternate between text and pictures. This was Tess' first book. The penmanship and the spelling grow more arduous with each page.

> *"bumpling, By Amytis*
>
> *once Upon a time There was a puppie His name was bumpling He was The most cutes puppie*
>
> *There Had evr Been. one day bumpling was Walking thow The forest When He sadnley wished He kod be long. He walked a little father until He saw a Blak Sadow.*
>
> *ran away bumpling want hom Suddely He saw That he wos Log and Livd hapaly avr aftr*
>
> *The aend."*

The pictures she has drawn are less agonized: a short dog, a longer dog, an empty field with flowers, more blowing leaves.

I am thinking of her delight with words, of her brilliance as a story-teller, and I am crying without restraint—not because she is dead, but for her suffering while she lived, and for all that she is now missing.

Even as I am crying, though, I am asking myself—why this grief? Why do I insist on it, pursue it even? It does nothing for her; she is beyond feeling, or caring what I feel.

We grieve to remember. To fight the forgetfulness that allows us to walk comfortably through this suffering world. To keep those who have vanished alive a while longer.

When Tess died, the World Bank told me to take as much time off as I needed. I left work for three months. I knew that going back to the office would divert me, and I didn't want that; I wanted to remember. I returned to Israel, where Tess and I had lived for three years; I traveled to England to see her old schools again.

And I visited my father. He said little about Tess, but I know he worried for me. By then, he was thinking about his own death. We sat in his study one day that winter, drinking tea by the fire. We were talking about the Second War, as we often did.

"Do you remember the gravestones?" he said, out of nowhere. "The ones in—where was it? Somewhere near that old school of yours."

"Walhampton? You mean the cemetery near Poppa's house? The one at Boldre Church? That was fifty years ago, Dad. What made you think of that?"

"Well, we need to remember the dead, don't we?"

"Yes," I said. "We do."

As we grow older, we lose much that we care so much about, and most of those we love. The student of Buddhism would say we should let such things go; they are painful distractions. The longing for the dead is insatiable. It is yet one more cause of suffering—and one that benefits the dead not a whit.

But I can't see it that way. The extinction of those we love is intolerable; forgetting them is to forget our proper selves, and to invite others to forget us too. Why else did we create the soul and its various destinations—heaven and hell, reincarnation—against all the dictates of sense and evidence? The reward of a great lama, surely, is not extinction through nirvana, but to be remembered: remembered long beyond the span of mere family memory. This prospect is indispensable to many writers. In the void to come, their words will remain, a living echo of the voice that once was.

I am writing this in memory of those I loved who have died, above all my daughter. My writing, inadequate as it may be, is my brief inscription on their gravestones.

—·—

There is someone outside my tent; Palden is calling me.

I compose myself. A man has come to see me—a wild man, his handsome face cut by sun and wind, hair gathered up on his head, red woolen plaits crisscrossing his brow. He is speaking Tibetan to Konzok.

"This father of the boy. Saldang boy? Crack head?" says Palden.

"You mean Chimi Tsewang?"

"Yes, suh."

He has a tan pony with him, saddled up, with colored tassels in its mane.

He steps forward unfolding a *khãda*, the Tibetan scarf of respect and welcome; thin green silk, it billows in the sharp afternoon wind. The eight auspicious symbols are traced in faint black outline—conch, thunderbolt, victory banner, lotus, lattice, vase, *dharma* wheel, paired fishes. I clasp my hands together and bow as he places it over my shoulders. Should I give it back to him? No—you only do that for a lama.

"He says thanks to you for helping his son."

"*Kehi chhaina*," I say. "It's nothing." And it really wasn't anything. As the French say, *c'est normal*.

"This pony is for you to ride over Kang La when we leave Shey Gompa."

I am touched; this is not the drunkard I had imagined. I thank him, and say no, I will walk. He is disappointed, and offers us some beer and a can of Red Bull. I accept them, and thank him again. He seems shy, looking at his ornate felt boots, then shuffles back towards the house of his dead mother.

This evening I eat little. I leave the kitchen tent into intense cold, and hurry to bed. I read, then doze, sliding in and out of sleep. I dream I am in a hotel in the desert. Dull sounds of hammering come through the wall. I go to see what is happening, and come upon an African chief, in tribal regalia, smashing the bowl of a toilet with a sledgehammer. He looks at me angrily and pushes past me to leave; somehow what has happened is my fault. I am eager not to be punished, so I set about cleaning up the mess of ceramic shards, paper, shit and water from the tiled floor. Once finished, I swing like a monkey up onto the roof, losing all sense of oppression, and lope across the corrugated iron surface. Red sunset floods the sands.

I wake up with a nasty headache; I didn't drink enough water today. I sit up and reach for my water bottle. My tent is aglow with a yellow light; what is this? I put on my boots and step outside. It's still dark. Up on the hillside, under the large, white moon, a fire is burning. This must be the funeral pyre; the lama returned, then, and this was what his *mo* said they should do. The house opposite is empty; everyone has gone to the hill. In the distance, spark clouds burst, as wood and oil are fed into the flames.

Christ, it's freezing. I feel I should keep watch tonight, of all nights—but the cold drives me back to my tent.

As I pull the useless sleeping bag around my shoulders, I hear an animal calling, a sound somewhere between a bark and a deep-throated scream. It calls four times, searching for something in these dead and desolate wastelands.

The calling ceases, leaving only the sound of the stream and the quiet light of the funeral pyre.

10

THE STERILE LAKE

**September 17, 2016—Day 29, Shey Gompa,
Dolpo District—14,150 feet.**

The fire has gone out; a few traces of smoke are still visible.

I get up, reluctant in this saturating cold, and go over to the cooking tent for my omelet. I ask if anyone heard that animal calling last night. Was it a wolf?

"No, suh," says Palden. "Jackal. Many jackal here."

We leave tomorrow. Today I will walk up to the *gompa* and take a few photos. I've learned that it was raided by temple thieves some weeks ago, and not for the first time; they cut a hole through the *gompa* wall and made off with valuable *thãnkãs* and statues. These will find their way to the houses of collectors in China, Europe or the US. Perhaps Buddha III will bid for an artifact or two.

I am thinking about last night's disturbing dream—the spiteful chieftain, the carefree monkey, that sense of guilt and exposure. Both the monkey and my discomfort take me back to a time I arrived in Kathmandu from Washington; it must have been 1991. Mandana met me at the airport in our Toyota Corolla—no driver that day.

"Let's go and do *kora* at Swyambhu, Nigel-*joon*," she said. She was relieved I was back; Tess had been fractious. It was late May, the air muggy. Mandana wore a yellow linen shirt, her face flushed, a slight sweat on her forehead. She drove with her usual abandon, up to Swyambhunath, a Buddhist shrine that has overlooked the north-western edge of the Kathmandu Valley for more than two thousand years. Literally overlooked: a fierce pair of eyes stares out from each golden facade beneath the stupa, as if some vast Roblox character is fused into the shrine.

We began to walk clockwise around the base of the hill, following other pilgrims brushing their hands over the prayer-wheels set into the circular perimeter wall. I had bought a bunch of bananas, thinking I would pass them out to the macaques that swarmed around the temple complex. The macaques had other ideas, though. A large red-faced male jumped in front of me, baring impressive teeth, mean little eyes fixed on my face. I started back, dropping my hands. Soft fingers pried the bananas away from me. I glanced down at the gentlest of faces, staring up at me with no hint of malice. The baby accomplice gathered the bananas to his chest, and jumped the guard fence into the jungle.

Mandana was laughing, then suddenly stopped and looked at me. "You are my oxygen," she said. "Do you know that? Do you understand?"

All these eyes on me. I smiled, and I looked at the ground. I was glad to be home, but I hadn't missed Mandana much; I was having an affair with someone else in Washington. I felt sharp shame then, at my irresponsibility towards both women—and yet I carried on this deception for several more years. Mandana never learned of it, so you could argue that it left no mark on her. But I was not fully present; I was distracted from the pain her depression was causing her and our daughter.

September 18, 2016—Day 30, Beside the Phoksundo Khola, Dolpo District, 12,254 feet.

We leave Shey, first climbing up towards the 17,647-foot (5,379-meter) Nagdalo La (Matthiessen's and Schaller's Kang La). This is the highest point of our trip—the pass that gave them so much trouble on their way into the Shey Valley. They crossed it on November 1, 1973, through ice rivers and snow up to their waists; for us there is almost no snow: mere dustings a couple of hundred feet below the saddle. The strength of those two again impresses me; ours was easy walking by comparison, and I was carrying less than twenty pounds on my back—not *"floundering through soft snow beneath sixty pounds of lentils."*[1]

In that long valley nothing grows; gnarly reefs of brown rock thrust above slopes of smashed slate—and yet the landscape is far from dead. The banks and shoals of rock, forced up from the bottom of the ocean more than fifty million years ago, are folded, lined, twisted like perished licorice, communicating the pent-up energy they still carry. I have wondered why people speak of "living" rock—now I can see it all around me.

The sun is furious, the shade icy, one side of your face burning while the other chills. The climb from Shey is only 3,500 feet, but we are already high, and the altitude soon begins to bite.

"Drink, suh," says Palden, handing me the Red Bull that Chimi Tsewang's father gave us. Perhaps it's the clean air, perhaps my growing headache; it is foul, smelling of over-sweetened orange and vomit.

"Where's that damn horse now?" I ask, as if it were Palden who turned the man's offer down.

We walk on without speaking, following a clear gray path through the slate. The last seven hundred feet are particularly draining; the ground is sodden, and gives beneath our feet like slipping shingle on a sea shore. I am dizzy and spaced out, and a fragment from Matthew Arnold's mournful poem *Dover Beach* comes at me out of some discarded pile of exam clutter.

> *"Listen! you hear the grating roar*
> *Of pebbles which the waves draw back, and fling,*
> *At their return, up the high strand ...."*[2]

I stop to breathe every dozen paces, and lag behind the others. Eventually I crest the ridge, into a gale. The mules are standing into the wind, manes and forelocks flying. My crew, hands in pockets, hang about as if on fucking Dover Beach itself, oblivious to the cold.

"Very lucky, suh!" shouts Palden, "Lord Buddha helping us today!"

"Bugger the Lord Buddha," I mutter.

That seems to do it, though; my mood lifts.

Ngima, the clown, has tangled himself into the mound of prayer flags marking the pass. As my breath stabilizes, I walk over and photograph him. It is an ominous picture. It shows twisted lines of colored flags and Ngima's disembodied head, tongue lolling out, as if severed, helpless against a blasted backdrop of rock, dust, sky and distant snow pinnacles.

It is too cold to stop, so I walk down out of the wind into sudden quiet, leaving the heart of Dolpo behind me—perhaps forever. Mostly I am relieved, but I am also frustrated at my inability to live inside my own experience.

Any further such reflections are curtailed by a descent of over five thousand feet, taking almost six hours, much of it frightening. There are long pitches of steep, slippery path strewn with pebbles too numerous and too small to step around, but too large for my cleats to grip onto, so I resort to holding Konzok's hand once again. This time, though, with the descent seeming so endless, I try to detach myself from my fear. It works, to some extent. Not through any equanimity at the prospect of sliding into one of the chasms that beckon beneath us: more from the repetitive nature of this endless shuffle down to the river, and the physical trance it induces. The simple sounds of our walking possess me. The crunch of my boots. The tinkling sound of my ski pole. Konzok's occasional cough. Wind buffets. Soft footfalls around me. Trickling water. Every few minutes, though, one of my feet slides, and my heart jumps again.

And yet I am glad we are not climbing, for this is a formidable hill when taken in reverse. Late in the afternoon we catch glimpses of red flesh ducking in and out of boulders below us. Three, four Westerners, aging, overweight, sunburned and sweaty, stripped down to beachwear—or, in one woman's case, a frilly black shift. They have no porters or guides, and they are struggling.

"Afternoon!" says the first one, squinting up at me. "We're from Brisbane."

"My Best Man comes from there," I say. Unlikely, but true.

To understand language, context is needed. This is the case today, I observe. The man looks blank. I repeat myself.

"Suh, he don't understand Nepali," whispers Palden.

Of course. I try again, in English.

Pleased to meet you, he says, I'm Alan. We two blokes, he says, have just retired. Kids all grown up, time for an adventure. Bloody marvelous here, isn't it? That lake Fok … Fok … whateveritwas—just amazing. Tough walking, though. This hill's a bit of a bastard. You on your own, then? Hoping to get to Sheer Gomby tomorrow. Best press on now, good luck to you too mate.

The other man and the two women remain mute; they are shattered. We watch them lumber on up, awkward creatures disappearing into the gloom.

A few minutes later, Konzok says "*Āja pugna sukdaina, saheb. Mānchhe*"— pointing back up the trail. They won't make it today, sir. I agree; I should have tried to stop them. Palden, instinctively kind-hearted, drops his pack and runs back up the trail.

"Sagar and Ngima can follow, bring their bags," says Konzok.

We are below the tree line again, the trail tunneling down through stands of conifers. Opposite and above us, across the hidden river, the edge of an ice flue pokes over the rim of a hill.

"Kanjiroba Himal," says Konzok. He is smiling.

"Thank you for everything," I say in sudden gratitude. "*Ma kahilye pāni birsine chhaina*. I'll never forget this."

And, after a strained pause, "Is everything okay with you and Sagar?"

"A little better. I will speak to Basant-sir when we get to Ringmo."

Palden returns, wholly unconcerned. "No problem, suh. They very happy. They say thank you."

I am not reassured; I should have gone myself. But we carry on our way.

Sagar and Ngima are far ahead; I saw them start running once they had opened a decent interval between us. Soon they emerge from the trees with mugs of hot tea and some Pashupati glucose biscuits. These are damp, but we have foregone *lonch*, and I can imagine nothing better. And such unexpected generosity.

We camp beneath yellow granite cliffs, on a gravel bed by the Phoksundo River. Across the stream, a squeezed moon shines on the steep ice-walls of the Kanjiroba massif. I lie on boulders, my sleep interrupted by violent dreams that leave no visual trace—just sensations of insecurity, like the body's memories of an earthquake.

September 19, 2016—Day 31, Ringmo Gaun, Dolpo District—11,879 feet.

You lose the sun early here too; it drops behind steep canyon walls by about three in the afternoon. The evening chill has set in, though with nothing of the bone-aching damp of Shey. We are camped on the southern shore of Lake Phoksundo, on the landslide that dammed up this valley some forty thousand years ago. Behind us is the village of Ringmo; beyond it, to the south, the ground falls steeply back into the original river gorge, and on into the middle hills of Nepal. We are at the edge of Dolpo. I am both relieved and sad—from here all is residue, an exit march towards Jumla.

Jamie and Carolyn left Shey before us, and arrived last night. I have been drinking tea with them and Chandra. Anxiety must have dehydrated me. I drank and drank, and am tight as a drum.

Did we leave Shey only yesterday? It seems much longer. Sixteen hours of walking will do that, punctuated as it was by interludes of fear.

We set off early this morning, following the meander of the river across gravel bars, among willows and pines. Looking forward to an easy day, I forge on ahead and soon find myself climbing steeply up the east bank of the river. I come to a huge fallen pine, resin from the torn bark pooling on the ground. I get stuck in its branches like a fat bluebottle in a spider's web, lose purpose and climb back down through the pine needles to rejoin the others. We walk on together. The meander becomes annoying; we double back, cross and re-cross. My boots get soaked. Then we glimpse the lake, a milky blue between thorn bushes. Suddenly an enormous gaggle of French hikers sweep out of the willows, ignoring us, gabbling continuously. We have become accustomed to walking in near silence.

We stop for lunch on a gravel beach where the river feeds into the northern end of the lake. This is Sallaghari, and several Germans are sitting around on the rocks. In the first three weeks of this trek, we met only four foreigners: two Dutchmen in Do, then Jamie and Carolyn. Since reaching Namgung six days ago, we have met about fifty others, all moving in the opposite direction. In 1973, Dolpo was remote. Now Shey has become an exotic three-week holiday destination for global tourists.

From here we must skirt the western shore of the lake. We set off into a thick silver pine forest; I go ahead, keen for some separation. An hour later I see yet another foreigner above me, seated by the trail with a notebook. This one is pretty ancient, and I plan to walk on past him. I stop, though, because he is accompanied by an attractive young Sherpa woman. This is most unusual: I have never seen a female guide in the Himalayas.

I chat with her in Nepali. Yes, I say, we have come from Shey. We came through Saldang. And before that, Do. Before that? Darbang. Yes, quite a long trip. From here? To Jumla.

"He looks much too old for this," I then say to her.

She smiles. "No, no—he is very strong. We have been walking two hours and we are far ahead of the younger ones."

"Hello," I say to the man, so as not to be offensive. He nods at me.

To her, in Nepali again—"Where is he from?"

"America."

Their trip will last a month; they are going to Shey. She has a couple of expensive cameras around her neck.

"Where are you from, sister?"

She is from here, originally—from Ringmo. But she lives in Kathmandu.

"Have you heard of *The Snow Leopard*?" she then asks me.

My mind begins to clock in.

"Yes," I say. "It's in my pack . . ."

She is nodding at me, and pointing discretely over her shoulder. I look at the man again. He is still writing in his notebook.

"This was Peter Matthiessen's friend," she adds.

I look again. "You don't mean . . . it can't be. George *Schaller*?"

She is nodding vigorously.

"Jesus wept," I mutter, and then quickly, "Doctor Schaller?"

"Hello," he says, unsmiling. And then, "Come and sit down. You speak Nepali. What brings you here?"

He is a big man, tall and lanky, a thick head of white hair. He is dressed in a bush shirt with pens in his pocket.

How to answer him? Er, I came because of *The Snow Leopard*? I'm following your journey (only I'm not, we got it back to front)? I have your book, *Stones of Silence*, in my pack, could you possibly autograph it for me?

No; none of that will do. "Well, I'm thinking about writing a book about Dolpo," I try. Which is far worse.

"That's good," he says, without looking up. "People need to understand Nepal properly. Have you read Ken Bauer's book?"

I have not. I take out a little notebook. I write "Ken Bower, *Higher Frontiers*."

"Write your name and address for me," he says, giving me his own notebook. This is odd; perhaps he is a little deaf?

"Virginia," he says, appraising my stilted handwriting. "I live in Connecticut."

"Nice part of the world," I say.

"What's nice about it?" he asks. I should have expected that from the austere, direct character in *The Snow Leopard*; I'm just having a little trouble with overlapping realities. The single-minded, lean and intent young man.

I concentrate, setting banter aside. I ask him why he is here. It's a memorial trip, he tells me. For Peter, who died two years ago. I tell him I have Peter's book with me, that this is why I came. I have *your* book too.

He seems uninterested that I do. "Peter's son, Alex, is here," he continues. "He's back up there. You should talk to him." Alex, the boy Peter left behind in 1973.

Has Dr. Schaller been back to Shey Gompa since 1973? No, this is the first time. He has been too busy. There is just so much to do. Quite a lot of work in China these days; and next year he's been invited to India to appraise their tiger conservation efforts.

"You won't find Shey much different," I say. "From when you and Peter were there. Except for the tourists, unfortunately."

"The fewer people, the better," he says often."[3]

"But there seem to be less houses nowadays. Comparing it with your photos, I mean."

"Yes, but life was different then. These days they have solar panels, cell phones and everything else. Quite different."

"Beneath GS's stern control are gleams of anger, it appears, although he talks little of himself—there isn't much to go on. Essentially, I think, he is a solitary; a certain shy warmth is most apparent when he speaks of crows and pigs. Last year in New York, he said, "Perhaps you can teach me how to write about peo- ple; I don't know how to go about it." This sort of open and lonely

remark redeems his sternness and an occasional lack of proportion brought about by sheer intensity."[4]

He tells me that the young Sherpa lady is doing her master's on snow leopards; that they hope to find some scat and scrapes on their trip.

"Could I write to you?" I then ask.

"Yes, of course," he says, with unexpected warmth. "I might be away, though. But my wife will know where I am."

He prints out two email addresses. Both have "kms" in them—this must be his wife Kay. Kay, who offered to look after Alex while he and Peter were on this trip. Of whom George wrote so touchingly in the preface to *Stones of Silence*:

> *"The fact that she not only waited, but also encouraged me in my work in spite of the pain my absences caused, that she raised our children through critical years of development, creating persons of whom I am immensely proud, and that, in the end, she edited and typed this book, a book about journeys she wanted to take with me but could not, can only elicit my admiration, devotion and love."*[5]

How has he found the trip so far?

"Much less dangerous," he says, referring to the trail, admitting to more than Peter Matthiessen had ever observed.

> *"...I am glad that the cliff corner hid my ignominious advance on hands and knees. Squeezing by, GS remarks, "This is the first really interesting stretch of trail we've had so far." How easy it would be to push him over."*[6]

It is time to move; Palden has caught up with me.

"How old are you, suh?" he asks George, to my embarrassment.

"I am eighty-three," George replies evenly.

"Very, very good," says Palden. "Strong man!"

"Hm," says George. And then, "It's a pity you aren't going our way. We could talk more."

I hesitate, but I'm unsure if this is just pleasantry. "I'll write," I say.

Why didn't I turn around and go back towards Shey with him?

Half an hour later a swarthy middle-aged man is coming down a steep part of the trail. This has to be Alex Matthiessen; the image of his father.

"Hello," I say.

"Hi," he replies, smiling.

He steps back so I can pass him. We continue with no further words. I've been meaning to say something like "Alex Matthiessen, I presume?" or "So you are the 'sun'!"–but it seems so lame, and I can't think of anything else. Moments later I am cursing myself for my reticence. How could I miss such an opportunity?

Soon after this, I see two others—another young Sherpa lady and an American woman. They are clearly part of the same group, and too late, my tongue unwraps itself. I tell them I am following Matthiessen and Schaller's 1973 route. They must have heard that before. I mention that we hadn't seen many *bharal* up at Shey—perhaps it's too early still, or perhaps the tourists have made them wary. They tell me Alex was looking at his father's book at the exact place where Peter Matthiessen had crawled on all fours above Lake Phoksundo. Yes, I say, smiling, I remember that bit all too well.

> *"Certain sections are so narrow and precarious that more than once my legs refuse to move, and my heart beats so that I feel sick. One horrid stretch, lacking the smallest handhold in the wall, rounds a windy point of cliff that is one hundred feet or more above the rocks at lake edge."*[7]

"Don't worry," says the American, whom I later find out is the well-known climber and photographer Beth Wald. "You won't have to crawl there now. It's much easier."

What she neglects to tell me, though, is that the section of the trail that begins just past where we are standing is the most frightening we will encounter on the whole trip.

—·—

We climb steeply out of the forest, onto bare hillsides. Perhaps it is the imminence of the still lake that makes me feel so exposed, as if any mis-step will pitch me into the water far below. From this angle the lake is a flat sheet of shining turquoise, as if cut from the stone itself. No fish live there; nothing does. It is cold, brilliant and silent.

"*…a lake without impurities, like the dust-free mirror of Buddhist symbolism,*" writes Matthiessen.[8]

For me, up here, it is quietly sinister.

Much of the path follows the contour—in places no more than a foot wide, notched into the rocks and earth of the dusty hillside. My legs tremble as I skirt the hill, and that icy tingling in the groin you get when you lean over a high balcony possesses me. Then, even more alarming, the trail descends into steep gulleys. The path is coated in dust, beneath which lie deceitful pebbles and glassy, packed earth. Disaster beckons, and I tiptoe down like a blind man.

After an hour of this nonsense, we reach the lake, cross a stream bed and come to cliffs that fall sheer into the water. It is here, in Éric Valli's film *Himalaya,* that a loaded yak falls through the timber road built around the mountain and disappears into the lake. This is the last mile to Ringmo, at a hundred feet or less above the lake; this is Peter's "*horrid stretch*"[9] —but it is, thank God, an anticlimax. The timber trail has been widened. You can keep to the rock wall, and you don't have to look over the edge. It is, indeed, far less adventurous than in 1973.

As we approach Ringmo, I am still beating myself up about Alex Matthiessen. As I step off the last of the rickety platforms, though, I can see that there's more to it than shyness.

For the last month, his father's silent words have accompanied me everywhere, drawing me into the present, doing what only a writer can do. To speak of a trance would be misleading, but his voice—a phantom voice that only I can hear—is woven deep into my journey. I want nothing to interrupt him; not even his son.

11

A PLACE AND A NAME

September 20, 2016—Day 32, Ringmo
Gaun, Dolpo District—11,879 feet.

This morning I said farewell to Jamie and Carolyn; they will travel south to the airstrip at Dunai, and will be back in Kathmandu within a week. I shall miss them.

I sit in the sun and rinse some socks in the lake, then wash my hair for the first time in two weeks. Last night there were a dozen tents here, but everyone has packed up and gone, save one couple. They are Israeli; I can hear them speaking Hebrew inside the most minuscule of tents. My misanthropy in remission, I go over and talk to them. They are young and fit, just out of the army. I invite them into our cooking tent for some tea.

They are shy, but friendly. Avi and Rachel. He is tall and bearded; she is tiny and blond. They are traveling alone, and Ringmo is as far north as they are going—the permits for Dolpo are too expensive for them. They came up the Suli Gad from Dunai; they are wondering where to go next. Maybe Jumla? Maybe Pokhara? They will decide tomorrow. And then? Kathmandu of course, but they hated the place. So crowded and so dirty, so much traffic. Back to Goa, maybe. They loved Goa.

I mention that I used to live in Jerusalem. They look doubtful. No, I say, I did. Am I Jewish? Yes, in part, but only one-eighth; I was working there. Who were you working for? The World Bank. You know it? I ask because many people know nothing of this institution.

They say they do, but I am skeptical, so I explain a bit.

You remember the 1991 Madrid peace conference? They nod, but again I doubt they know what I'm talking about: they weren't even born then. Well, after that, in 1993, the World Bank began work in, er, the region (I was going to say Palestine, but no point in offending them). The cosponsors of Madrid—the US and Russia—asked the World Bank to report on the reconstruction needs in, um, the Territories (I remember this term works for everyone. The official UN title is the Occupied Palestinian Territories; the Israelis leave out "Occupied" and, of course, "Palestinian". They usually argue that they are not strictly an occupier: the West Bank was never part of any state; Jordan's 1950 annexation was not internationally recognized, etc.).

Which, I continue, we did. The study, I mean (I am losing my train of thought as I reach back for this rusty vocabulary). And after that, we began funding projects in Gaza, and then the West Bank (which would be Judea and Samaria to them, though not to me). Roads, drainage, education reform, pensions, housing finance, and the budget deficit of the Palestinian Authority (which to the Palestinians is the Palestinian *National* Authority, though not to Israelis). I worked on the Bank program from 1994 to 2006, I explain, for the last five years as the director, based in Jerusalem (I try not to say "the Bank"—it's both arrogant and confusing, since the employees of any large bank, from HSBC to the African Development Bank, also refer to themselves as "the" Bank . . . but how easy it is to slip back into old habits. The "we", too). West Bank program? asks Avi. No, World Bank program I say, illustrating my own point.

"Where in Jerusalem did you live?" asks Rachel. I sense that she wants to walk past the minefields; they must have had an earful over the course of their travels.

"In a hotel at first—the American Colony. Then in an apartment—in Dahiyat Al-Barid?"

"Of course," says Avi. "My grandparents live in Neve Yaakov."

"Right next door," I say. "On top of the hill, near the communications tower. The fence ran down the side of our driveway." Neve Yaakov is one of the oldest Jewish settlements in Jerusalem, Avi tells me; it was founded in the British period. Some of my Palestinian neighbors remembered those times, I reply; one old lady told me her father used to invite the settlers over to pick lemons in their orchard. Maybe she knew your grandparents. That was before the 1948 war, of course.

"Hard to believe, now," says Avi sadly.

Rachel then tells me that she was stationed near Ramallah during her military service. What was that like? She pauses. "Uncomfortable," she says, smiling. "They hate us so much." Do I know Ramallah? I do. In the '80s, she says, before the *intifada*—the first *intifada*—her parents used to go and eat hummus there at the weekends. It's so different now.

We leave it there; they are on holiday after all. We exchange addresses, and in the early afternoon they pack up and leave. As they wave goodbye, I am reminded of something that struck me when I first went to Israel. My Israeli friends would sometimes speak about Palestinians as if there was something exotic, immutable, or childlike about them. This was oddly familiar, but for a while I couldn't say why. One day it came to me: this is how my mother's friends would refer to their African houseboys. It didn't mean they were bad people: it reflected a colonial relationship, one in which those who possess power don't need to understand those who do not.

— · —

In the afternoon I decide to wander over to the *Bön* monastery, out on a nearby promontory.

Dolpo is known for the prevalence of *Bön*, a form of tantric Buddhism followed by about ten percent of all Tibetan Buddhists. Some claim it is a separate religion, originating in the ancient western Tibetan kingdom of Sh'ang Sh'ung, and predating modern Buddhism. To others, this seems doubtful. Although distinct *Bön* divinities such as the Sky Guide and Shen-God White Light seem to recall an older shamanic religion of wind, earth, and natural calamity, David Snellgrove believes that *Bön* is in reality a latecomer—a derivative of tantric Buddhism that nonetheless insists on its unique origins.

To the non-Buddhist outsider, *Bön* is all but indistinguishable from other forms of Himalayan Buddhism; the rituals, statues, and temple art differ only in detail, much as High-Church Protestant iconography might differ from that of Catholicism. And so followers of *Bön* will pass a prayer wall to the right, not the left, while *Bön* swastikas face left, and not right—but they are still prayer walls and swastikas.

In 1956, Snellgrove found a community of fourteen practitioners living on the monastery's land, only two of whom were literate lamas. He found the *gompa* dusty and run down, the religion slipping from sight. By the time Peter Matthiessen arrived, the monastery was locked up, with no one living there.

The buildings are not shut today, and there are fresh prayer flags strung between the *gompa* and other buildings, and on tall poles above the lake. A couple of monks are busying themselves sweeping, and though some of the wooden roofs have fallen in and there are weeds everywhere, the place is neither deserted nor unused.

There is a wooden bench of sorts out in front of the *gompa*, next to an ancient juniper tree, its trunk doubled over and gray as rock. Beyond lies the surreal turquoise lake, the color thick and impenetrable.

I take out *bumpling, by Amytis* from the file in my daypack. Reading it today is just as devastating as it was in Shey.

I find myself thinking about someone I knew in the World Bank many years ago, when he was a director and I a junior staff member. It must have been the mention of Goa—he was Goan. Somebody Pinto—a well-liked manager. One day his son was mowing the lawn outside the family house in Bethesda, in the Washington DC suburbs. A stranger who'd just been released from a psychiatric facility came walking by, stopped, pulled out a handgun and shot his son dead. It was a crime without any meaning, or any possibility of comfort. The boy's mother, I was told, became a recluse. The father became gray and bitter, his personality as distorted and aged as the tree I am sitting next to.

This didn't happen to me. My life wasn't laid waste by Tess' death. Is there something wrong with me? Didn't I truly love her? Such questions pursue me, and this is why I am in part comforted by my reaction to her booklet. Perhaps I am not heartless; perhaps people just deal with grief in different ways. I have avoided looking at the booklet for many years. I have also avoided going through the many old Sony videotapes I have of Tess as a young girl.

My daughter is never absent from me, though her presence is less vital now than when she was alive, when I worried constantly about her; or in the months after her death, when my mind would admit little else. For me, though, extreme grief proved unsustainable. Now her presence is a constant, low hum—a part of me, always there. There are moments when she is silent, but that silence is instantly sharp, and strange.

"Time is no healer: the patient is no longer here," T. S. Eliot wrote[1], and he is right; it isn't time that heals, it's the mind's inability to retain perfect information, buffeted by new impressions, sensations and the business of daily living. The rapacious success of our species is built on such forgetfulness, along with our limited empathy: how else could we remain calm amid the suffering that we create? The moral psychiatrist Jonathan Haidt says that 90 percent of our DNA comes from the self-absorbed chimpanzee. Empathy is a sideline.

And yet—it is essential to me that my daughter should not be forgotten. Those who believe in the eternity of the soul have higher hopes than I do; some believe the names of those who have gone before us can be preserved for ever. This premise animates the Holocaust museum in Jerusalem, *Yad Vashem*: thus the Book of Isaiah, chapter 56, verse 5 says

> *"Even unto them will I give in mine house and within my walls a place and a name [yad va shem] better than of sons and daughters; I will give them an everlasting name, that shall not be cut off."*[2]

The remembrance falls to me; who else knew her so well? Her mother; but she is dead too. Alex can't remember her at all; he was two when she died, and all he knows of her are the photographs, the videos, and her absence from his life. There is Alex's father Bryan, and his grandmother, with whom Tess lived for two years before and after Alex's birth—they hold many memories, and part of her lives in them. And there are her friends, but much as her death hurt them, they will remember her only in flashes; flashes that will grow fainter and less frequent, as lightning from a disappearing storm. Coded shards of her live on in the literal sense, in her son Alex, but they lie beyond the realm of consciousness.

When I think of her now, I think mostly of difficult times, perhaps because there is nothing I can now do to help her.

A few months after Tess died, I visited Jakarta on a publicity tour for a World Bank report I had helped write. I stayed in a hotel near the house of my Lebanese friends Lara and Imad. Unlike most people, Lara wanted to talk to me about Tess. Is it unbearable? she asked, in the manner of one acquainted with the unbearable. It's getting a little easier, I replied.

"As a parent, you let your children down all the time," she said. "But you always have tomorrow."

"Yes," I said. "And now I don't."

In a sense, a person is dead to you whenever you are no longer together; all that exists of them is memory, giving them an equality with the dead. The difference, though, is that you know that you can see them again.

September 21, 2016—Day 33, Ringmo Gaun, Dolpo District—11,879 feet.

Tomorrow we leave for Jumla—the last leg of our journey. We will go south briefly, turning west to cross the Kagmara La. We have sixteen days to get to Jumla before Sarah arrives from Kathmandu, for another two weeks of hiking around Lake Rara.

It is almost four. The sun is hot, reflecting off the lake, but my shaded arm feels chilly. Behind the steep hillsides a few rag clouds are shredding in the afternoon wind. I have done little today, and will be glad to get moving again. Sarah has been in touch. I texted her about meeting George Schaller, and she emailed Kay Schaller at the address he gave me. Kay wrote back at once, not the least bothered by the kind of email she must often receive.

There are few mentions of Kay in *The Snow Leopard*, but they are revealing of both husband and wife, married now for nearly sixty years. She met him at the University of Alaska, drawn to a man shouting at his pet raven to return. Peter Matthiessen reported that *"He often says this—'Kay gets wild at me'—as if to remind himself that his wife may have good reason."*[3]

Sarah and I are hoping to meet George in Kathmandu when we all get back there, but the dates may not work: he leaves Kathmandu on October 18, and we will probably miss him by a day. The contact is made, though, and I shall write to him once I get home.

I dreamed of Tess again this morning—a confused, uncomfortable dream. She was riding a pony across a green English barley field, a duck under one arm. The field was sloppy, sedgy, with crocodiles basking on its surface. I struggled to keep up. The tail of an airliner poked up through a beech wood, smoking lightly: a Vickers VC10, a plane from the 1970s. My father was nagging me. We were late somewhere again.

So little of Tess is left. Her body, of course, in a bright cemetery in Arlington—but I cannot bring myself to imagine her lying beneath my feet when I visit her grave; unlike Milarepa, I have no desire to make peace with destruction by contemplating my daughter's corpse.

At home I keep several drawers of her things. Many diaries, but I don't feel I can read them. A purple cardboard box, a school project, with her baby teeth inside. A plastic band from Georgetown Hospital, no more than three inches around, fastened to her foot a few minutes after she was born. A box of Japanese ceramic figures which I bought for her in Tokyo. Lip gloss. A battered blue Eeyore. Two old cellphones, one a fancy LG flip phone with keyboard and interior screen. *Twenty-Four Hours a Day*, a book of prayer and meditations given to members of Alcoholics Anonymous (and, as far as I can see, unused). Her first British passport, issued on April 14, 1989, to Miss Katrina Amytis Roberts. Her World Bank medical insurance card. A red Target glasses case (that girl lost so many pairs of glasses). Books and videos from her apartment in Falls Church—William Boyd's *Brazzaville Beach*, Jane Austen's *Pride and Prejudice*, Stephen King's *Skeleton Crew*; Gus van Sant's movie about the Columbine killings, *Elephant*, and *The Ballad of Jack and Rose*, starring Daniel Day-Lewis, about a devoted, codependent relationship between a father and his daughter. A Smashing Pumpkins DVD. Her wallet—mine actually, given her to help her organize her coupons, credit and discount cards. Plus some clothes I remembered her wearing—a yellow swimsuit, a pair of high heels, an Alice band, a plaid shirt, some pink pajama bottoms, a gray pullover. I could once smell her hair in that pullover, but six years later only the scent of mothballs remains.

Tess had a room in Mandana's flat in London; after Tess died, Mandana left it unchanged, as bereft parents do. There was the furniture suite Mandana had bought her, an old boom box, some drawings a graffiti artist boyfriend had given Tess, a few clothes in a wardrobe of empty wire hangers. The same duvet and sheet set remained on the bed, and only I was allowed to sleep in that room. When Mandana died, the apartment was refurbished and rented out, and all traces of mother and child erased.

These were the material things. Of her dreams of acting and becoming famous, of her fiction, which her last English teacher told me was better than anything she had seen from a girl of her age (though atrociously mis-spelled)—of these, nothing remains.

The light is failing as I wander around the village for the first time; we are back on the edge of governable territory, in a place where officials can serve all year-round and where shops once again exist. I come across a small helicopter beneath a tarpaulin; pieces of the engine have been removed, stranding it here since May of last year. This potent machine has become as useless as a ladder without rungs, and parts of it have been commandeered for other purposes. The tires, I notice, are gone—and later I see what looks like one of them up on the corner of a roof, filled with soil, home to a pumpkin plant

The houses are similar to those in other Dolpo settlements. They are built up in sections: a squared layer of planks as a platform, a two-to-three-foot layer of stones and mud, another layer of planks, a raft of pine trunks to support floorboards, then another layer of stones and mud rising to a beaten mud roof held up by a final row of close-knit pine boles, cut longer than the wall-line and supporting slate stone eaves. At this time of year, the roofs are stacked high with millet and fodder grass.

I smile as I imagine myself detailing all this out to Tess, knowing how much it would bore her—trying to persuade her to appreciate things I don't truly appreciate myself. This purposeful, redundant parenting: that I can laugh about.

Other memories, though, still fill me with dread.

It was late 1987, she was just three, and we were staying in the Himalaya Hotel in Kathmandu. The World Bank had posted me to Nepal; we had just arrived, and were looking for a house. Tess' early childhood had been a happy one. Back in the US, Mandana had masked her depression by hiring a live-in nanny who stepped in when she was incapacitated; here we had not yet hired anyone. By her thirties, Mandana's bipolar depression had mutated into a particularly nasty variant of the disorder.

"Classic" bipolar disorder manifests as cycles of depression and elation, with each cycle lasting days, or weeks. In Mandana's case, the cycles were short, and her moods would sometimes shift several times within one day; nor was there any elation—depression was replaced by anxiety, and by intense irritability. "It's like fire," she once said. "Fire burning through your veins."

Mandana did her best to conceal her moods from her daughter. Tess had seen Mandana withdrawn, in bed, erased by mute suffering—but that could be explained as sleepiness, or Mama not feeling well that day. To this point she had not seen her loving mother transformed into something else.

It was early winter; the empty rice terraces beyond the hotel window were shrouded in mist. Mandana was dressing Tess. She wanted her to wear a particular hair clip—one with a rabbit's face on it.

"No, Mama," said Tess. "This rabbit has been squashed. I don't like him."

"Ah," said Mandana. "You don't like what Maman bought you?"

After seven years of marriage, your ear is tuned to the slightest changes in your wife's voice. I stepped into the bathroom, my heart dropping.

"And here comes Daddy," Mandana said, turning a savage face towards me. "Your so-called 'Potector.'"

"Tessie-*joon*, wear the clip," I said.

Tess, though, was unaware of what was moving beneath the surface.

"No, no, no," she said, laughing, inclining her face from side to side in the mirror.

"You disobedient child, put it ON!" screamed Mandana.

Shock and fear register below the heart—a slow, cold fall. To me this was frightening, but for Tess it was more: something had been taken from her. She froze, her eyes widening. I could see her struggling to connect this apparition with the person she knew. She hunched down into herself, and said quietly "Where's my Mama gone?"

Mandana managed to check herself, turning away and leaving the room in tears.

There would be many such explosions, but this was memorable because it felt like the first tiny fracture on perfect glaze.

Tess remembered it too. Many years later she wrote asking me to send her a photograph she kept beside her bed at home. She was sixteen by then, a student at the Academy at Swift River, a "therapeutic" boarding school for troubled kids, up in Massachusetts. The children in her peer group had been asked to recall a perfect memory, and this is what that photograph meant to her: a time before scars. Mum took it, she wrote, in some hotel in Nepal.

In the photo, Tess is standing in our bedroom in the Himalaya Hotel. She is facing the camera, in front of opened, unpacked suitcases, wearing a red dress with a white collar, frilly socks, and buckled black shoes. Draped round her neck and trailing on the floor is one of my ties; under her arm, a thick blue paperback novel by Robert Graves, her mother's book, the title hidden; hanging from her wrist, a small party gift bag. She is smiling shyly, her eyes deep black, her head tilted to one side. She is off to work, like me that same morning. Today this picture sits on my hall table in Virginia, along with two pairs of Tess' glasses and her small brass statue of Ganesh, a god who is supposed to remove obstacles and bring you good fortune.

Every parent feels anguish as they realize they cannot shield their children from the nastiness of strangers; the world will have its way with all of them, whatever we do. But we do not expect such malice, however fleeting, in our own home—nor to feel so helpless before it.

And then there was Goa (once again). It was just over two years later, in January 1990. We were on a brief holiday from Nepal. The first two days were hot, languorous, and untroubled. We visited the weathered sixteenth century Jesuit church of brick and straw, the Basílica do Bom Jesus, and swam between rain showers on the beach outside our hotel, a beach littered with scraps of burnt driftwood and pitted by wandering cattle. Tess excavated a hollow for herself, and sat inside it drawing the sea and feeding the cows roasted corn cobs; a framed picture in our Virginia basement shows her bent forward, her hair falling across her face, elbow on the ground, wrist cocked over the paper, a couple of green marker streaks on her thigh.

By the third day, though, Mandana's mood had darkened. Unknown to me, she was using this vacation to wean herself off Ativan; the soothing effects of this powerful, addictive benzodiazepine would fade, requiring a tapering off period and a switch to something else. I am not sure why she lost her temper that morning; perhaps she was reducing her dose too quickly. The memories that remain thirty-six years later are patchy and blurred, but I can taste the despair I felt, and I can see my daughter's terrified, angry face. I picked Tess up and took her from the room. We sat on an outside staircase, watching a rising wind scour sand off the beach, unsure what to do next. As a thatched umbrella disintegrated, I knew I should take Tess away from her mother. But the prospect was daunting; and anyway, I told myself, Tess was the strong one; her mother needed me.

For many years I have regretted my lack of insight, and my weak resolve. As I now think back on that sad day, though, I am no longer so confident that a happier outcome was mine to bestow—on either of them.

12

HÃMRO PÃLA ÃYO

**September 22, 2016—Day 34, above Pungmo,
Dolpo District, 11,548 feet.**

Easy walking. We are making quicker time than expected. In just over six hours we are far past Sanduwa, the village we planned to reach today. Everyone is rested, and at this pace we will be in Jumla by the end of the month. There's an end-of-term feeling about this stage of the journey; we don't have long left.

I've spent much of the last month dodging the past I came here to explore. Since Shey, though, it has become much more assertive.

During the years we spent in Kathmandu, I still believed our family would muddle through—that I could protect them from mishap while preserving most of my time for my job. Tess had many friends, and there were few signs of the learning difficulties and emotional turmoil that would erupt a few years later. Mandana was happier than she had been in America. She loved Nepal and its casual spirituality: the corner shrines, lingam stones and sacred trees around which Kathmandu's new roads and tower blocks had wound themselves; the abundance of spirit healers, oracles, monks, itinerant sadhus. Indignation with her illness and constant questioning of her life's purpose drew her to Tibetan Buddhism, and to a community of loving friends. Yet her illness stalked our lives, erupting every few weeks in intense, bed-bound depression or episodes of crazed pain: screaming, emergency pharmacy visits to buy codeine, menacing drunkenness, a barbiturate overdose.

We returned to the US in 1993, and I began more than a decade of work on the World Bank's Palestine program. Life in McLean, Virginia, was anonymous; we were just another suburban family in a dormitory community. Much of Mandana's life was lived in cars. It was isolating, and began to drain hope from her.

She had been shouting at Tess about something that winter evening before she retreated to our bedroom. Usually I would try to distract her, do anything I could to defuse her rage, and recapture some temporary calm. This time I was angry; I said "You have to stop this. You're like a stranger in our home."

To feel rejected was, for Mandana, quite unbearable—and these words were enough. After I had read Tess her bedtime story and made sure she was asleep, I went to our room. Mandana wasn't there; nor was she anywhere in the house. There were no cellphones then, so I had no way of calling her. I assumed she had rung for a cab, and would return. I spoke to a couple of her friends, but she wasn't with them. I tried to sleep.

I took Tess to school the next morning: I told her that Mama had gone to visit her friend Nadereh. I called my office, telling them I was sick. By mid-morning I was thinking I should contact the police; then the phone rang. It was the Emergency Room at Fairfax Hospital. Your wife is in recovery, they said; you can come and see her.

I was shown into a room with two other patients. There were bandages on Mandana's wrists.

"Nigel-*joon*," she said. "It didn't work, I've wasted everyone's time. The doctor is furious with me."

"I'm sure he doesn't understand anything. He's young."

She was drowsy, but she wanted to tell me what had happened.

"I thought no one in the world wanted me. I was just a burden. You said so."

She had gone to a small motel on Route 50, somewhere in the strip mall wastelands of northern Virginia. She bought a bottle of vodka and some old-fashioned razor blades. She ran a hot bath. She thought of writing a letter to me. She'd wanted to tell me none of this was my or Tess' fault, but she hadn't had the strength.

"It didn't hurt then. It hurts now. I watched the blood in the water. I was so happy. I went to sleep. And then, goddamit, I woke up. The bath was empty, there was blood all over the place, I was freezing cold. So cold. And I couldn't move. I called, but the highway was next to my room and there was lots of traffic, so no one heard. I managed to pull myself out of the bath, I don't know how, but I couldn't stand. I couldn't even crawl. I was so thirsty, Nigel, you wouldn't believe how thirsty. I licked the moisture from the floor. In the end the maid came to clean the room and heard me."

She was contrite, affectionate, her old self—but the impostor soon returned.

I decided that Tess would be safer in a boarding school: the only other choice was to leave Mandana, but that was unthinkable to me then. So Tess lost her home, and much of her belief in me: I had chosen her mother. Her exile, and her growing frustrations with school led to anger, alcohol, and depression.

Over the next seven years, Tess drifted. She went through three English boarding schools, and a day school with us in Ethiopia. She began to drink, and to disappear at night. In desperation we sent her to a wilderness camp for troubled teens in North Carolina, and from there to a remedial boarding school in Massachusetts.

And during this chaotic period I did leave Mandana—for another woman, not on account of Tess. By then it helped neither of them.

Tess joined me in Israel in 2003. She lived with me in Jerusalem, and afterwards in Washington, until she was twenty-two. She never completed high school. In late 2006 she agreed to try rehab once again: the third time. She was admitted to a two-week program at Father Martin's

Ashley, at Havre de Grace in Maryland. There she met Bryan, who was trying to deal with an addiction to the opiate oxycodone. By midsummer they were living together, and she was pregnant with Alex.

After Alex was born, the three of them moved into an apartment in Falls Church, Virginia. Tess seemed more settled than she had ever been, delighting in her child and in her first adult home. She was good-humored and patient. She spoke of going back to school to study literature, or perhaps training as a nurse. Mandana came over and visited her in January of 2010; it went well.

They had done much to repair their uneasy relationship the year before. Tess and I were both in the US then, and Mandana was in London. Mandana's sister Mina called me one evening: Mandana had been found unconscious by her cleaner, and was in intensive care in the Chelsea and Westminster Hospital; she wasn't expected to live. We scrambled for tickets; Tess got an earlier flight than I was able to.

By the time I got to the hospital the next morning, the crisis had passed. Mandana, it transpired, had collapsed, lying insensible on the floor of her apartment for several days. She had almost died of dehydration, but with IV fluids she was recovering rapidly.

When I entered Mandana's hospital room, Tess was sitting on her bed, chatting to her. I was struck by the warmth between them. Apart from a bruise on her left cheek, Mandana seemed little the worse for wear, and was already agitating to be discharged.

Later on, Tess and I ate in a nearby restaurant. For the first time I could remember, she showed some sympathy for her mother.

"Poor Mama," she said to me. "She's had such a painful life."

"I know. I feel bad. I should come over more often."

"I wasn't talking about you," Tess said, slightly impatient. "I'm glad you left her. You should have left much earlier."

"For your sake, you mean."

"That too. She knew she could behave how she did because you let her. She never learned to figure things out. Mind you," she added, rolling her eyes, "look who's talking."

"You seemed so comfortable in there."

"It's all different now. I thought she was going to die. I used to think I'd be glad. I wasn't. It's that baby of mine. He drives me crazy, but I miss him so much. I can see what Mama must have gone through, that's all I'm saying."

—·—

We left Ringmo through pine forests, the path thick with brown needles, our footsteps muffled. Arriving at Sanduwa before 11, we ate our lunch and decided to push on. We are on the opposite side of the Kanjiroba massif we encountered after our descent from the Nagdalo La, four days ago. Then we saw a wall of glaciers, building toward the 21,700 foot peak; now the icefields lay unseen above a steep-sided river valley.

In mid-afternoon we reached Pungmo, a stone-built village in an apple orchard. The trees were laden with black-spotted fruit—flyspeck, probably. Could we buy some of them, Konzok asked? No, replied an old lady from inside a gloomy doorway, flapping her hand at him and covering her mouth with her headscarf. You can just take them, there are too many for us. Ngima dropped his load, shimmied into one of the trees, and shook it until a dozen apples dropped to the ground.

A couple of other Nepali trekkers arrived, youngsters, one stocky with shorts and a thick black beard, the other thinner, his features less distinct. Both were carrying packs and wearing windbreakers by The North Face.

"*Yo khāna sakinchha?*" asked the thin one, inspecting one of the apples. They didn't look that appetizing: but the flyspeck was superficial, so I said "*Sakcche-ni, thikai chha*"—you can eat them, they're fine.

"You speak Nepali?" he asked, in very good English.

"A little."

"*Mero saheb sabai kurā bujhchha,*" said Palden, predictably: my sahib understands everything. By now I know that my language skills, such as they are, enhance his status—but their English was better than my Nepali, so I didn't push my luck.

I asked them where they were headed; towards Jumla, they said, like us. They had come from the airport at Jufal, down the Suli Gad. They would go on to Gamghadi, north of Jumla and east of Lake Rara; it was a long story, but one of them had promised to help his sister stage a play there in a week's time.

A play?

"Shakespeare-style, but set in Nepal," said Blackbeard. "In the time of Bhimsen Thapa. One of our *great* statesmen," he added, sitting down on a stone wall and swinging one of his legs from side to side. His English was even better than his friend's. "But a villain. They all were, if I'm honest. I am Rajib, by the way. This is Ashok."

Ashok nodded slightly, smiling, looking at the ground. He folded his arms.

"You know our history, right?" asked Rajib. "A little? It's extraordinary, really. Very bloody. And, in the end, well—depressing. Greed, court intrigue, you know. The play, it's about a feud. Between the Pandeys and the Thapas. Two of the big families of those times? Still, actually. The feud began in 1804—"

"1805," said Ashok, not looking up, parting some grass between long fingernails.

"1805 then."

"Battle of Trafalgar," I said automatically, and then "Sorry—please go on."

"Bhimsen Thapa arranges—no, contrives. Contrives the execution of the prime minister, Damodar Pandey. Huge slaughter of his rivals. In the Bandharkhal."

"The what?"

"A sort of garden. And *dozens* get slaughtered. I mean, children too, the whole nine yards. Their bodies are left on the bank of the Bagmati River. No burial allowed. The wives are given to Dalits—you know, so-called untouchables. Totally degrading—in those days, I mean. The royal family is put in house arrest. Meanwhile, Nepal is expanding. It ends up much bigger than today. That was Bhimsen's doing, more or less. A great leader. But he overdid it."

"'From the Sutlej to the Teesta,'" said his friend, making quotations marks with his fingers, as if apologizing for this aggrandizement.

"They were fighting the East India Company for control of the Terai. The Brits. You're British, right? Thought so. Very nice. A dumb thing to do, looking back on it. The same applies today, with India. Don't put your foot in India's mouth. Nepal loses the war, and much of the country too. Bhimsen survives that, but the wheel turns. Long story short, he gets locked up and tortured. Tries to cut his throat. With a *khukuri* which is in his jail cell somehow—weird, that. But he's still alive. So the king and queen have him dragged to the bank of the Bagmati, and leave him there to die. In the same place as his own great massacre of however many years before. He lasts for nine days. What comes around goes around."

"And the play?"

"The author is brilliant."

"She's your sister," said Ashok.

"So? She really is fantastic, you think so too. You do. This play is, sort of a Nepali *Macbeth*. Bhimsen is a man of big ambitions, but with a conscience. And women play a big part in all of this. My sister is a feminist."

The sun had left the valley, and there was a perceptible darkening; we would soon lose the afternoon. I was fascinated by this man, his voice, his movements, his energy—and by the strangeness of the conversation.

Shadows from the sickly apple trees were darkening their faces. "We should go on," I said reluctantly. "Let's talk more this evening."

—·—

We are camped beside the Pungma Khola, an hour and a half above Sanduwa, and well-positioned to cross the Kagmara La tomorrow. It's late, but I am wakeful.

Konzok noticed that Rajib and Ashok were carrying no cooking equipment; they were hoping to buy dinner from a village house along the way. But Konzok knows this trail; no one lives above Sanduwa. So we invited them to eat with us.

After dinner they build a fire outside their tiny pup tent, and ask me over to share some rum with them. I haven't had any alcohol in five weeks.

The Pungma is shallow here, and loud. As we listen to the stream, I realize how little silence there is in these mountains. We always camp near running water; and once we climb out of any valley, we are assaulted by wind. We are enveloped in sound, so much that I am scarcely aware of my tinnitus.

Both my new friends are modern Brahmins, as different from Konzok, Palden, and Ngima as I am. Like me, they were raised as inheritors, not quarry; the kind of people who assume that the policeman in the squad car is there to help them. They are urbane, self-aware, apologetic about their privilege, confident of their place in the world. Rajib's father is a professor of history at Tribhuvan University in Kathmandu, Ashok's is the director of a private bank. They both recently graduated from the States—Rajib with a bachelor's from a liberal arts college in Michigan, Ashok with a master's in plant biology from Temple.

Last year Nepal suffered one of its periodic earthquakes. Although not quite as bad as the magnitude 8.0 Bihar-Nepal earthquake of 1934, which devastated the cities of the Kathmandu Valley and killed twelve thousand people in India and Nepal, the 2015 earthquake came close. It killed more than nine thousand, flattened parts of Kathmandu and nearby Bhaktapur, and destroyed villages, roads and bridges to the north and east of the capital. Rajib and Ashok had just come back from the US, and wanted to help. They used their college contacts to raise money in the States, collecting over $10,000—enough to rebuild a couple of shattered schools in Rasuwa District, a few hours from Kathmandu on the highway to China.

"Our first experience of corruption," says Rajib. "Totally open, no effort to hide it. None. The district engineer said we needed to give him ten percent. Or he wouldn't approve the technical drawings."

"Ten percent of the construction costs," says Ashok.

"Like, this is totally normal. And he became super-pissed off when we said no way, this is donated money, we have to account for it."

"What did you do?"

"We told him to fuck off. Nepali version, of course."

"We said we'd carry on *without* his permission."

"Right. Without. And you know what he said? He said, he said he would take *us* to court for not following government procedure! *And*—if we thought the judge would listen to *us*, we knew nothing."

"So what did you do?"

"We had bigger 'source and force' than him, so he had to back off. But what if you have no connections?"

"These scams are organized by the politicians," says Ashok. "They chase after an NGO with a foolish accusation—like 'you are pro-Dalai Lama.' Some people end up losing their own money. And even go to jail."

"*Umalé* is the worst," says Rajib, referring to the Unified Marxist-Leninist Party.

"No, they all do it," says Ashok.

"Even the Maoists?" I ask.

"Of course," Rajib continues. "This is our politics—elitists make money. This is our history. From the time of Prithivi Narayan Shah, before that even. Ask your porters what the Maoists did for *them*."

"This country is cursed," says Ashok. "After Bhimsen Thapa was killed, his widow should become *sati*. Strictly, widows go of their own wishes into the husband funeral bonfire, but Bhimsen's body was left by the river. They built a big fire anyway, and threw her inside. Just before she died, she cursed Nepal. For all the cruelty and wickedness to her husband, not her. That's important. That curse remains with us today."

"Do you know the phrase?" asks Rajib. "*Sati-le sãrãpeko desh*. The country cursed by the *sati*."

— · —

I return to my tent, happy to have met these two, with their youth and their energy. They are here to explore their own country, something few urban Brahmins would have done when I first came to Nepal—something I certainly haven't done in either the US or the UK. And they got those schools built.

Their talk of corruption takes me back to an evening in 1990, just after the People's Movement had forced King Birendra to cede absolute power. In Europe the Berlin Wall had fallen, and East Europe was freeing itself from Soviet occupation. Here in Asia, a democratic revolution was underway. It was July or August, during the monsoon. An interim government had been formed, led by the Nepali Congress Party but including communists and royalists. A new constitution was being drafted.

Dipak Gyawali, who twelve years later would serve briefly as minister of water resources, had invited me to his house for dinner. "You should meet Congress younger generation," he said. Sher Bahadur Deuba was there, then a rising politician from Dadeldhura in the far west, to this day a recurrent prime minister. There was whiskey, beer, chicken curry. The room was dark and sparse; outside, wind and rain. Tales of jail time. A mood of great satisfaction, and of open horizons. An uplifting evening—until Laxman Basnet got too drunk. Laxman was the president of the Nepal Trade Union Congress, and a key organizer of the spring street protests that had toppled the monarchy.

"*Abā Nigel*-sir," he said to me, raising his glass, laughing. "*Hāmro pāla āyo!*" But Nigel-sir, it's *our* turn now.

We had been talking about corruption under the Panchayat system and among the king's family and supporters, and of how things would be different under a democracy.

Everyone else laughed, not without some embarrassment—the man was drunk, after all. But he wasn't lying.

In 1991 the social anthropologist Dor Bahadur Bista published his classic essay, *Fatalism and Development*, in which he argued that the double bindings of class and religiously-sanctioned caste engender a "*absolute belief in fatalism*" among Nepalis—the sense that *"no-one has personal control over one's life circumstances, which are determined through a divine or powerful external agency."*[1] Fatalism, he wrote, leads to passivity and to the practice of *chākari*, or sycophancy—serving a person who will reward you for your loyalty rather than your skills. This in turn means that your political leader is expected to channel public resources to his *āphno mānche* [own people]. For some, it isn't corruption per se that is so reprehensible: as the Nepali proverb observes, "*Jasle maha kādchha, usle hāt chātchha*"—whoever collects honey gets to lick his hand. What incenses them is when none of that honey falls their way.

September 23, 2016—Day 35, below and to the west of the Kagmara La, Jumla District, 14,382 feet.

I've never been as cold as I was this afternoon.

With a long day ahead, we pack up and set off before 8 a.m., leaving our Nepali friends to follow us.

We are walking in wet mist, the gradient at first gentle, through a forest of dying pine trees, past ruined and abandoned houses. It's like a ravaged set in the wars of Westeros. I feel quite strong today, and push on ahead of the others. I'm trying to put some distance between myself and Palden, who hangs on me—this is his job, after all.

After three hours we stop briefly to eat our packed lunches. Unpicking the tinfoil, I find a clump of my favorite orange cocktail sausages, folded into one another like baby mice. Along with a boiled egg and salt—quintessential picnic food. Clouds are scudding overhead, breaking up occasionally and revealing fresh snow on the Kanjirobas behind us. We move quickly on, the wind rising and tugging our faces.

Soon there is rain, driving hard at us down the valley. We are walking up a wide bowl of rough sedge grass and rivulets, dotted with dirty sheep—no shepherds in sight. The rain intensifies, but Palden has been carrying my umbrella these past few days and I don't want to stop and wait for him; besides, I can see as I look back, he is using it—though it has inverted itself. This stops me for a moment, and I gesture to him through a gathering mist, mimicking the act of bending the umbrella ribs back into shape again. He ignores me, dueling with the wind, the umbrella thrust forward like some crazy, oscillating shield.

I am dressed in shorts, a T-shirt, and an uninsulated rain breaker, and every time I stop I am colder, though I hesitate to take out my pullover: I must keep moving. What was dust is now mud, becoming sloppy snow as the rain turns into sleet. There is no clear path; we are high, close to the summit, but ahead are banks of cloud, and soon we are inside them. I have no idea where I am, but I keep moving, reluctant to wait for anyone, let alone cede even a foot by turning back down again. Now it's snowing. I check my InReach; 16,220 feet. We have already come up nearly 4,700 feet; today's climb will be our longest. My energy is undiminished, but I am shivering now, and I can't control it. I've left my gloves with the mules this morning, and the pockets of my rain breaker offer little protection.

I climb on, seeing nothing ahead. The wind is increasing, a sure sign we are nearing a ridge—but where on the ridge are we? Turning around, there is no sign of Palden.

This is stupid, and dangerous; I am unsure where I should be going, or how to go back down, but I carry on still, taking smaller steps now.

The air is thin, and my breathing is heavy; I hunch into my clothes to trap what is left of my body heat. The snow is at least a foot deep now. After a few minutes I stop, put on my pullover, and continue—but I am chilled to the bone, and the pullover makes no difference. I stop, looking down at my soaking shorts, suddenly tired.

Just then I hear a rhythmic plodding behind me; it's Bukhé, the white lead mule. She is streaked with brown mud. She steps on past me without turning her head, and disappears up into the cloud. I follow. Behind me I hear the bridle bells of another mule. Sure enough, a few minutes later Bukhé reaches the pass. She doesn't stop, but walks right on down, steering sharply left, following an invisible path through the snow. She's been here once before, in bright sun, many years ago. I am amazed.

We are at 16,780 feet (5,115 meters)—the Kagmara La, the last of our four five-thousand-meter passes. *Kãg mãrne* is Nepali for "crow killer"—akin to *Hindu Kush*, which some say is Persian for "Hindu Killer." So named, Palden told me last night, for a flight of dead crows found in the summit pass by a villager in times long lost; dead, one assumes, from some unexpected blast of arctic air.

Palden comes up, Konzok close behind him. I try to speak, and realize I can't—my mouth is frozen. "I am c-c-c-c-cold," I manage finally. Palden laughs uproariously, his way of showing concern. I hustle over the pass to escape the wind, not bothering to leave any prayer flags. The view from this pass is said to be one of the best in Nepal—north-east to Kanjiroba (22,582 feet), and north into a host of other twenty-thousand-foot mountains. Photographs of this northern panorama on a clear day show a line of serrated rocks, shot with snow drifts, floating between bright sky and shadowed blue hillsides. For us, though, it was sleet, mist, and a view no more than ten feet ahead.

Across the pass, Konzok extends his hand to me as we move down through deep snow, the rocks of the path concealed from us. A thousand feet later the snow becomes mud, the cloud thins out, and the wind drops. Below us lies a brown and desolate hillside.

An hour later we call it quits—we are short of our destination, a riverbed some fifteen hundred feet further down, but where we are is sheltered from blast and just about flat enough to pitch the tents. I sit, exhausted now. We've been going eight hours, but it's the cold that's done me in. Once my tent is set up, I climb inside and pull out my sleeping bag. It's damp, but I crawl in to warm up and quickly fall asleep.

—·—

I awake suddenly, with no sense of where I am. I put my head outside the tent—the sky is clear again, the evening light disappearing. I can hear Rajib's deep voice from the kitchen tent, which glows like a yellow lantern in the dusk. Attracted by the appearance of warmth, I shuffle over. Palden, Konzok, Kedar, Ngima, Sagar, Rajib, Ashok—all are sitting round the hissing primus stove, eating, maneuvering large hunks of rice around battered metal plates with their hands. The air smells of kerosene and damp clothes. Rajib is in shorts, a bandage around his knee. I am greeted by laughter and cries of "c-c-c-c-cold!!!"

"Yeah, yeah," I say, smiling. "What happened, Rajib-*ji*?"

"Overdid it," he says. "Should be fine by tomorrow."

I make to sit on the floor too, but Konzok and Palden look alarmed and usher me to my camp seat at the trestle table. I peck at my dal and paratha, but I'm not hungry, just tired, and I lean back against the side of the tent and listen to the conversation. I'm happy to be ignored; it's a situation I relish, and one many other travelers do. I am the stranger, yet everyone is here because of me; there's no need to impress or compete; no unease.

I can't follow everything, but Ngima is speaking in a low and pained voice, telling Ashok about his childhood. His father died when he was a baby, he says. Then his mother, Palden's sister, married again. The new husband didn't want Ngima and his brother, so one day his mother brought them to Palden's house in Kathmandu and said he must take them. And Palden did, though Ngima doesn't sound too happy about this.

"My sister no good suh," says Palden, shaking his head. "Bad mother."

Do you ever see her now? asks Ashok. And Ngima becomes angry, clenching his big fists and screwing one of them into the ground between his feet. "*Kahilye pãni!*" he says with quiet venom—not ever.

After a while I return to my tent and climb fully clothed into my sleeping bag. The wind has disappeared. I am still cold. I don't want to read, and I shut the Kindle back down again; but sleep eludes me.

I haven't asked my crew what they think of the Maoists, but this evening Rajib did. Last month Pushpa Kumar Dahal, a.k.a. Prachanda [the fierce one], chairman of the Communist Party of Nepal (Maoist Centre) was elected prime minister for the second time since the end of the ten-year Maoist insurrection. Now he heads a parliamentary coalition of Maoists and Nepali Congress, deadly enemies during the civil war.

"What about Prachanda's new watch?" Rajib asked. "And his fancy new double bed?"

No one rose to this, but he persisted.

"And his big house in Lazimpath?

"*Hajur*," said Konzok. "You think we support him?"

"No, just asking."

Konzok usually says little, and I thought he was finished. But after a couple of minutes he continued.

"They fought for the right things. Many people believed them. They were Bahun, but they seemed different—like *hajur*, I mean. They did bad things, but I believe they cared for us. After the war, they lost their way. *Bãto bhuliyo, hajur*. Now they are like all politicians."

"Konzok-*ji*, they didn't lose their way. They planned this from the beginning."

Rajib's opinion is shared by historian John Whelpton, in *A History of Nepal*: for him, the Maoists' revolution was designed to break into Nepal's "magic circle" of personal wealth and prestige, a road denied them when their predecessor party, the United Left Front, won only nine out of 188 parliamentary seats in 1991, in Nepal's first democratic elections of the post-Panchayat era. The ballot box had not worked, so they defaulted to the gun.

I play several rounds of *Plague, Inc.* on my Samsung 7 smartphone, exterminate all of humanity three times, and sleep soundly.

September 24, 2016—Day 36, Toijum, Jumla District, 10,185 feet.

It's Mum's birthday—today she would have been 94.

My mother died a week after my daughter. I'd just been to London to tell Mandana about Tess; I couldn't do it by phone. We came straight back to the US for the funeral. A couple of days later, my sister Mandy called; she'd been visiting Mum in Maidenhead. The ambulance has just taken her to hospital, she said. Severe breathing problems—her emphysema. I told Mandy I'd try to get a flight that night. No, don't do that, the doctor says you should wait, Mum might not make it through the night—your trip would be wasted, you have so much to do in Washington. If she lasts another day, she should be fine—that's what he says.

I called Mum's room in the hospital early the next morning; no one picked up. Mandy then called, and a nurse answered. She's sitting up in bed, she's drinking a nice cup of tea, oh yes, and she's chatting with us; she seems a bit better this morning, she does. So Mandy relaxed, and said she'd come in at 11 a.m., the beginning of normal visiting hours: but Mum suddenly faded, and died before Mandy got there. I hadn't managed to speak to her.

So I flew back to London again; first I would bury my mother, and then my daughter. We held a wake for Mum at Monkey Island in the River Thames, near the village of Bray. That name is a corruption of Monk's Eyot [island], a corruption embraced by the fifth Duke of Marlborough, who in the 1730s built a wooden fishing pavilion with an interior dome painted *en grotesque* by the French artist Andie de Clermont—scenes of monkeys in fashionable Regency costume, punting, hunting, and fishing the nearby river. Mum had spoken of this place, telling me the apocryphal story of insane King George III's confinement here with his own pet monkey.

"I bet he faked his madness," she'd said. "So he could escape there with his monkey and get away from all those frightful people at court."

In her later years, my mother had come to prefer the company of animals to that of most humans. This was a good place to remember her and her unlucky life.

Much had conspired to chip away at my mother's emotional generosity. A childhood fouled by her mother's alcoholism. The death of her beloved fiancé during the war. An unhappy marriage to my father. A stellar university career that promised much, but which she abandoned to join the Women's Royal Naval Service (the WRENS), leaving her with no higher qualifications and restricting her to mundane jobs after her divorce. A second husband who, like her own mother, was a depressive alcoholic.

Throughout her life, my mother wrote to me every two weeks, and though she was incapable of saying so, I knew she missed me. When I could, I would take her on holiday to various places. In 1990, when she was sixty-eight and I was thirty-nine, we went back to her beloved Nyasaland. By then she was a bitter version of her younger self, and the week I spent with her wore on me. She was shocked by the physical decay in post-colonial Malawi—as if her precious memories had been rifled through by an intruder. To me, it felt more like a slow, kindly dissolution.

We found our old house, standing empty, its corrugated iron roof battered and its whitewashed walls stained by rust. The garden had reverted to brush, but the terraces my father had built into the hillside nearly sixty years ago were still visible.

Down the hill, the old Zomba Club house had also survived, if barely. We walked through the collapsing building into the old cinema hall.

A dozen misaligned desk-chair combinations were scattered about; the parquet floor had been softened by flooding. I remembered smooth concrete—that was me, slithering behind the back row on my tummy; I had wanted to see *War and Peace*, the Audrey Hepburn and Henry Fonda version, forbidden to seven-year-olds then. I had lain at 90 degrees to the screen, on my side, my arm stretched out along the cool floor. In front of my nose were a shoe, and a lady's leg. The shoe was black with a solid heel. The leg was enclosed in a white stocking and smelled like my mother's lingerie drawer. Perhaps I touched the lady's leg; I was always fiddling with things. I was discovered and hauled out long before Napoleon got to Moscow.

On our last night, we were eating dinner in our hotel in Blantyre when Mum said "I'm so sad about Zomba. Everything's gone. I mean, the houses are there still. But all the energy. All that activity. Just gone."

"Perhaps you should write about it."

"Most of our friends are dead now. The Finnys, the Simmonds. Hugh Norman-Walker. I wish *someone* would write about those days. I wish I'd kept a diary at least... now I've forgotten so much. It's the silly little things that come back. Like Ursula Hobson falling over a balcony at a cocktail party with no knickers on. Or the day Jane Norman-Walker and I learned there was a human leg on sale at the market (of course it was gone by the time we arrived). Or when we were staying at the Simmonds' and they had to pump the drains and found they were clogged with condoms. Kenneth's 'liaisons', of course. Poor Ruth."

She then looked directly at me, something she didn't do much any more.

"You know, there were some very decent, dedicated people here. They did their best for the Africans. No one mentions that now. These days everyone thinks we were 'colonialists.' Oppressors. You too, I suspect. It's unfair. But what can you say that makes any difference? Who's listening?"

A mother's gifts are impossible to measure: you cannot winnow them away from the person you have become. A parent, though, can only give what is left to them to give. When I was a boy, my mother hid from me the pain of her own childhood and her marriage, and tried her best to show love and approval. Children are hypersensitive, though, and the effort was apparent, leaving me with an unease that never quite disappeared.

The reserves of strength and insouciance that still animated her when I was a child deserted her later in life, and her growing bitterness was reflected in a fractious relationship with my adolescent sister Mandy. It was my good fortune that I came first.

—·—

Today is surprisingly hard going, perhaps because the terrain is so broken, perhaps because of yesterday's exertions. For the first two hours we thread our way through boulders littering the sides of the Galpung Khola, climbing, descending, crossing and re-crossing the freezing stream. In time, the sun rises over the hillsides and we stop to dry off, eating *lonch* near a livestock bridge. Rajib and Ashok press on, though Rajib is limping painfully; they need to reach Gamghadi by September 28 or they will miss the play.

We follow the Galpung all day. The valley widens and the switchbacks lengthen, taking us several hundred feet above the river before bringing us back down into the gorge again. Depressing walking, this— made awkward by rocks, and devoid of trees. By late afternoon we reach the confluence of the Galpung with the south-flowing Jagdula Khola, and we climb out of the steep-sided valley onto a grassy bluff overlooking the two rivers. Palden suggests we stop for the night, but I dislike the place and insist we cross the Jagdula towards the distant roofs of the army post at Toijum.

I imagine order and good company there, and the thought of this sustains me through a nasty descent down steep, muddy foresters' paths in a close-packed larch wood, and then sharply up and out of the ravine again. By now it's raining, and the light has gone. We arrive in darkness at a mean collection of thatched huts, and halt in a fallow millet field. The cut stalks are overrun with fibrous groundcover; this is Himalayan balsam, *impatiens glandulifera*, brought to England in the nineteenth century as the poor man's version of a hothouse orchid, and praised at the time for its invasiveness. Today these open-mouthed, pink "policemen's helmets" infest British woods, riverbanks, and back gardens—as they do our field, a wide stand of them concealing the paper, plastic, and cow shit on which we pitch our tents. I sit morosely on my groundsheet; a couple of strangers squat in a doorway, looking at me without interest. The night is warm, pungent with nectar and manure.

Sleep is difficult, so I turn on my Kindle. I've started *An Unnecessary Woman* by Rabih Alameddine. It's a beautifully-written story about Aaliya, an aging, single bookworm in Beirut whose drab life is transformed by what she reads. Her neighbor Fadia is preventing Aaliya's brother from foisting their aging, hateful mother on her.

> " *"Take her back," Fadia keeps repeating, "take her back," in an unrelenting tone that brooks no discussion, no disagreement, a tone that grows stronger and more insistent with each repetition. "Take her back."*
>
> *"Let me go; take back thy gift."*
>
> *Of all the lovely phrases and images, the bright jewels embedded in Tennyson's "Tithonus," this sentence, "take back thy gift," is my favorite. Lodged in my memory from the moment I first read it, it quickens my essence.*
>
> *"I wither slowly in thine arms,*
>
> *Here at the quiet limit of the world."*[2]

The poem laments the curse of Tithonus' immortality: he once asked his lover Eros, goddess of the Dawn, to give him eternal life, but forgot to ask her for eternal youth. It is really about Alfred Tennyson's lasting grief at the death of his beloved Arthur Hallam; the poem was first drafted in 1833, rewritten many times and published only in 1860. It reads like a plea for release from the other-worldly identity that grief induces, in which the one who has died remains eternally young and the mourner, disconnected from the warm ambience of daily life, grows thin and brittle:

"...hold me not for ever in thine East:
How can my nature longer mix with thine?
Coldly thy rosy shadows bathe me, cold
Are all thy lights, and cold my wrinkled feet
Upon thy glimmering thresholds..."[3]

Here at the quiet limit of my world, I shut the Kindle back down.

In the summer darkness I can still make out the blue of the tent's walls.

Yesterday was the sixth anniversary of Tess' death. I find myself thinking of a time I was reading Genesis to her, in her bedroom in Kathmandu. She must have been five, perhaps six.

"And God created great whales, and every living creature that moveth, which the waters brought forth abundantly, after their kind, and every winged fowl after his kind: and God saw that it was good..."[4]

"But who made God?" Tess interrupted.

I was silent.

"You did," she said, turning towards me. "You made the sun and the moon. And the stars. You made everything."

For a few brief years, you are your child's universe. I found this frightening; I wasn't ready for something so momentous. In time, as it always does, her rapture dissipated. I will never be so essential to anyone else again, but I am grateful that once I was.

13

AT THE EDGE
OF THINGS

September 25, 2016—Day 37, Balasa,
above Chaurikot, 10,150 feet.

We pick our way carefully out of shitty Toijum and carry on down the
Jagdula Khola. The hillside gradients continue to flatten and the valley
to broaden, and for the first time in weeks I can walk without watching
each footfall. Here there are fewer conifers, more willows, beech and
oaks, then the first cultivated fields since Ringmo: stands of ripened yellow millet fringed with blue-green hedges of tangled hemp. Many fields
lie fallow, though, and several houses have been abandoned; there are
few people about.

"What's going on here?" I ask. "Where is everyone?"

"Gone, suh," says Palden. "No good here. Too much poor."

"Gone where, though?"

"Hurikot," said Kedar, pointing with his finger. "And Sim, Thapagaun"—
now with his chin—"*ausadhi jadibootiharu*—everyone is out collecting
jadibooti."

He means medicinal plants. Near here the Bheri Nadi swings west in
an arc of about six miles, between the latitudinal Bharbhare and Khame
ridgelines. In gulleys folded against the wind, accumulated soils have

nurtured a great variety of trees, shrubs and flowers valued by India's vast Ayurvedic medical market. There you can find *nardostachys grandiflora*, spikenard, a flowering valerian used as an anti-convulsant; *swertia chirata*, a plant from the gentian family that kills intestinal worms and cures skin diseases; and *zanthoxylum*, the prickly ash, which dampens the pain of toothache and aids digestion.

Over the last generation, as motorable roads have pushed closer towards these gulleys, collecting *jadibooti* has become far more profitable than scratching away at field crops—and this new prosperity is evident in dozens of corrugated iron roofs in Hurikot, some blue, others gunmetal gray.

"Also *yārsagumba*," adds Palden.

In Tibetan, *yārsagumba* means "summer grass, winter worm," a poetic way of describing one of nature's nastier transactions. Each year, ghost moths lay their eggs in the high Himalayan meadows, and their larvae develop underground. Those caterpillars unfortunate enough to encounter the parasitic *cordyceps* fungus, however, are body-snatched by spores that suffuse, and finally kill them. Small, yellowish mushroom stems then burst through the heads of their dead hosts, poking almost imperceptibly through the ground: the harvesters commonly crawl through the grass to search them out. *Yārsagumba* are only found above eleven thousand feet, and in the summer months whole villages in and around Dolpo empty out into mountainside harvest camps. They are worth enormous sums in China, mainly due to their aphrodisiac properties. The anthropologist James Fisher, in *Trans-Himalaya Traders Transformed*, estimates that a family of four harvesters might expect to gather a kilogram of worms in two months; in 2011 this was worth perhaps 400,000 rupees, or $4,700—twenty times what the same four family members could earn from two months of agricultural laboring. In the Shanghai market, the same kilogram would sell for as much as $35,000 (we have heard figures of up to $100,000 per kg for this year's harvest).

Like most windfall enrichment schemes, the *yārsagumba* business has malign side effects. Each season brings up to 20,000 outsiders, all hacking away at the fragile alpine turf, hunting the *bharal* for food, at times murdering one another and local villagers.

We walk through the short main street and descend into the grounds of a monastery. This *gompa*, Palden tells me, is a famous center of *Bön* teaching. After we drop our packs I go with Konzok into the temple hall. My eyes adjust only slowly to abrupt light changes these days, and coming in from the bright sun I can at first see nothing. Standing still, I feel dizzy, and back against a glass case for support. There is a harsh smell of burned butter and incense smoke. I can hear a soft, disembodied voice, its direction uncertain. As my eyes adjust, huge statues of the Buddha emerge from the gloom like ships from fog. For a moment I am quite disoriented; the air around me throbs. Where are we? Who is this, and what is he saying?

"He is head lama," says Konzok, perhaps sensing my distraction. "He is asking you for donation."

I can see him now, a tiny man on a crimson cushion beside the altar. He smiles and beckons to me. I fish out my wallet. No small notes, only a 500 rupee bill—far too much. I hesitate; but they have both seen it. I make to insert it into the glass donation box in front of the altar, but the lama holds out his hand and takes it from me. It disappears into the folds of his cloak.

We sit. He speaks in Tibetan, and Konzok translates into English. There is a school here, he tells me; the monastery hosts about thirty children from poor families and gives them a five-year education, up to the end of second grade. It's free—and probably more important to their parents, the monastery feeds them.

I ask him about *Bön*. How is it different from Buddhism? It isn't, he says. It's older, that's all. As you are older than the young man standing beside you, he adds, gesturing to my left. I look around—there is no one.

"He means you," says Konzok. "He sees you as a boy. He says you have the gold hair." As I did, when I was little.

When a child grows up, the lama continues, he no longer sees devils—he sees people. "In *Bön*," said Konzok, "there is wind, fire . . . *tuphan*?"

"Typhoon."

"In Buddhism. . . . sir, I am not understand him well. In Buddhism, the yogi sees the true world. No spirits, no *Bodhisattvas*, just—stones, he say, water, animals. No—no more. . . . I don't know in English. No *chitrakalā*."

"No paintings?"

"Yes."

"He sees the mountain," I added.

The lama looks puzzled.

"Never mind," I say. We leave it there.

Out in the sun, I take off my boots and socks and lie back on the grass.

Curious kids surround me, some giggling. I smile, close my eyes and throw an arm across my face, shutting them out. I've not heard anything like that before. I have always found Tibetan Buddhism a bewildering riot of imaginary beings—endless manifestations of the Buddha, the obese fanged demons, the bright green consorts, the cadaverous ghosts, the funky little monsters crawling around the edges of the *thãnkãs*. . . . but is it *deliberately* absurd? Is that the point? To force you back into the visible, the material, the only *real* world?

—·—

Before we leave, I check my InReach for incoming messages. One from Mandy, cheering me on to Jumla. Another from Sarah—"only twelve more days!" And one from Bryan, Alex's father. Two days earlier he'd visited Tess' grave, and he'd seen Mandana's memorial—a small black marble plaque installed at the foot of Tess' headstone late last year. An oval photo medallion has been cut into the marble; it shows Mandana holding Tess on a beach on Skiathos—a beautiful photograph. Taken in 1986,

Tess is not yet two. She is wrapped tight in a towel, squinting into the sun from beneath a floppy beach hat. Mandana's hair is short, her face calm and somewhat dreamy as she leans into the camera, her arms light around her child.

At once we find ourselves climbing an impossibly steep path, so steep you can only laugh, up through red sand, bamboo, and a coruscating sun, back onto the valley slopes again. Here the trail flattens, contouring the valley. This is easy walking, and we press on through a goat market in the large Chetri village of Sim. With the sun disappearing over a low horizon, we reach the pass at Chaurikot and set camp, sheltered from the wind by the wooden buildings lining the village's single street. Up the last part of the trail and around the camp field stand weathered wooden fence posts, human faces carved casually into them. These spirit-wardens seem to welcome strangers. A few skillful cuts of an adze leave deep eyes, flat cheeks and parted lips; above these faces the post-tops stand like pillars of dense hair, reminding me of the red crowns of volcanic stone found on the heads of *moai* on Easter Island.

Jumla is no more than four days away now; this will leave nine more before Sarah's arrival. Sick as I am of walking, I begin to wonder how we can use up this spare week. Perhaps we can go on up into Humla District, to Simikot and back, and visit Konzok's mother? He hasn't been there for almost a year.

In my wallet I am carrying Mandana's last note to me, written in February 2014, the month before she died. I unfold it and read it again by the light of my head torch.

> *"I'm wondering why I stop hurting when you are here. If you can, imagine a piano that can feel. For twenty years it is tuned one way. Then suddenly many of its notes go so badly out of tune. When you are here, it seems, feels, as though the notes are in tune again, and so the piano does not hurt so much. Can you understand what I am saying?"*

Although I had left Mandana, we never divorced: it was important to Mandana to maintain this connection, and Sarah accepted this as part of what I carried with me. After Tess died, I saw Mandana often, either in London or in Virginia—she came and stayed with us so she could see Alex.

Depression still crippled her; with a few brief exceptions, she had remained impervious to the effects of anti-depressants, and by the end of her life was undergoing an astonishing last-gasp drug regime based around DFF 118 Forte, or dihydrocodeine tartrate 40 mg, an opiate. If I take one DFF 118, I get high. Mandana would build up to as many as fifty tablets each day—all under supervision—before detoxing for several weeks with methadone, and then repeating the cycle.

That day in February 2014 I was visiting Mandana in London, and she asked if she could come and live with Sarah and me. "You know I like Sarah. I'm just lonely. I'll just live out in your annex there. Then I can see Alex much more."

No, I said, I don't think that'll work. Come and visit us often, like you have been doing. Please. And I can come and spend time here with you—two or three weeks, every few months. I can do that. I can come back in April.

Four weeks later she fell in her bathroom, hitting her head on the edge of the sink. The concussion was mild, but she fell awkwardly. The opiates coursing through her system suppressed her breathing, and she suffocated.

Some of her ashes are buried in Columbia Gardens, near her daughter. Sarah and I took the rest to Nepal last year. We hiked up to Lawudo Gompa, near Mount Everest. This was the spiritual home of Lama Zopa Rinpoche, her teacher in Kathmandu two decades earlier. Lama Zopa built the monastery around the meditation cave of Lama Kunzang Yeshe, who died there in 1946. Zopa was born to a farm family nearby, and from the time he could crawl would constantly set off towards the cave, though he had never seen it, and as soon as he could speak would insist he *was* Kunzang Yeshe. In time he was formally recognized by the lama of Thangboche as Kunzang Yeshe's reincarnation.

Not knowing what to do with the ashes, I walked around the monastery in the early morning. Then I saw the meditation cave and knew this was the right place. I scattered the flask over an ancient juniper bush on top of the cave, which is set into a steep hillside and overlooks an uncountable succession of snow peaks. High above the cave sits the Bragridkarpo [White Cliff] rockface. The cliff is said to mask the entrance to one of the Himalayan *beyul,* those sacred valleys blessed by Guru Rinpoche. Like the hidden door to the dwarf kingdom of Erebor, I thought, and Bilbo's inspired discovery of the keyhole in the moonlight at the end of Durin's Day. Mandana didn't live to see *The Desolation of Smaug.* She'd have loved that movie.

September 26, 2016—Day 38, Ghan Khola, Jumla District, 11,578 feet.

The day begins with some infuriating terrain: an immediate sharp drop of 8-900 feet over slippery rocks down the throat of a river gorge, and a steep climb to get out again—all to cover a distance you could shout across. From there begins a shallow climb, one that lasts the whole day, millet and marijuana slowly giving gave way to sand and pine again. We walk up through a Domay village, a village of tailors, "untouchables," or Dalit: to my surprise, a village of broad millet fields below sturdy houses—so unlike the homes of Dalit in the east, where blacksmiths [Kami], cobblers [Sarki] and tailors [Domai] usually live in hovels, isolated from the main village. Up on top of a tall *chir* pine, a faded blue triangular flag marked with a golden cross.

"Is that ... ?"

"Yes, suh—Crishun. Many Crishun here."

It makes sense—a religion in which caste has no place, and which offers spiritual equality to all believers. Christianity has always been seen as subversive by Nepal's high-caste rulers. When I first worked in Nepal, missionary activity was forbidden, and for a Hindu to convert to Christianity was a crime. The constitution that followed the 1990 People's Movement did allow Nepalis to change religion, but still prohibited any proselytization. This position was sustained in the 2007 post-monarchical Interim Constitution, even though it characterized Nepal as a secular state. The new 2015 Constitution reiterates Nepal's secular status—but then reels it back in with an Orwellian definition: *"'secular' means protection of religion and culture being practiced since ancient times."*

I fumble about for my earbuds. Spotify deserted me in the Tarap River canyon: the downloads have to be refreshed every two weeks, and there is no Wi-Fi in these parts. I'm reduced to a few dozen old iTunes purchases; one of these is Bob Dylan's 1965 album *Highway 61 Revisited*, which ends with *Desolation Row*.

As I listen, I find myself witnessing quiet, creeping desolation. We are well away from the *jadibooti* valleys now. Here the fields are emptied of life, the communities hollowed out. This was never prosperous land, but its ability to sustain a rural way of life has decayed quickly since Peter Matthiessen was here. Throughout the middle hills, public health programs have helped double Nepal's population—thirteen million then, twenty-eight million now. Roadheads have moved up and in, reducing the prices once paid for traditional crops. Seasonal migration, always a feature of rainfed hill agriculture in Nepal, has increased massively since the civil war of 1996–2006, when young men were targets of forced Maoist recruitment, or objects of suspicion by government forces.

In the villages we are passing through, we see old people, children, and a sprinkling of young women: much of the intervening generation has gone, absent for years at a time, in India, the Gulf, or Malaysia. The markers of their disappearance are the radios, the trainers, the gas cookers, the odd household generator—belongings that signify hard-earned membership of the mercantile world.

The year after Peter Matthiessen and George Schaller visited Dolpo, three lecturers from the University of East Anglia launched a series of household surveys in mid-western Nepal, initiating a body of research on Nepal's political economy that remains relevant nearly fifty years later. Piers Blaikie, John Cameron and David Seddon's best-known work is *Nepal in Crisis,* a book that prefigures much of what you can find in Maoist socioeconomic writing. They depict a stagnant rural economy in which caste and property relations had remained almost unchanged since the Gorkha conquest of the late eighteenth century. To them, Nepalese "development" meant the extraction of rural surplus by Kathmandu elites, acting on behalf of metropolitan capitalists in India—leaving the rural poor as peripheral actors in a peripheral country. As you would expect, the role played by roads was extractive: sucking out products and people, and returning cheap consumer goods from Kathmandu or India.

—·—

On we go, now passed by a shiny young Nepali woman in jeans and backpack, hitching a ride on a Tibetan peddler's cantering horse. A few minutes later we find her sitting beside the trail, drinking from a tin of Fanta. *Namaste,* she says, where are you going? Like Rajib and Ashok, she is from Kathmandu, her father in this case an ambassador-in-waiting. She has two weeks of vacation from her job with an image consultancy and she too has decided to see something of her country, flying in to Jufal Airport southwest of here, and due to fly out again from Jumla in four days' time. Yes, she is on her own. Doesn't that worry her?

"Should it?" she asks me. She is a tall and commanding woman, and her society confers on her class and caste an authority that few young women in the US would carry outside their immediate environments.

She walks with us to the ridge town at Maure Lanya, at 12,800 feet the end of our long climb. It's late, but the place is cold, windy, and filthy, and my judgment is clouded by some codeine I've been taking for my hip, which has begun to play up. We press on, dropping down the western slope, looking for a sheltered campsite. The shadows are thick, the deep red soil turned muddy by rain. Ngima and Sagar both fall heavily. I misstep and wrench my hip. It takes another two hours and over a thousand feet before the slope evens out enough to camp; we stop by a stream, feeling sorry for ourselves.

Codeine can leave a bitter aftertaste, and tonight it is my father's dead face I see as I lie in a tent battered by the wind.

When he was ninety, my father broke his hip for the second time. I flew in from the US to find him comatose. I spent that night with him, and although I have no idea whether he could hear me, I reminded him what a good father he had been.

He was the last British chief justice of both Hong Kong and Brunei. He was genuinely unimpressed by himself. "*As a young man, I did not make much of a living at the bar*," he had written, in the twilight of his life.

> *"For this I cannot blame the chambers I was in, though they were not that good, nor the absence of legal aid, which was introduced in the High Court in 1950 but which proved of little use to me. The real truth is that I was not a competent advocate. If I had stayed on, perhaps I would have earned an adequate living in the 1960s and become a circuit court judge when the bench was expanded in the 1970s, but I do not regret having left Britain. My second-class talents looked better abroad, thanks to a combination of hard work, good luck and scant competition.*"[1]

Some might think that Sir Denys was indulging in fashionable self-deprecation when he wrote this; he was not.

Successful men can intimidate their sons, but he would always tell me that his career proved anyone could get ahead with hard work and a slice of good luck, and there was no reason I shouldn't too—whatever getting ahead might look like to me.

"Fifty years ago," he had once said, "You'd have been a district commissioner in India. What you do in the World Bank is about as close as you can get these days."

He died the next morning, and he was laid out in the Welsh manner, in an open coffin in his curtained study, the mirrors covered. I sat alone with him.

His wife Fiona had dressed him in a gray pin-striped suit, white shirt, and MCC tie; on his finger, the family signet ring, a confection of his upstart father's: a phoenix rising from a coronet, wings folded, above its head a furled banner bearing the motto *Toujours Pret*. Ready for what, though? The undertaker had perhaps struggled with this before lighting on a rather dubious answer. The face powder, the rouge, the lipstick—more than a hint of debauchery; think Peter O'Toole in *Caligula*. My real father, long departed, would have loved the absurdity.

September 27, 2016—Day 39, Guthichaur Sheep and Goat Research Farm, Jumla District, 9,450 feet.

We are all in pain. Tomorrow, though, we will reach Jumla, only seven days after setting out from Phoksundo. We have all been impatient to get there, and we are paying for this imprudence: everyone is now carrying some sort of injury. Konzok is wretched, his ear infected. Palden has sprained a knee, and Sagar is hobbling. Kedar was finally kicked by Bukhé in a moment of carelessness; he has a swollen heel. Ngima has a sore shoulder and couldn't lift anything today.

Peter Matthiessen also walked from the lake to Jumla in seven days. He took a more southerly route, down the Suli Gad to its confluence with the Beri Khola—the cliffs of which I last saw from Tarakot in the evening light of August 31, four weeks and a lifetime ago. His route is a bit hard to figure out—a combination of different names on my maps, and his imperfectly heard Nepali (like Balasco for Balangchur). On the fourth day of each of our journeys from Ringmo, his route up the Bheri intersected with ours at the village of Hurikot (Sonrikot for him) as we descended in a southwesterly direction from the Kagmara Pass. It then took him just over two days to reach Jumla; it will take us closer to three. He was in a foul mood as he finished off his journey. He was *"coming down too fast,"* and felt *"mutilated, murderous: I am in a fury of dark energies, with no control at all on my short temper."*[2] He wondered if this was due to a precipitate loss of altitude.

In fact the trails in this area hover around the ten-thousand-foot mark, which is only some four thousand feet below Shey. A more likely cause of his ill-temper was his reluctance to reengage with the crowded world he left behind when he walked out of Darbang two months earlier: a reluctance expressed through a distaste for Indo-Aryan Nepalis, and Hindu society in general. He was now re-encountering the edges of the populous world, home to southern despoilers who threatened the wilderness and the cultures of his Tibetan plateau. Jumla was sour with *"the intricate hostile deference of Hindus, so many of whom—even the children—seem to be frowning"* and

> *" ...the litter of Chetri villages, ubiquitous police, dogs, human excrement, the hard blare of transistor radios, and finally Jumla, once a great kingdom of north-western Nepal, now a frontier town littered all across the eroded hills on the far side of the river ...with most of the vices and none of the virtues of the twentieth century."*[3]

Matthiessen's distaste for Indian intrusion was shared by many Westerners who came to Nepal in the 1970s, be they climbers, Gurkha officers, or my former colleagues at the Britain-Nepal Medical Trust. For us, the true nobility of the country were the indigenous tribes of the middle hills, the Rai, the Tamang, the Limbu, the Gurung, the Sherpa, forcibly assimilated into the Hindu caste system, and losing their land and their livelihoods to clever, unmanly Brahmins. However plausible it felt, this construct relied—as do most forms of prejudice—on caricature and simplified dramas of injustice.

Most of us carry tribalism in our hearts; give us license and the right company, and out it comes. When I would walk out of the hills down to BNMT's headquarters on the Indian border, I would find the sudden heat, crowds, and argumentative confusion of the Terai distasteful; I would long to return to cooler air and slower speech. Listening to my colleagues disparage hill Brahmins, I would enjoy watching them surf on the back of Nepali caste antagonism. I doubt any of us reflected on how similar our casual typology was to the worldview of our colonial predecessors in the Indian Army, with their love of the "martial races," and their disdain for educated urban Babus.

Unlike Peter Matthiessen, though, I am glad to be back in the middle hills again, at altitudes I am familiar with; this is the world I once knew. Where maize grows. Where there is thick grass on the hillsides. Where you can walk without precipices.

More disquieting to Matthiessen than the friction of reentry, though, was the stinging perception that his quest had failed; or, rather, that he had set himself up to fail. The journey had not changed him; he was beset by *"that aching gap between what I know and what I am ...For all the exhilaration, splendour and 'success' of the journey to the Crystal Mountain, a great chance has been missed and I have failed."*[4]

A travel book comes with its own structure—the journey itself. *The Snow Leopard* builds to a climax in the Shey Valley, and subsides as the author reenters the world of the lowlands. What distinguishes it from most such memoirs is the bitterness of the return journey. There is no comfortable ending; instead, there is frustration and disappointment with himself. No excuses are offered—there is no clean resolution.

I too set out on this journey with a clouded mind. I told myself I would use this time to think about Tess and Mandana—but in truth, the picture of me remembering them is what I found most attractive. From the first day of this trip part of me has longed for it to be over, so I can return to my comfortable, clean American life, and then recall the walk in mythical form. I too feel little self-satisfaction as I reach the outer rim of my journey. I have wasted the opportunity of immersing myself in this harsh country, and in the lives of my companions. I have evaded true mental discipline, and have nibbled only half-heartedly at the tough questions.

—·—

I begin the day in discomfort. Kedar can see I am hurting, and kindly takes my pack for me. Once again, the lunch stop helps, as does some paracetamol (no codeine left). We follow the Ghan Khola downstream for most of the day, gradually dropping to below ten thousand feet. In a gentle afternoon sun we pass through villages surrounded by hemp plants.

We find a teahouse beside the trail—the first we have stopped in since the tent in the Tarap Valley that laid me low at the beginning of the month. The building has a red hammer and sickle painted on the white-washed outside wall. I ask the owner what he thinks of the Maoists, assuming he is a supporter. He is not, and the conversation is brief. The wall was not his doing. He doesn't know who put "that thing" there. He doesn't approve, but he's reluctant to paint it out; today it would bring no retribution, but he carries sinister memories.

Below the teahouse a large family is harvesting millet, squatting in the fields tying sheaves. This could be Thomas Hardy's Wessex, the Dorset of my schooldays. And, as in Hardy, the timelessness of the image is deceitful. Writing at the end of the nineteenth century, Hardy under-stood how insecure rural life had become in an age of mechanization; it was a place of caprice and injustice, a place of erratic harvests, depressed prices, and forced migration towards urban slum life.

As the shadows lengthen we turned up the Khunku Khola into a wide, gently sloping meadow, up to this research station. We are camping outside the cafeteria. It's the first time we have slept below ten thousand feet since we were in Tarakot on August 31, twenty-seven days ago. How pleasant it is to sit outside my tent without feeling cold, or even damp! Konzok and I have our backs to a wall, catching the last of the sun.

Tomorrow we will be in Jumla—once a center of medieval power, now a medium-sized district capital of no great significance.

Most of history is unwritten, and quickly forgotten, and this is so here. Apart from the archaeological record, we are left for the most part with odd pilot lights scattered by the wealthy and privileged. From this loss of collective memory only scraps remain—a list of the kings of Jumla from 1404 until the kingdom was extinguished in 1789, tax receipts, and a few self-congratulatory royal edicts.

By the early fifteenth century, the extensive Khas-Malla kingdom of far-western Nepal was breaking apart; Jumla became the most potent of the shards. At its seventeenth-century apogee, Jumla controlled much of northwest Nepal, and collected tribute from the distant hills of Uttarakhand, north of modern-day New Delhi.

In 1787, Jumla was attacked by the armies of the expanding Gorkha state. Subduing Jumla took two years, achieved in part by brokering alliances with rivals, and in part by choking off Jumla's trade routes to Tibet. The kingdom never recovered its former status. An estimated 125,000 people lived in Jumla before annexation. Even by 2011, with the population of Nepal as a whole at least five times greater than in 1789, Jumla district—heartland of the former Khas empire—was home to only 109,000 souls.

September 28, 2016—Day 40, Jumla Bazaar, Jumla District, 7,850 feet.

Today we begin with a small climb out of Guthichaur, some four hundred feet, and then spend the rest of the day sidling up to Jumla along a motorable road (never a pleasant thing to walk on). A sprawl of villages snaking along the Dochal Gad Khola announces the larger town: first Garjyankot, then Depalgaun, then Dansaghu. Motorbikes, dust, and noise increase as we get closer, as do the crowds of people walking along with us towards the bazaar. We are lower down now, and harvesting is underway—mostly sorghum and millet, though there are signs of cut maize as well, even an abandoned tractor. A roadside stall, the first we have seen for a month, then several more.

We stop beside the river for *lonch*. While the crew eats man-food, I am treated to the last of the *kuhiré* cargo—little pasties filled with cheese and tomatoes, fries, orange cocktail sausages, and coleslaw. Palden then leads me off in the wrong direction—there are several dirt tracks here. We are patiently rescued by the others, and soon find ourselves underneath Jumla's runway, which is aligned exactly east–west (090°/270°). From there we walk through crowded streets to a compound to the south of the airport, and to a half-built hotel.

I am sweating, and the sight of the town makes me feel dirty—what a strange reaction! The compound is surrounded by a wall, behind which people congregate and stare. We are inured to this by now, and go about our business. The mules, liberated from their loads, at once roll on the ground and rub their necks on the grass, free again.

They are then staked by the ankle in a line, and given extra piles of grass. They jostle, bark, eat and fart in abundance.

There is even a warm shower in the half-built hotel; I go for it. It is six weeks since I have taken my clothes off. I am quite stunningly dirty, the grime only accentuated by my efforts to wash it away. What I had thought of as suntan is, in fact, an ineradicable plumb line of filth ending at the tops of my thighs. I scrub a while, then decide this must be done in stages; I will resume tomorrow.

We made it . . . today took about six-and-a-half hours, a normal sort of day, though it felt much longer under the hot sun. I am thankful we don't have to walk tomorrow—my hip hurt for the first couple of hours, and an aching persists. Yet here we are. Back home in Virginia, in March, I was doubtful I'd last this long. We have come about 460 miles.

The tents are up, and we sit together to talk about the coming week. Sarah *madum*, I say, is coming in nine days. We have two alternatives. Either a mini-trek of five to six days—after a couple of days rest, mind you—getting us back here on October 5. Or perhaps I could go to Kathmandu and surprise *madum*, and then fly back here with her. What do you all think?

Oh, but suh, says Palden, such a *good* idea for you to go and meet *madum*! And you are anyway so tired, you are also old man, excuse me suh for saying so, and your hip, *dherai dukche*!! Fffff, so painful! Can be *very* bad injury if not rested! No, no, we will not get bored at all resting here nine days—so much to do, so busy! Ticket? Very easy, Konzok knows airport staff here so well, they are like brother to him! If you are not here, we don't need to worry about you—please, no offense!

So that is that. Besides, Konzok is in pain and I need to have his ear seen to: he will not ask it of me, but it is expected. Just as his risking life and limb on those foul trails was expected. Plus, my hip really could use a rest.

I sit against another warm wall, ignoring the crowd of distant onlookers, and watch the sun go down. For once I feel no need to be anywhere else, or to do anything. With all that exercise under my belt, I can eat without remorse for weeks.

I'm glad I came. I'm even more glad it's over. Reflecting on his decision to write *Tales of the South Pacific* immediately after the Second World War, James Michener had this to say:

> *"Clearly, almost clinically, I calculated that if you ordered all the young men of a generation to climb Mount Everest, you would expect the climb to have a major significance in their lives. And while they were climbing the damned mountain, they would bitch like hell and condemn the assignment. But years later as*

they looked back they'd see it as the supreme adventure it was, and they'd want to read about it to reexperience it."[5]

I'm not suggesting this trip compares to climbing Mount Everest, let alone fighting the Japanese—but I know that my bitching will be re-formed by recollection, in ways that my tired mind can't yet grasp.

Most stories talk of the opportunities we confront, and the choices we make. For me, the intrusive question has been whether I would fail a test of physical courage—would I, like Joseph Conrad's *Lord Jim*, jump from the sinking *SS Patna*, leaving its cargo of pilgrims to their fate? Would I be able to do what my father did in Normandy, avoiding disgrace under fire?

For those of us lucky enough to escape the melodramas of war and violence, the real tests are often much quieter ones. They creep up, unheralded and mundane, and can slip us by without our quite knowing they were here. Like the youth that Conrad wrote about, they can pass before us *"unseen, in a sigh, in a flash,"* unrecognized, stealing away as we look *"anxiously for something out of life, that while it is expected is already gone."*[6]

My tests were no great dramatic trials by fire, but the continuous need to protect two people who depended on me, me above anyone. I faltered, wrapped up in myself, my timidity an intimate part of their tragedies. Now they have gone, and there will be no second chances. I have done better by Alex, but Alex is not my child; nor can you write over the past. People who know tell me I was a caring father and a patient husband, that I did all that I could have done—but what else would they say?

"I have neglected my children and done myself harm, and there is no way back," Peter Matthiessen wrote;[7] and more than anything else, this is my point of connection with his great book. Leaving his children a year and a half after their mother's death felt wrong to him, but what I did was far worse. I did not protect my daughter, nor did I help my wife. I took refuge in my work, and in secretive sexual affairs that hurt the women I became involved with.

—·—

The sun sets early, over the high hills and the ugly concrete houses to the west. The air chills. The crowd disperses. The flies have gone and the mules are still, their raggedy tails limp behind them. I fish a packet of Pashupati biscuits out of my daypack and take it over to them. They light up like a clutch of vampires, heaving at their ankle-stakes, baring their teeth and whistling. I remember you have to hold food in an open hand or you can lose a finger. I step carefully up the line, leaving Bukhé to last. Malevolent as ever, she contrives to nip the corner of my palm.

I sit back down and look for a dressing, thinking how set in my ways *I* have become. But where did my subtle brand of cowardice come from? I wasn't born that way. I wasn't like that in Africa; it happened in England. Like the proverbial Hindu, I crossed the *kãlo pãni*, the black water, and in so doing lost both my family and my caste. In England I no longer felt unique; in England I felt rumbled. As with the origins of the fatalism that Dor Bahadur Bista describes, the unmediated force of school authority bred in me passivity and emotional evasiveness. To be fair, my mid-century upbringing was poor preparation for the turbulence that dominated the lives of my wife and daughter—but this can only be partial mitigation.

Here, in Nepal, I do not feel rumbled. I feel at home, or more at home than anywhere else. *Not* being able to blend in here is the whole point; it reproduces something of the status I left behind in Africa.

Enough of all this; Konzok is calling. It's dinner time.

14

WHEN I WAS A GROWN-UP

April 24, 2017—The Plains, Virginia.

We have been home for five months. It's morning, and Max has his paws on my face. I must get up. Sarah is already working in the garden. As I head for the shower, I remember that I am going to write to George Schaller today. I've wanted to contact him since we got back home in late November, but I haven't known what to say.

Last night, though, we watched the *Mountains* episode of Sir David Attenborough's new series, *Planet Earth II*. It begins with views of the Karakorum, and then of a snow leopard patrolling her territory on a high, barren pass. As the titles come up, the leopard stops, gazes past the camera, and howls from deep inside her chest—five deep, mournful cries echoing across the snow and the rocks. The sound is unmistakable. This is what I heard under the full moon at Shey Gompa; what Palden told me was a jackal.

How incredible this is! And on that of all nights—the sixth lunar anniversary of my daughter's death. Now I want to ask George if he heard or found traces of this leopard when he arrived at Shey. His young Sherpani guide told me they were going to look for snow leopards up there.

I've dug out Dawa Palden's account of George Schaller's 2016 trip in the *Nepali Times*.[1] It recalls how George successfully campaigned to protect Upper Dolpo after his 1973 visit, and that his efforts led in 1984 to the establishment of the 1,372 square mile Shey-Phoksundo National Park. His recent trip was sponsored by the Werth Family Foundation, which has funded a number of energy and education projects in Dolpo; in addition to honoring Peter Matthiessen, George wanted to assess the changes that had taken place over the forty-three years since he had last been there.

Much of what he found depressed him. The management of the park is, at best, negligent—the handful of rangers based in the comfortable urban environs of Dunai rarely visit any remote communities, while the two hundred-some soldiers assigned to protect the park idle away their time in barracks near Ringmo, and do little to manage the annual *yãrsagumba* frenzy or suppress the illegal logging we saw evidence of in Tinje. In theory, the money collected from tourist fees and from *yãrsagumba* harvesters provide a useful income stream for village development: but George's team saw no evidence that these funds were reaching their intended beneficiaries.

For George Schaller, snow leopards were less metaphor than part of the job. In *Stones of Silence*, he writes of months spent tracking them in Pakistan. Observing them and recording their habits required stamina, perseverance, and precision—a cast of mind that seems at first glance to have little in common with Peter's metaphysical conception of the creature. But discipline and fierce concentration can open the mind to unexpected insights. In one particular encounter in the Hindu Kush, George seems almost to become one with what he was so intently studying:

> *"Then the snow fell more thickly, and, dreamlike, the cat slipped away as is if she had never been ... the snow leopard represented not just a rare and beautiful cat whose habits I wanted to study,*

but also the symbol of a search for something intangible that seemed forever elusive."[2]

Reading this again today gives me the courage to write what I so far have been unable to.

—·—

My daughter died in the early hours of September 23, 2010, the night of the full moon.

She was just shy of twenty-six. After years of estrangement, she had reconciled with Mandana: as she had told me that day in London, having her own son helped her see how hard it could be to deal with a child when your own mind is battering itself like a caged animal.

By the late spring of 2010, depression was clouding Tess' life. In the past it had been hard, for her and for others, to distinguish depression from anger and alienation—but it had always been there. She had been drinking since she was fifteen; alcohol was her refuge. There were periods of remission, but none lasted long. During her pregnancy she cut back, albeit with a couple of serious lapses. About a year after Alex was born, though, intensifying depression began to bleed through her like a detonating bruise.

Mandana's mother Mahin and her grandmother Shahin had both lived with depression; Tess' illness was passed down to her through four known generations. She had inherited her mother's form of bipolar disease, depression alternating with, or sitting alongside anxiety. The depression was one thing; this she could manage by drinking again. The anxiety was less bearable. She found a young psychiatrist who prescribed her Klonopin, a benzodiazepine; this helped, but it helped less as the weeks passed. Mandana told me on the phone that this doctor was far too cautious, and should be prescribing higher doses. So I persuaded my doctor to prescribe *me* Klonopin, and I used this to augment Tess' prescriptions. I hired a nanny to look after Alex for a few hours each day.

Still Tess' irritation grew. I spent as much time with her and Alex as I felt I could, waiting for relief—waiting in the same kind of dread suspense with which I had witnessed Mandana's lifelong illness.

In August, I visited friends in Canada for a few days. I was trying to help Tess cut back on Klonopin—she was worried about dependency, and about withdrawal. She now knew that Mandana's terrifying rages had been caused when she had tried to wean herself off other benzodiazepines. Tess asked me to hide her daily dose around the grounds of the Skyline Towers apartment complex before I left. Each day I texted her the location.

In early September, desperate by now, she asked her doctor to refer her for electroconvulsive therapy treatment. ECT is used when a depressed patient is treatment-resistant. I learned that roughly a half of bipolar patients can expect significant relief from a course of ECT, at least over the near-term. I also learned that it's safer than most people of my generation believe: my impressions of ECT came from *One Flew Over the Cuckoo's Nest*, where shock treatment was administered to Jack Nicholson's character without empathy, explanation, or anesthetic, convulsing him and turning his face bright red. Mandana had once tried ECT, though Tess didn't know this. I remembered it hadn't done anything for her; but ECT had been considerably refined since then, I was told, and was now a lot more effective.

The early morning of Wednesday, September 22 was still, blue, and windless—one of those lovely East Coast fall days, heat still polishing the air, humidity low. I was up early, dropping Tess off at Virginia Hospital Center in Arlington for her second ECT session. From there I drove to the World Bank, planning to see her that evening.

Tess called me at about 10:30 a.m. Her voice was flat. "Dad, can you come and get me from the hospital? Can I stay with you today? Bryan has to work. I'm not feeling good."

I left a team editing meeting and picked her up; she looked washed over, and a bit dazed from the ECT ("the doctor told me it was a good seizure").

In the car she turned to me and said "Don't worry, Dad, it's not the ECT—I'm hung over."

I breathed deeply, but said nothing. I felt angry, and helpless. "I had a big fight with Bryan last night," she continued. "I needed a drink and he wouldn't get me anything. I just left and went to a bar. I was a total bitch."

We drove to my girlfriend Jill's house in the Palisades in DC; Jill was away on World Bank business in Sri Lanka. I made Tess some tea, and after a while she brightened. She walked about the house, smoking and looking at Jill's recipe books. I'd bought that month's *Vogue* for her; there was an article on Carey Mulligan and her new movie, *Never Let Me Go*, adapted from Kazuo Ishiguro's novel about clones who are bred to be organ donors. We planned to go and see it when it opened on Friday. I called the office and made a few edits over the phone; work, as ever, was a relief from my daughter's pain.

I heard Tess calling her psychiatrist, and then her ECT doctor, urging them to let her have more Klonopin. She came back frustrated. "They don't get it," she said. "'*Be positive. You're stronger than you think.*'" She pushed a 2-mg tablet through its tinfoil strip and swallowed it. "At least this is my first today." Her doctor was reducing the dose; she was officially on 3 mg each day.

"I'm going to run out in a few days, and she won't give me a break. You don't have *any* left?"

"I really don't. Try and wait a bit," I added, knowing she would need a second pill soon. "Come, sit here a moment. Let's get back to the wedding. What else do we need to do?" Her wedding was six weeks away.

She smiled. "We're almost done. There's the cake, though. And...." She was looking at me, head on one side.

"The ring."

Mandana had given her one, a twisted gold band inlaid with tiny diamonds, a nineteenth-century Rana ring from Nepal. She didn't want to say anything to her mother, but she was uncomfortable wearing something this large and arresting. I said I'd get her one she could wear when her mother wasn't around; Bryan would pay me back later.

We headed out to the Mazza Gallerie on Wisconsin Avenue. She leaned the car seat back and seemed to be sleeping. Stopped at a traffic light, I looked across at her. She was unusually pale, faint blue shadows beneath her eyes.

We found a jewelers, and sorted through their stock of platinum and white gold rings; she picked out a couple of thin bands she liked. They were each upwards of $3,000. To cover my alarm, I suggested a third priced at $4,200.

She tried them all on, twisted them, asked some questions, then put them back in their velveteen boxes and thanked the sales assistant.

"They're expensive, Dad."

"No—it's fine. It's your wedding." I warmed to the idea. "Honestly."

She smiled and leaned her head against me. "We'll look somewhere else." Tess' smile forced you to smile too—it illuminated her face, though she would often cover her mouth, as if she was letting too much of herself be seen.

We bought some slippers and eyeliner instead, then walked arm-in-arm across the road to a nearby Japanese restaurant, Yosaku. A few months ago she would have chided me for still taking her hand in traffic, but not today. Tess wanted a beer; I could see she was suffering, and with a heavy heart I ordered one, and, in time, a second.

She was able to relax a little.

"Dad, I know you're disappointed I didn't get a degree and I don't have a career or anything. It wasn't what you wanted."

"No," I said, "no, I don't think like that. Really. I want you to be happy, that's all. I just want us to get you through this depression."

I meant this; but I wish I had said something else that day. That the greatest gift a child can give a parent is unconditional love, and she had given me that. That the rest was detail.

"Dad," she said. "Promise me, now I remember it. Promise me you'll tell Alex stories like you used to tell me when I was little."

"Of course I will. But you can do that too. You tell great stories."

"I want him to hear your stories. The true ones, and the ones you make up. Like the monkey's wedding. Especially that one."

She looked at me without blinking, a slight, crooked smile across a blank, faraway face.

"Dad, I don't want to go home," she said, her finger tracing a circle of beer foam on her side plate. "I can't look after him when I'm feeling like this. The thought of clearing up . . . ." she shook her head.

"Listen," I said, "I really have to work tomorrow. But after that—from Friday—I can take time off and we can do things together. Maybe go to the beach with Alex. Like you were saying."

But she wasn't listening.

"I want to die," she said, looking straight at me again, this time focusing. "I can't stand this. It's unbearable. I feel—flat, just flat, like there's nothing of me here. And so anxious. It's killing me."

She must have seen my face. She had never said anything like this. "Dad, don't worry, I'm not going to do silly shit like that."

We drove back to the house. She took two more Klonopin, felt slightly better, went upstairs and started trying on Jill's T-shirts. "Look," she called out. "I'm a perfect weight for once. Ninety-three pounds." Tess was tiny, barely five feet tall—though no one remembers her as short.

"Did you know Mum said she'd give me $2,000 for clothes? As a wedding present?"

I began to feel easier, and drove her home. Only much later would I see the texts she was sending Bryan.

5:30 I want to die. I think im in a good place with god now and hes telling me to kick the bucket

6:09 Alex is too small to even remember me. i dont want this shit anymore. im my mom trust me. i'm crazy

On the way she begged me to buy her a bottle of wine. "I'm so sorry, I'm desperate Dad." I argued with her; she began to get angry, I gave in—a familiar, sinking feeling, a feeling of shame and desolation, of trying to keep things from tipping out of control, of looking for anything to ease her pain. We drove and parked, took the elevator up to the seventeenth floor, and knocked on the door of the apartment. I knelt on the ground: I knew what was coming. Bryan opened the door and Alex launched himself at me like a rocket. Tess' delighted laughter. The apartment dim, a bit messy. Their white cockatiel upside down on his rope, staring at us with one eye.

I played hide-and-seek with Alex to give Tess some space; she sat on the sofa, her face bleak. "I'm in a foul mood," she warned. Bryan showed me some photos on his phone, one of Tess from the day before, with the cockatiel balanced on her foot. The focus is on the bird; her face is blurred in the background, and carries a resigned smile. Like an athlete after a long, grueling race.

I found Tess in the kitchen, preparing Alex's dinner. Are you OK? No, not at all, but I'll manage. Thanks for helping with Alex, it makes such a difference. Bryan's tired—he's been working really hard, I can't keep asking him to watch Alex. When I'm like, doing nothing.

I sat with Alex while he ate; Tess and Bryan began watching *The English Patient*, a favorite of theirs. I said I'd put Alex to bed, and took him to his room. I lay down with him and started telling him a story about three tiny fleas, Bim, Bam and Bom, who traveled all around the world in the creases of my trousers and bit people's butts when they got bored. I began to lose the plot and doze off, though Alex was still wide awake.

Tess was shaking me. "Dad," she said. "Please talk to him. Like you said." She picked Alex up and carried him around the bedroom, then came to sit next to us in the living room. I'd promised I'd talk to Bryan about bipolar disease; Tess said he just couldn't seem to understand she was ill, not just crazy and moody. So I spoke to him about how hard it had been for me to understand Mandana's illness, and how long it took to accept that it wasn't some character issue, it was as real as an injury, or cancer. I mean, you wouldn't tell someone with a broken leg to try a bit harder to walk to the car, would you? Bryan listened, taking it in, nodding his head. "It feels like I'm living in a storm cloud," he said, smiling ruefully. "Just me and the storm."

At some point that evening, just to make sure, I told Bryan to keep an eye on the balcony door: not that I really thought anything would happen.

I went back to Alex's room and lay beside him again. Presently Tess came in and told me they were going out for a few minutes; she needed some money for another bottle of wine. I knew this was a mistake, but I knew she would grow angry if I refused. I gave her money. By now Alex was asleep. I lay beside him, staring at the ceiling, wondering how we would get through the evening.

I awoke in alarm. It was almost midnight. Blinking, I went into the living room. The lights were dim, but Tess and Bryan were still up. Tess came and hugged me. She seemed much calmer. "Dad, you go home, I know you're really busy. Daddy, thank you so much, it's all okay now."

I felt I should stay, but I wanted to go, to not feel so responsible for a while. I was exhausted, and tomorrow we'd have another marathon editing session at work. I'd see her on Friday; we'd have several days together then.

I drove home and went straight to bed; it was just past midnight. I fell into a deep sleep.

—·—

The phone rang; I switched the light on—2:17 a.m. Someone was shouting at me, come, come, please come. It was Bryan. Tess had fallen from their seventeenth-floor balcony.

All I remember of that drive was the sense of horror, and of how unreal it felt, of how this surely couldn't be—how I was watching someone else, or a movie in which I was acting. It took perhaps twenty-five minutes; by then there was police tape, flashing yellow lights, and a sheet over a still form on the sidewalk. The police wouldn't let me near her body. Bryan was shirtless, howling, literally howling, under a bright full moon. "It's not your fault," I kept telling him, feeling detached from myself and hugging him. "It's not your fault. It's not your fault." Like a mantra, separating me from the scene and from myself. "It's not your fault." The lines of some movie, I didn't know which one, but what else can you do? Now I remember; this is Robin Williams talking to Matt Damon in *Good Will Hunting*, telling him he mustn't blame himself for the way his stepfather abused him. Matt Damon, Tess' favorite actor, the one she said Bryan looked so much like.

We waited, for hours. The police were measuring things—how far away from the window she'd fallen, how far the branches had diverted her fall. Bryan was told to stay where he was. I sat alone under a tree and cried. From time to time I looked towards my daughter's body; my mind wouldn't allow me to imagine what she must look like. I remember leaves and small snapped branches around her on the sidewalk, and the cold, brown, unmarked concrete paving in the neon light. I called Jill in Sri Lanka, but couldn't say anything; I too howled like an animal. After a while I said "Tessie's dead. Come home. Please come home."

Bryan's mother arrived, and Bryan went to sit with her in the foyer. A female officer went to fetch Alex. He arrived, cheerful in her arms, and called to me. No one knew what to say to him, so we pretended nothing had happened—and this helped us all get through the next hour.

Much later, after the police had gone, I drove back home once again. I drove, but the car seemed motionless. I went back to bed—it was after six. I couldn't sleep, so I got up. I'd been watching *Defiance*, a film about Jewish resistance to the Nazis in Poland during the Second War. But the thought of violence disgusted me, so I switched off the TV and sat on the sofa, listening to the street waking up around me, knowing everything once clean was suddenly filthy and ruined, like the contents of an overturned car spilled across a highway.

—·—

You carry on. Your body still operates. Jill came home the next day, saying little but doing everything she could for me. I alternated between silence and a determination to make sure Tess would not be forgotten. I would write a book about her. We would start a scholarship fund. Every year we'd have a memorial service.

There were things that couldn't wait. Doctors' appointments to be canceled. Ambulance bills; yes, believe me, several of them, though she had died instantly. Canceling the wedding, returning the wedding dress. Arranging the funeral, deciding what she should be buried in.

Should she be made up? We can do a great deal, but I have to advise you—it won't quite be the same. It's the right side of her face. Do you want to see her? No, I don't. *I think that's the right choice. We have this catalog here?*

Coffins, all ghastly, impossible for this elegant child. Just that one— yes, the plain rosewood one. I know it's the cheapest, but I'm sure, thank you. Being polite and sympathetic to so many awkward, well-meaning people. You have to do this; you feel sorry for them.

Worst of all, I had to tell Mandana. And not by phone. So three days after Tess' death, Jill and I flew to London. Mandana's old friend Nadereh was in London; we planned it so Nadereh would meet her at a nearby café. Nadereh brought her to her flat; I had a key, and I'd already let myself in.

"Nigel, what are you doing here? This is a nice surprise!" And "What? What's wrong?" Then jokingly—"Has Tess had an accident or something?" One close look at me, and she collapsed to the floor. Even as Nadereh and I picked her up, she was saying "Oh God, it's a mercy, a mercy." Mandana knew what Tess had been suffering; Mandana had often wished herself dead.

A while later she asked me to please call Keith Casburne, a "sensitive" she knew well and often consulted about her purpose here, and why she must continue living in pain. "Please, Nigel, I can't talk to him now." She told me Keith had stopped contacting the departed—it was draining his own life from him. But she would ask him this once, and she knew he'd agree. I emailed him. He rang that afternoon.

"Tell Mandana her daughter is still close," he said. "And there is a stillness and a calm. She gives me this sense of, of purposefulness. About where she is. There's no confusion, no sense of dislocation. She knew where she was going before it happened. Don't misunderstand me—this was not premeditated. We are talking about the higher soul. Sometimes a soul knows its destination, even in life .... I have no sense of why this happened, no communication. In fact she doesn't want to communicate now. Don't be alarmed; this is often the way when someone passes. Mostly because the process of assimilating the new life is—so intense. She can be reached, but she is not responding. This is so unlike my father's death. There is calm, a silence so to speak. In his case, he was so confused and frightened. I had to intervene .... she is experiencing a great sense of freedom. She doesn't wish to break the silence. It's an *extreme* composure she has, most unusual in such circumstances .... you should wait about six months before you try to communicate with her. She needs that time, for healing and resolution. I can sense her surprise—at her own peace of mind."

Of course, this was reassuring.

Jill and I brought Mandana back to stay with us in DC. Tess' funeral was held at St. John's Presbyterian church in McLean, near her first school, and near the house she had lived in when we came back from Nepal. In my eulogy, I said

*"I have the strongest feeling that Tess' spirit, or soul, or essential
personality, is intact. I also believe that her spirit is well, and safe.
Is that the wishful thinking of a grieving father?"*

I now think it was; my awareness of her presence has vanished. Last
year, I heard my old friend Julian say much the same when he spoke at
his wife Anthea's funeral, in the very same church. She is still with us, he
insisted; I can feel it, and no one can tell me otherwise.

—·—

Soon afterwards, I went back to Tess' apartment. Everything was so
familiar—the hallway, the sounds of the elevator, the grip and then slide
of the hall carpet beneath my shoes. The air was close, the place slightly
untidy, one of Tess' sweaters and a stuffed green elephant (Babar) on the
floor; the cockatiel was gone, back in the pet store. I looked out at the
balcony and the low railings through the half-closed balcony door, but I
couldn't approach it. So I sat on the sofa, my back to the window. I could
feel the TV remote underneath me. I stared at the empty screen.

I'm not sure how other minds work, but my consciousness is managed
by a version of myself unknown to anyone else. An anxious, censorious
self, one that seeks to shield me from the inspection of others—from
letting them see what it suspects is a poverty of spirit.

On that day, this other self had disappeared. A lifetime of distraction;
now nothing.

I must have been exhausted; I slept, and dreamed that Tess and I were
back in Yosaku, the Japanese restaurant, facing one another across the
yellow pine table.

"Do you know what I just dreamed?" I was saying. "I dreamed you
were dead!"

"You didn't think I was dead just because you couldn't see me, did
you?"

"Of course not."

Slowly my mind coalesced again. The remote was still underneath me. The afternoon sun had caught Alex's fingerprints in the dust on the TV screen; he used to stand right in front of it to watch cartoons. One of Tess' earrings lay on the carpet. I picked it up and left the apartment. The dream lingered; she was still out there, somewhere. She had to be.

—·—

It's New Year's Eve, ninety-one days since she died. I'm taking Alex for a drive, to help him sleep. He's fractious. "Car, car, Papa car," he insists; and then "Seat! Drive!" As usual, I give him his monkey, a Curious George I bought when he was a baby, and as usual he throws it with a mixture of frustration and delight across the car: "No monkey!"

I came over to read him a bedtime story, but I was unable to calm him. It's ice cold; the sky is clear and the roads empty. Just my blue Honda and Tess' motherless son, bundled in the car seat, me holding his hand awkwardly behind me while I drive. "No home," he says. He doesn't want to go back, he just wants to drive.

Most days I visit Tess' grave in Columbia Gardens. Although I don't like to think about it, I know she's wearing the pink shift she chose for her engagement photos, the gold ring her mother gave her, and the orange slippers we bought on her last day. After those photos were taken, she was radiant. I didn't even notice the cold, she said—but you can see the goose bumps on her arms. I have her autopsy report. I can't read it; it's in my safe. I don't want to know about her broken bones, or how much her heart weighed.

Alex is asleep at last, his face calm; we must have been driving around Manassas Airport for the past hour. I have no clue what he's feeling, or how we can help him; the responsibility is daunting. He still asks for his mother; he still keeps looking for her.

July 10, 2017–The Plains, Virginia.

I've accepted a job in Myanmar for six months, as a stop-gap director of a peace and reconciliation program.

I've been telling myself it's okay for me to be away, though when I came back from Dolpo Alex asked me not to go away again—ever. Since then he has grown more distant. I still make sure I see him at least once each week, and he comes and stays here every second weekend. When he was tiny, he wanted to be with me more than with anyone; now he misses his dad when he's here for more than a day.

He's nine now, but he still insists I lie in his bed with him until he falls asleep. He resists sleep's onset, asking for one more story, and then just one more. I have long exhausted the ones he likes best—the accounts of all the naughty things I did when I was a little boy in Africa. Like the time I decided to give Oliver Simmonds a haircut, without first removing his father's trilby (I cut the top of the trilby off, like opening a can, so I could get at his hair). Or the time that Johnny Woosey and I contrived to get ourselves locked into his father's sweet shop for the night.

Alex rarely speaks to me of his feelings now, nor does he say much about his mother. When he does, it's usually on the very edge of sleep. I was thinking about this today and remembered I'd made some recordings of us a few years back.

Where were they? I rummaged through a box of dead electronics, checked a couple of old dictaphones. Not there. Perhaps I'd used my cell; but that would have been my iPhone, before I switched to a Samsung. I opened my MacBook and looked for the old iTunes folder. Yes—voice memos. There were a dozen, all from 2013, when Alex was five. I listened, one by one. I couldn't remember any of these conversations: I daresay I'd been half asleep when I recorded them. Several were quite short, a couple were longer, with lots of empty air—I must have left the recorder on after we'd both fallen asleep.

But there was one . . .

"You know what a TMT is?" Alex asks me.

"A what?" I reply.

"You know what a TMT is?"

"Yes, it's an explosive."

"No, it's a bomb."

"That's right. A bomb."

"A TMT can explode the whole world, can explode half of a world. So God must make sure that doesn't happen, right?"

"Yeah."

"But sometimes he wants to control it to happen actually, to the enemies, but sometimes it happens to the good guys, no matter what. He controls it to do that. No matter what. He makes the good guys die sometimes. No matter what. It's just gotta be sometimes like that."

"So why do the—why do the good guys die sometimes?"

"They just need to sometimes, they do. And that's just how it goes."

"Yes, it's very sad when that happens."

Long pause. Eventually Alex yawns.

"When I was a grown-up ... when I was a grown-up and I understanded it all, did I say ... when, 'Where—,' when, when I was big, did I say 'Where's my Mummy?'"

"Yes, you did. When you were little, you mean, when you were ... at that time?"

"No, when I was probably free years old something and, that's when she was already died, and, and I didn't know that—right?"

"Yes, you didn't really understand at the time what had happened. Thought your Mummy had disappeared but you didn't know where she had gone."

"I want her back."

"So do I. I miss her a lot."

"I don't want—I want her back. No matter what, I want her back."

"Of course you do. She was your Mummy."

"What you mean, of course I do? I love, I so much, so much I want her."

Long pause.

"I want Mummy back. I want Mummy."

"I know."

Long pause.

"What if they never … what if everybod … what if a bad guy gets to read all of my Mummy's pictures and I never know what she looks like again?"

"No bad guy's going to get all of your pictures, we have too many of them and they are saved in all sorts of safe places. I've loads of pictures of your Mummy and so does your Daddy and your Nana. It's not going to happen."

"Does Sarah know my Mama?"

"No, she doesn't know your Mama. Your Mama died before I knew Sarah."

"Does she know her name?"

"Yes, of course, because I talk to her a lot about her."

"Does she know what she looks like?"

"Yes."

"Can you tell me what she doesn't know?"

"Well, she knows quite a lot because I talk to her about your Mummy a lot."

"Does she know her voice?"

"No, she doesn't know her voice, except from the videos. There's some videos we have, she knows her voice from that."

"What's stuff she not knows?"

"She know, she doesn't—well there's lots she doesn't know. About how, how she was as a person, and how she was with you."

"Can you tell me?"

"Well. She doesn't know how your Mummy used to sing to you in the morning. Because I never told her that. And she doesn't know how your Mummy used to laugh and play with you because she never saw that. And she doesn't know how your Mummy was when she was a little girl because she wasn't there. It's just me and Manani know that."

"And me?"

"You know a lot about your Mummy from when you saw her. . . ."

"If I was a girl, a baby would—if I was still a little kid, a baby would be in my body, and it would be a real little baby, and then it would change into me."

Pause.

"Can you tell me more people that didn't meet her?"

"Well, your friends at school didn't meet your Mummy. They didn't have the chance to meet your Mummy."

But he was asleep.

July 11, 2017—The Plains, Virginia.

I've just heard from Basant. Palden has decided to return to Dubai on another four-year contract. Sagar is qualifying as a guide, and he and Konzok have become one of Basant's best expedition teams; the foul argument they had in Saldang, it seems, laid the basis for a relationship of understanding and respect. Kedar Roka is getting married, and his wife-to-be wants him to give up mule-wrangling. Ngima is drifting in and out of view, working different jobs, sticking with none of them. He is talking about going to Dubai.

And Chimi Tsewang, the boy with the fractured skull, is doing well. His operation was a success, and his uncle (a monk) has managed to get him into the primary school at Phulari Monastery in the north of the Kathmandu Valley, where he can study for free. He is bright, and naughty, as the most promising young novices often are.

I am ending this book where it began, at home in Virginia. It's a midsummer's evening. By July the meadows have begun to burn beneath their green topcoat. Our cats bask on the back lawn like sea lions. We have acquired a fourth—Sarah found her on a recent visit to Guyana, a tiny feral kitten thrown away in a gunny sack beside the road.

John Bunyan is said to have written *"It is always hard to see the purpose in wilderness wanderings until after they are over."*[3] Recognition is at the heart of Peter Matthiessen's book—getting back to the place where we began, and knowing it for the first time: homegoing. The strange places are a form of detour; the destination is wakefulness.

Did my journey—or rather, writing about that journey—awaken me? Did it help me see more clearly what happened to my daughter, my family, and myself?

In some ways, yes: but if seeing things more clearly means you would act differently should the same events recur, or as new tests arise, then I am less certain. To be awake is not just to realize what you did not see, but to do something about it—and to do it in time to avert disaster. It is all very well to finally see a mountain for what it is: but if that insight dissolves as soon as you cease your contemplation, it isn't worth much at all.

Being awake also means letting go of the romance of your illusions. In my case, so I am told, it means accepting that the lives of others lie beyond my control; that I could not save those who would not save themselves. I *know* this, but I cannot accept it.

My desk faces north, across a slanting meadow that runs down to our boundary fence. A groundhog colony lives there. Unlike their Himalayan cousins, they are very wary of humans. If I keep my head still, they stand erect, paws up, thinking themselves invisible. The slightest move and they are off, rollicking through the grass like ships in a swelling sea.

I've decided to look at Tess' school book again—*bumpling*, the booklet that reduced me to tears in Shey and at Lake Phoksundo. It's almost a year since I last read it, and I don't expect the same reaction now; this is our tranquil home, after all, not the supercharged Himalayan uplands.

I don't often dream of my daughter now, much as I wish I did; nor am I so often moved to tears by memories of her. Time erases continents, species, peoples, memories—and even grief.

The door behind me is open, the household calm. I can hear Sarah's voice from the lawn outside, speaking to her father on WhatsApp. But once again I am overcome, my stomach in spasm and my throat like a sore fist.

I welcome these tears, really. Even though I don't now believe Tess is aware of me, of her life, or of anything. I don't want to "get over" this. I don't want to "pass through the seven stages of grief," or "find closure." Nor do I wish to accept that the cause of my suffering, of my craving, is illusion—an illusion I should strive to be free from. Such notions repel me; they reduce my daughter to a number among the numberless dead.

As I had sensed at the outset, it wasn't the journey to Dolpo that mattered; it was making myself write about that journey. In doing so I have learned things about my family and myself that I had forgotten, or had understood poorly.

This is the real conceit of travel writing: the journey may not change you, but recollecting it just may. Writing about an experience transforms it, into a story releasing emotions that were absent, or latent at the time. The writing has been the real journey: the hike took weeks; the book, years.

Perhaps I really had hoped for absolution, for my failings as an enabler, as a flawed father and husband, and for my coldness towards my parents in their old age. The writing has eased the pain of losing them, but it has not made me see my own weakness as anything other than it was. And in this—in this, there is some consolation.

But there is more. There is the most secret of all the emotions of the bereaved—relief; relief that I am no longer responsible for a family I was unable to manage. Relief that I am no longer walking barefoot across a meadow seeded with hidden glass. Relief, God forgive me, that those I loved have departed.

—·—

Sometimes you remember the small sensations—and you treasure them, as a parent, because they are gone; their loss gives them value. The smell of her arm when she was a child, lying beside me in her bed in Kathmandu.

"Papa, tell me the story of the monkey's wedding."

"Really? Again? Alright . . . *then listen well, my dearest one, for this is a story of Africa, and of the early mysteries of the world. Of the days before lions ate meat, the days when monkeys walked the earth upright, like you or me, and did not need to venture up into the trees. This is the story of the greatest of all the monkeys, Sun and Moon, and how they outwitted Mkango, the terrifying, wicked lion.*"

"When it rains and the sun is shining, we call it a monkey's wedding."

"Exactly."

Today my daughter's voice surrounds me once again, her words like fireflies in the hot Virginia night. They flame, then they fade, but they leave me with a sense of temporary magic. Her voice holds her in the world of the living for a while longer—until no one is listening, and all traces of memory have been erased.

EPILOGUE
IT'S NOT YOUR FAULT

November 22, 2022—Route 29, Virginia.

It's a fall day, and the early part of the drive back home from Rustburg runs up the eastern edge of the Shenandoahs. I have the windows open; the air is humid, the temperature in the 70s. Great banks of rusty autumn foliage climb off the road as it winds towards Lovingston.

I'm coming back from a hearing at the Campbell County District Court in Rustburg. I went there to argue that the case brought against me by Alex's grandmother should be adjudicated in my court district, not hers. She has petitioned for joint custody of Alex, and I am resisting this. As expected, the judge determined that the case should be heard in Warrenton, not Rustburg. Alex has been living with Sarah and me for more than six months, and for the purposes of this case his domicile is The Plains.

His grandmother was furious. She was representing herself; it will be far more difficult to do this 150 miles from her home, in what she sees as hostile territory.

—·—

In late February this year I was back in Kathmandu, about to set out on a trek across the breadth of Nepal. Konzok and his team had already gone ahead by bus to the far-western border, in Darchula District, and I was set to follow them two days later. Then Alex called; things are crazy here, Papa, he said to me; there's fighting, and drugs, and the police are outside. Please come and get me. I can't live here anymore.

Since his mother had died, Alex had been living with his father and his two uncles, all in his grandmother's house. It was a fractious place; Bryan and his older brother both struggled with addictions, and the youngest son suffered from schizophrenia.

I'd told Alex before I went to Nepal that I'd come back if he needed me to. In the immediate aftershock of that evening, both Bryan and Alex' grandmother agreed that Alex could take a short break with us. Sarah drove straight down to Lynchburg and picked him up; I flew home. I hadn't realized quite how far Alex's relationship with his grandmother had deteriorated: now that he'd "got out of jail," as he put it, he spoke more freely about her. I negotiated with Bryan, and a week turned into a month, a month into three. Alex transferred to a local middle school, and would complete the academic year here.

Then Bryan told me he was moving out to his own place, and said he was willing to let me have legal custody. "You can probably take better care of him than me," he said, "and of course, I'll see him a lot." His grandmother hated the idea, but in June I made my first visit to the Rustburg courthouse, with Bryan and Alex there in support. The judge gave me sole legal custody. Alex would live with us now; that seemed to settle his immediate future.

It did not.

Less than two weeks later Sarah, Alex, and I flew to Nepal; we were going on a short trek to Lo Mantang, capital of the remote northern district of Mustang. The walk begins in Jomosom, north of the great Annapurna-Dhaulagiri gap on the Kali Gandaki River Gorge. Getting there, sadly, exposed Alex to the worst of Nepal—a development wasteland stretching all the way along the battered Kathmandu-Pokhara road and up toward Mustang. As they reach into every part of Nepal, motor roads bring opportunity and human vitality—along with the chaos that implies: rough, half-built concrete houses, tatty billboards, shredded tires, plastic bottles, sticky dust. As if a giant punk has shuffled across this majestic landscape, ripping furrows with his pointy shoes and seeding them with cascades of junk from his pockets.

While we were in our hotel in Jomosom, his grandmother called. It was late; Alex was asleep. She was distraught. Bryan had died, a few hours before. An accidental overdose. She was terrified that Alex would hear from one of his cousins. I'll tell him, I said; I'll take his phone until tomorrow. It was an accident, she said—you must tell him it was an accident.

Bryan had never got free from his oxycodone habit; he had tried, and there had been long periods of relative sobriety—but he couldn't quite escape. He'd been scheduled to go into rehab the next day, but he'd driven off that night on his own, seeking one last moment of relief before the pain of detox. It all went wrong; there was fentanyl in whatever he took, and the police found him dead in his car.

The next morning we ate breakfast together; I dreaded telling Alex, conscious that every minute I delayed meant his father was still alive to him. Eventually I took him to the empty bar. We sat overlooking the Kali Gandaki, a small stream up here in the high desert. Cloudy, snow-veined mountains surrounded the river plain.

Alex is fourteen now; he can be rough, and is anything but sentimental. When I was his age, I was in boarding school, learning submission; his response to bullying is to resist, to become intransigent—it's a healthier reaction, and will serve him well in life once he can calibrate it. Today, though, faced with such impossible news, he was composed, and thoughtful. He asked for details. His immediate reaction was sorrow for his father, and for his father's troubled life—not for himself.

"I never realized he was so sad," he said.

And "I just keep thinking of all the things he'll never get to do."

We abandoned the vacation and came home. I watched him carefully for signs of disintegration: interrupted sleep, strange new behavior, loss of appetite; and although his sarcastic humor darkened even further, he held himself together. I know the memory of his father sits with him constantly, but after the first few days he hasn't spoken about him. I don't press.

Soon after we returned from Nepal, his grandmother approached me saying she believed that we should now share legal custody of Alex; she wasn't suggesting that Alex go back and live with her, but this, she said, was what her son Bryan would have wanted—besides, she knew Alex better than anyone else, and his teenage years were bound to be rough.

What could be more reasonable, you might think; and what could give greater comfort to a grieving mother? But I knew it would be entirely unworkable. She craved control, and had a lightning temper: this is why Alex could no longer live with her. I had spent a decade tiptoeing around her so I wouldn't lose access to him.

—·—

I'm a couple of hours from home when Alex calls me. Nana texted me, he says. She said I should ask you about my Mommy's last day. If you don't dare tell me, she said she will. What's she talking about?

Unbelievable, I think, fear draining through my stomach like cold water. I know exactly what she means. Bryan's persistent grief after Tess' death led her to blame me for what happened. Five years after Tess' death, she emailed me saying that as far as she was concerned, I had killed my daughter through my *"asinine need to do whatever she asked for no matter what."* That by giving Tess money for alcohol that last evening, I had as good as pushed her off that balcony.

Hurtful as this was, there was some truth in it; what she is doing now, though, is much more damaging. She knows she's losing her court battle, and she's lashing out. Irrespective of how this might affect Alex.

"Nana's talking about me buying wine for your mother," I tell Alex. "I made a big mistake that day. I'll explain once I get home, I don't want to do it while I'm driving. Just tell her that if she hassles you."

I have a long time to think as I drive through the gathering dark. I pull up, walk to my study, fetch my computer.

"Let's sit on the steps," I say to Alex.

It's a mild November night, temperature in the upper 40s. A sliver of moon, no clouds. Across the valley, most of the trees are bare now; winter comes quicker in the north of the state.

"I always wanted to know what happened that day," Alex says—but his tone isn't angry.

"Well," I say, "since you've asked me, I'll tell you. As it happens, I wrote about it. I think the best thing I can do is just read it to you."

"Sounds good, Papa."

And so I do. I find Chapter 14 of this book. "*My daughter died in the early hours of September 23, 2010, the night of the full moon,*" I begin. I read him the next eight pages. I finish at "*I switched off the TV and sat on the sofa, listening to the street waking up around me, knowing everything once clean was suddenly filthy and ruined, like the contents of an overturned car spilled across a highway.*"

"That's how I remember it," I say.

He has been unusually attentive. He nods his head. He doesn't look at me. "Can you text that to me?" he asks.

"Of course."

There's a long silence. I don't want to look at him.

Then he says "It's not your fault, Papa. You can't blame yourself. It was her life. Not yours. Her decisions."

I am hugely relieved. But I am also wondering how this boy learned such compassion. This, after all, was the formative tragedy of his life.

"You ate dinner, right?" I ask him eventually.

"No, I was waiting for you."

Sarah is watching TV. "There's chicken fried rice on the stove—and some broccoli," she says as we come back into the house.

I watch him eating at the kitchen bar; I want to tell him I will never forget the kindness he's just shown me—but I see he doesn't want to drag this out, so I leave it unspoken.

"January 8th, right, Papa?" he then says. He just wants to make sure; he knows it's a good time to lock this in.

"I'll get the tickets tomorrow," I say, smiling. "I'm looking forward to it." He's been wanting to watch the Packers' last home football game this season. Green Bay's almost nine hundred miles from here; it's a long drive—but I'm up for it.

He is so like his mother sometimes.

A BRIEF POLITICAL
HISTORY OF NEPAL

I thought that readers not familiar with Nepal might be interested in a summary of its fascinating political history.

I am no expert, and am relying on the work of more impressive scholars—in particular Aditya Adhikari, Dor Bahadur Bista, Father Ludwig Stiller, John Whelpton, Mahesh Regmi, Prasant Jha and Tom Bell.

My apologies to all of them.

⸺ · ⸺

Nepal's intimidating physical geography, the threats to its sovereignty posed by powerful neighbors, the successful domination of internal politics by high-caste elites: these are the persistent themes.

Beginnings

Nepal is the product of one of the earth's most dramatic geological collisions: somewhere between 59 and 33 million years ago, the Indian tectonic plate began driving into the Eurasian continental mass, buckling the earth into folds, ridges, mountains and a vast elevated plateau behind them. As human civilizations arose, this creased stretch of rubble—stretching from modern-day Afghanistan in the west to Myanmar in the east—presented formidable barriers to movement. Large states and empires consolidated elsewhere, in plains fed by the rivers that drained out of these mountain ranges. What is now Nepal lay along the margins of the settled world, and early Nepalese history is largely a history of the Terai, the southern flatlands and low hills bordering modern-day India. This history includes the small sun-worshipping Shakya republic of the fifth century BC, home to a discontented young prince, Siddhartha Gautama.

The Khas State: the 14th to the 18th Centuries AD

The middle hills of Nepal became home to immigrant bands who traversed the mountains from the Tibetan plateau, or moved in laterally from both east and west. They settled beneath the snow-line, and above the mosquito-infested jungles. In time, small coalitions of villages began taxing herds, land and the movement of traded goods, accumulating enough capital to build small fortresses and monasteries. The early part of the first millennium saw the emergence of the Khas people in western Nepal; their origins are disputed, some even suggesting that their name carries echoes of the Caspian sea.

By the medieval period, a Khas feudal state ruled over most of modern western Nepal, as well as parts of Tibet and India; its language, *Khãs Kurã*, is the forerunner of modern Nepali. The Khas were originally nomadic, and animist. In time their rulers came to adopt Hinduism; in the words of Nepali anthropologist Dor Bahadur Bista,

> *"Their tribal character began to change from around the latter part of the 14th century when Brahmin pandits began arriving at the court of the Khas kings. The illiterate kings and courtiers with their rustic lifestyle must have liked the idea of a Hindu caste framework based on the principles expounded in Manusmriti, as*

this would give them a permanent high status based on birthright rather than on personal ability and competence."[1]

The Indian influx was not limited to pandits: when the massive Rajasthan fortress of Chittoor fell to the Sultanate of Delhi in 1303, the exodus of Hindu Rajput aristocrats into the Nepalese hills accelerated, and these arrivistes began infiltrating Khas politics. *"Though they were relatively few in number,"* writes Father Ludwig Stiller in *The Rise of the House of Gorkha,*

> *"they were of higher caste, warriors and of a temperament that quickly gained them the ascendancy in the princedoms in the Jumla Kingdom; their effect on the kingdom was centrifugal. They strengthened the old feudal states and helped them pull free from the centre."*[2]

By the early fifteenth century, the Khas confederation had weakened, fragmenting into 22 fiefdoms west of the Kali Gandaki River (the *bāise rājya*), and a further 24 (the *chaubise rājya)* to its east; all were now run by families who had, or who at least claimed to have Rajput connections. One of these pocket handkerchiefs was Gorkha, birthplace of Prithivi Narayan Shah.

Further east still lay more than 20 other principalities, most controlled by *Kirāti* people of Tibeto-Burman heritage. The wealthiest of these, by far, was a valley then known as *Nepaul*, a wide, temperate bowl, once a great lake, where irrigated cultivation was ubiquitous, and through which flowed much of the trade between India and China. The inhabitants of the valley were known as Newar, a variant of *Nepaul*. The Newars are of mixed Indo-Aryan and Tibeto-Burman heritage; they came to practice both Hinduism and Buddhism, and created the distinctive brick and tile pagodas that, until the 1980s, formed the skylines above the valley's main townships. As with the Khas, so with the Newar: Hindus fleeing the Muslim south, this time from Mithila in the foothills, intermarried and came to dominate the elites. In 1201, a family calling themselves Malla [wrestler] assumed the kingship and united the valley, though by the eighteenth century this unity had fractured, into three substantial but antagonistic kingdoms.

Prithivi Narayan Shah and the Creation of Nepal: 1745–1775

Modern international relations theory uses the term "defensive realism" to describe why some states pursue aggressive foreign policies. When in 1743 Prithivi succeeded his father as "king" of the 95 square miles of Gorkha territory (an area one-seventh the size of London), he might have been thus motivated: if he didn't expand, he could well disappear.

He set his eyes on the rich and powerful *Nepaul* valley to his east, and after 25 years conquered it, through a combination of persistence, savvy diplomacy, the award of generous land grants to his soldiers and the inability of the feeble-minded Newar kings of the valley to unite against him. Within the next thirty-five years, his successors would complete the absorption of all sixty-plus former mini-states, plus a slew of territories far to the west, stretching through Uttarakhand—an empire of 97,000 square miles, one thousand times larger than Gorkha itself.

Prithivi Narayan Shah died in 1775, mid-conquest. Expansionist though he was, he understood that preserving his family's gains required astute management of relations with the great powers to the north and the south. For him, China represented the greater threat; a small East India Company force dispatched in 1767 to help the despairing Malla king of Kathmandu had been confounded by a lack of supplies, monsoon floods and diarrhea. In the testament that he dictated to his courtiers just before his death, the *Divya Upadesh*, he famously compared what he now called Nepal to a *"yam between two stones"*—China and British India. China was straightforward enough: *"keep strong friendship with the Emperor of China,"* he insisted. His advice on dealing with the British was more ambiguous.

"Maintain friendship with the Emperor of the Sea in the south. But he is very cunning. He has suppressed Hindustan. He is eyeing the plains area of Nepal… They will surely arrive here one day. Do not attack them, but if they attack, fight with them. They can be beheaded at the crossings of the Churia hills, and we will be able to collect treasures sufficient for five to seven generations. And the border can be extended up to the Ganga River."[3]

He seems to have fancied his chances with the Company—not the last time that a Shah king would misjudge the power to his south.

State Expansion, Domestic Instability: 1775–1846

Prithivi Narayan was succeeded briefly by his pampered first-born son Pratap Singh Shah: Father Stiller reports that Prithivi had been distracted by conquest while the boy was growing up, leaving him to suspect Brahmin tutors who schooled him in the *"mysteries of Tantricism"*; these, we are told, *"led him down the path of sensuality."*[4] This royal sexualist died in 1777, after only two years of kingship, probably from smallpox, and was succeeded by his infant son Rana Bahadur Shah—the first of three successive child kings. Despite them and the murderous chaos that their minorities gave rise to, the fledgling state survived and continued to grow, until two ill-judged wars stopped, and then reversed its expansion.

Pursuing Prithivi Narayan's territorial ambitions fell largely to his younger son, Bahadur Shah. Between 1786 and 1790, Bahadur completed the subjugation of the *chaubise* and the *bāise rājya* fiefdoms. As had his father, Bahadur coopted the armies of conquered princelings with promises of land they would acquire through further conquests. This was a formula requiring continuous war, one that self-destructed when it butted up against the region's apex predators—first China, and then British India.

Bahadur Shah invaded Tibet in 1788. Tibet appealed to its overlord, the Qing Emperor. A Chinese army arrived, chasing the Nepalis out of Tibet and on down the Trisuli River valley to within a few days' march of Kathmandu, where it ran out of steam. A chastened Bahadur Shah signed a non-aggression treaty that required payment of a nominal tribute, and an acknowledgment of Chinese suzerainty over Nepal (a humiliation that would pay unforeseen dividends a generation later).

In the turbulent half-century following Prithivi Narayan's death, the framework of elite politics was set by underage, weak and/or mad monarchs, and by those who took advantage of the power vacuum they created. The most prominent actors were three aristocratic strongmen—first Bahadur Shah, then Damodar Pandey, and finally Bhimsen Thapa. The women who produced or moulded the feeble kings also played determinant roles, as queens and/or regents: first Rajendra Lakshmi, mother of the infant King Rana Bahadur Shah; then Lalita Tripura Sundari, mother of the next infant king, Girvan Yudda Bikram Shah; and finally Samrajya Lakshmi, simultaneously King Rajendra Bikram Shah's queen *and* regent. As one might expect, the historical record tends to view these powerful women with distaste, and their characters are variously described as over-emotional, duplicitous and lustful. The rivalries and blood-letting caught up with each of the three strongmen: Bahadur Shah was imprisoned in 1797, and boiled in oil; Damodar Pandey was imprisoned in 1804, and beheaded along with his two eldest sons; Bhimsen Thapa was imprisoned in 1839, attempted suicide and was left to die in the Bandharkhal, a garden beside the Bagmati River where he had overseen the execution of nearly a hundred of his rivals 33 years earlier.

The three women all died of natural causes.

Bhimsen Thapa was Nepal's de facto ruler for thirty years. He oversaw the final territorial expansions, westwards to the banks of the Sutlej River in modern-day Pakistan; in 1809 the army pressed further, aiming to conquer Kashmir, but was driven back by Ranjit Singh's Sikh armies. In 1814, growing competition for the fertile floodplains of the Himalayan rivers, the Terai, led to war with the East India Company. This time the Gorkha kingdom wasn't as lucky as in 1767. After two years of hard fighting, Nepal capitulated, and under the 1816 Treaty of Sugauli lost about 40 percent of its territory: Sikkim in the east, Garwhal and Kumaon in the west and, for a time, all the land it laid claim to in the Terai. Nepal also had to submit to the indignity of a British Resident in Kathmandu. The country retained its sovereignty, however, since the Company was unwilling to antagonize China through outright occupation of its vassal (Beijing had in fact dispatched a precautionary army to Lhasa during the Anglo-Nepalese war).

Despite this disaster, the Gorkha state managed to avoid re-fragmentation. Prithivi Narayan Shah's governance formula remained intact until the middle of the twentieth century: an aristocracy controlled through conditional land grants, an isolating hill terrain that negated organized resistance, and limited contact with outside powers.

The Rana Regime: 1846–1950

Out of this treacherous world emerged Janga Bahadur Kunwar, a minor aristocrat known initially for physical exhibitionism (lassoing wild elephants, jumping down wells, etc.) He came to power by murdering over thirty of his noble enemies at a night-time assembly in the *Kot*, an arsenal next to the royal palace in Kathmandu, and contriving the dispossession and exile of 6,000 of their family members—on the orders of Queen Samrajya Lakshmi, who seemed to believe she was in charge of the coup. She soon found herself exiled to India with her submissive husband-king; Janga Bahadur then replaced him with the crown prince, an 18-year old, who was promptly put under house arrest in his palace.

Perhaps grasping that the life of the Gorkha strongman lacked a viable exit strategy, Janga Bahadur changed the rules and created what was, in effect, a parallel royal family. For the next 104 years, the Ranas ruled the country through a system of hereditary prime ministerships; the titular Shah kings were confined to their palaces, under guard, and trotted out only on ceremonial occasions. This was Nepal's version of Japan's Tokugawa Shogunate. In 1856 Janga Bahadur had his captive king grant the Rana family the right to inherit the prime minstership, under an agnatic line of succession (i.e. one that ran down through the brothers, then through their sons, and on to the nephews if required). Janga Bahadur ruled for thirty years, and died in his bed. His family were given all the important posts in the army; in time, Ranas came to inherit army ranks as well as the premiership, with important male heirs promoted to the rank of general at birth. John Whelpton describes how internal stability was maintained by keeping courtiers in constant uncertainty: nobles were required to spend most of their time in court, under the eyes of the Rana ruler; all appointments were subject to annual review; the locations of the *jagir*, the land grants that provided the aristocracy's income, were frequently changed.

Janga Bahadur appreciated that preserving Nepal's independence meant cultivating a less fractious relationship with the East India Company, and this understanding spurred him to an act quite astonishing for a high-class Hindu—in 1850, four years after he seized power, he requested permission to visit England. He was the first Hindu ruler to make such a trip; it involved a voyage over the *kālo pāni*, the black water of the oceans, risking a loss of caste from all the impurities he would encounter. Like Isoroku Yamamoto, the twentieth-century Japanese warrior-visitor to the USA, Janga Bahadur's time in Britain impressed on him the stupidity of tangling with the world's foremost industrial powerhouse; unlike Yamamoto, he was able to control Nepalese foreign policy. In 1857, after waiting to see who would win, he intervened in the Indian Rebellion on the side of the East India Company, sending a force that helped break the siege of Delhi. This prompted the British to return the western Terai to Nepal, and thereafter Nepal enjoyed a degree of subcontinental independence only otherwise permitted to Bhutan.

There were nine Rana rulers in all, ten if you count Janga Bahadur's brother Bam Bahadur, who subbed for him for a year in the 1850s. After Janga Bahadur died in 1877, another brother, Ranodip Singh, ruled until 1885. At that point, tired of waiting for a turn at the premiership that would likely never come, Janga Bahadur's nephew Bir Shamsher Rana murdered Ranodip and Janga Bahadur's two sons. Bir Shamsher was succeeded by six more "Shamsher" Rana rulers: four of his brothers, and two of their sons.

Today the Rana regime is remembered for its repression, and for isolating Nepal from the rest of the world. This negative characterization is more appropriate to the later years of Rana rule than to its beginnings. A key reason for limiting external contact in the 1850s and 1860s was to safeguard the country from British domination. Nor was early Rana extractive behavior different from that of other contemporary Indian rulers, or any European monarch before their middle classes began to constrain them. John Whelpton argues that Jang Bahadur was less predatory than his British neighbors: the underpopulated western Terai areas returned to Nepal after 1857 were settled largely by Indians, whom the Company allowed to be dispossessed by moneylenders in ways which Nepal's civil code of 1854 (the *Muluki Ain*) did not. Taxes under the Ranas were less onerous than under the Shahs, amounting to somewhere between a third and a half of the grain crop, and were sustained at this level up until 1900.

The Shamsher Ranas, though, directed most of Nepal's income to themselves, as witnessed in surviving photos of palaces stuffed with ornate furniture, imported crystal, carpets and pianos, culminating in the 1,700-room Singha Durbar palace built by Chandra Shamsher in 1903—in a country without schools, public irrigation systems, hospitals or roads. Even when compared with the princes of the Raj, the Ranas fell out of step with the early twentieth century. They clear-cut swaths of Nepal's teak forests for export to India, repressed all political activity, shot thousands of tigers, and upscaled themselves through marriages to Indian royalty. Like the über-rich of our times, theirs were lives of competitive consumption, their status reaffirmed by environmental and fiscal wastage, and by visible disdain for the poor. Today's yachts, private jets, serial wives and empty, echoing mansions find their parallel in Rana Nepal, in vast stucco palaces, legions of wives and concubines, trunkloads of jewels.

The early twentieth-century Ranas were, if anything, encouraged in their greedy insularity by a Raj that now saw Nepal, like the Indian princely states, as a counter to increasingly strident calls for independence by the Indian Congress Party. The British had long recruited Gorkha soldiers for its Indian armies; now Nepal provided 100,000 soldiers and policemen to aid the British in the First World War. In return, the Raj paid the Ranas a personal subsidy of a million rupees per annum, and in 1923 signed a Treaty of Peace and Friendship that explicitly recognized Nepali sovereignty for the first time.

The Monarchy Restored, and Democracy Hobbled: 1950–1960

By the end of the Second War Britain's sub-continental star had burned out, and Congress soon ruled an independent, democratic India—one that felt no more sympathy for Rana autocracy than it did for the governing traditions of the 560-plus princely states it was busy absorbing. Nor did China, recovering from Japanese occupation and embroiled in civil war, offer any meaningful counterbalance. Nepalis educated in India and influenced by the independence movement founded political parties in exile, culminating in the creation of the Nepali National Congress in 1947; this was led by educated Brahmins, such as Bishweshwar Prasad (BP) Koirala, and by dissident junior Ranas. Despite concerns over potential instability along its northern borders, post-colonial India gave tacit approval to armed incursions from its territory by Nepali Congress.

With power slipping from their grasp, the Ranas in 1950 felt compelled to sign a Treaty of Peace and Friendship with India. It is no coincidence that this treaty bore the same name as the Ranas' 1923 agreement with the Raj, though the purpose of the new treaty was to emphasize India's hegemony. A country that had always tried to resist external influence was now obliged to

"…grant, on a reciprocal basis, to the nationals of one country in the territories of the other the same privileges in the matter of residence, ownership of property, participation in trade and commerce, movement and other privileges of a similar nature."

Nepal was also *"free"* to *"import, from or through the territory of India, arms, ammunition or warlike material and equipment necessary for the security of Nepal"*—an implied Indian monopoly made explicit in a secret 1965 protocol to the treaty. A significant Indian military intelligence presence in Nepal soon followed; an Indian Advisory Military Group at Nepal Army HQ, and seventeen Indian-manned observation posts on or near the Nepal/China border.

This capitulation was not enough to save the Ranas. Shortly after the treaty was signed, Jawaharlal Nehru's India helped King Tribhuvan escape to Delhi via the Indian Embassy in Kathmandu, breaking over a century of royal confinement. The restoration of the Shah dynasty and the abdication of the Ranas soon followed, as did the introduction of a limited form of democracy. The initial cabinet comprised Nepali Congress and Rana leaders, but the power to appoint and dismiss governments, direct the executive, sign legislation and command the army lay with the king.

A fractious decade ensued, in which the nascent democratic parties struggled with a revived monarchy (first King Tribhuvan, and from 1955 his son King Mahendra). The period was marked by frequent cabinet changes and punctuated by interludes of direct royal rule. One might expect that Nepali democracy would sit well with India, the US and Britain in a Cold War context in which communist China had just reasserted control of Tibet. In truth, India et al. saw an empowered mon-

archy as a better guarantor of Nepal's internal stability. The 1951 and
1959 Constitutions, both of which were drafted with outside help, left
decisive residual power with the king. According to Mara Malagodi,

*"... the constitutional settlements of the 1950s translated the king's
political hegemony into legal dominance, while retaining a democratic veneer and deploying the language of modern constitution-
alism."*[5]

In 1960, following a general election in which BP Koirala's Congress
party won 75 of 108 Lower House seats, King Mahendra took advantage
of elite alarm at BP's land reform and taxation proposals, declared martial law and dismissed the government—as the Constitution permitted
him to do. Mahendra assumed full governing powers and replaced the
1959 Constitution with one that enshrined a new governance creation:
the "partyless" Panchayat system of "guided democracy," in which all
those standing for office at all levels did so as individuals, and were vet-
ted by the Palace for their suitability. BP and many other "anti-national
elements" were jailed, or went into exile; independent political parties
were banned. For Mahendra, the Panchayat system would protect Nepal
from foreign influence-buying, which he saw as Nepali democracy's great
weakness. It also encouraged personal loyalty to him.

The Panchayat Regime: 1960–1990

India was nonetheless wary of Mahendra and his son Birendra, who succeeded him in 1972, seeing them as nationalists who were less malleable
than their original protégé King Tribhuvan. Relations between the two
countries waxed and waned, depending on how far India was prepared
to put up with Nepal's efforts to resist its embrace. After losing the 1962
Sino-Indian border war, a less confident India gave Nepal a freer hand
to trade with third countries and reduced, though never terminated,
its support for Nepalese politicians who took refuge in India after the

"royal coup" of 1960. In 1969 Nepal was able to insist on the withdrawal of Indian military advisors and the closure of the frontier observation posts.

The early 1970s saw India re-asserting itself forcefully in South Asia, with the invasion of East Pakistan in 1973 and the absorbtion of Sikkim two years later. The Palace became uneasy. In 1975, in an attempt to buttress international support for Nepali sovereignty, Birendra proposed that Nepal be recognized as a neutral "Zone of Peace," an attempt at non-alignment which sounds stranger today than it did then: by 1989 the ZOP proposal had been endorsed by 106 countries, including China, the USA and the UK—but not, of course, by India.

This attempt to build international collateral was irritating enough, but further Nepalese policy initiatives turned Indian annoyance into active hostility in 1988. At that time India was still protecting its economy with high external tariffs, but exempted Nepal from most of them. Nepal, though, unilaterally raised duties on certain Indian manufactures, and reduced import taxes on various Chinese goods—some of which were then smuggled into India across what had, for years, been an open border. Nepal also signaled that it would require Indians working in Nepal to hold work permits, something that neither country had ever required of the other's citizens. Of greater significance still was Nepal's purchase of a token quantity of arms from China. Not only did this breach the 1965 security protocol; Nepal had gone to India's prime enemy. For Indian Prime Minister Rajiv Ghandi and his China-sensitive security advisers, Birendra had now crossed a red line.

In 1988 Nepal's trade and transit treaties with India were due for a routine 10-yearly renewal. India let them lapse on March 23, 1989, claiming this had occurred because Nepal no longer wanted a bilateral trade treaty. At the same time, India refused to deliver existing stocks of fuel in transit from Calcutta Port. By 1989, trade with India accounted for only 10 percent of Nepal's exports and 25 percent of its imports: almost everything else, though, travelled *through* India. Within days there were severe shortages of petrol, diesel and kerosene, and traffic in Kathmandu all but ceased. India's illegal blockade did attract some international protest, in particular a letter to the Indian Ambassador in Washington from 50 United States members of Congress. This described India's actions as "*unwarranted,*" and "*threatening the stability of the subcontinent.*"[6] No serious pressure was applied, though: India was of much greater importance to Nepal's friends, whether or not they supported the Zone of Peace proposal.

The First People's Movement: 1989–1990

The Panchayat system, established as a one-party autocracy by King Mahendra in 1960, gradually expanded general education; this hastened its downfall. The system became increasingly unpopular with educated, urban youngsters. In 1979, student demonstrations led to nation-wide anti-Panchayat protests, forcing King Birendra to agree to a national referendum on whether the system should continue, or be replaced by multi-party democracy. The result was a 55/45 vote in favor of the Panchayat—though by setting the minimum age of participation at 21, many of the protestors and activists were excluded.

Established autocrats tend to surround themselves with sycophants; Birendra was slow to see the danger to his prestige from India's blockade, and allowed himself to be carried forward on a tide of imagined nationalist support. The economic recession was significant: Nepal's hitherto booming 1987-88 per capita GDP growth rate of 15 percent contracted to minus 1.5 percent in 1988-89, and remained stagnant in 1989-90. This recession exposed the regime's powerlessness against India, and its clumsy management of the bilateral relationship—signs of weakness that emboldened the monarchy's political opponents.

The Movement for the Restoration of Democracy (MRD), a.k.a. the People's Movement or the (first) *Jana Āndolan,* launched its campaign on February 18, 1990. For the first time, a number of Nepal's fractious communist parties (seven of the twenty or so) came together to form a United Left Front, and allied with the Nepali Congress Party. All parties had been banned in Nepal since 1960, but now they would come out onto the streets. The MRD's launch date was announced after an unlawful meeting in January, one which the government had known about but hadn't bothered to prevent. Among the guests was the Indian politician Chandra Shekhar Singh, who would briefly become India's Prime Minister later in the year. Cassette tapes of his speech circulated widely in Kathmandu. He left little doubt about India's position—though the Indian government would steadfastly deny it had any views on the struggle (*"No man can consider himself a God,"* Chandra Shekhar said; *"We should take courage from downfall of Ceausescu, Marcos and the Shah of Iran. The Indian people understand the agonies of Nepal these days."*)[7]

Protest spread across the country, culminating in huge demonstrations on April 6, and the shooting of a number of demonstrators as they approached the gates of the Palace. Birendra was unwilling to use the degree of force now needed to repress the movement, and lifted the ban on political parties. Within a year, Nepal found itself with a new democratic constitution in which sovereignty was vested primarily with the people. The Panchayat regime had fallen to a genuine popular revolution—an Asian counterpart to the contemporaneous demolition of the Berlin Wall and collapse of the Soviet client regimes of East Europe.

A Disappointing Democracy: 1990–1996

Widespread frustration with the political system that emerged from the *Jana Āndolan* soon followed. On reflection, the return of democracy after 30 years of Panchayat autocracy raised public expectations beyond the gift of any regime.

The record shows that the various governments of the 1990s did a reasonable job with the resources at their disposal: between 1990 and 2000 the road network doubled from 7,300 to 15,300 kilometers, irrigated hectarage expanded by 30 percent, and literacy rose from 40 to 60 percent of the population. The subsistence farming economy, though, lay largely beyond the reach of public policy, and here livelihoods continued to stagnate. In the rapidly-growing urban areas, unemployment rose among increasing numbers of secondary-school leavers, as did their sense of grievance. The press, finally free to speak, focused incessantly on government bungles and shortcomings, on the continuous bickering and coalition-mongering of Kathmandu's political elites—and on what John Whelpton calls *"the 'democratisation' of the corruption that had marked the final Panchayat years,"*[8] as the bribes, commissions and contracts once restricted to a relatively small circle were now shared more widely. Patronage and corruption had re-emerged in overt, more virulent forms: politics was openly competitive, but it lacked all accountability and had become much more expensive.

The Maoist Civil War: 1996–2006

The 1991 general election, the first genuinely democratic exercise in Nepal since 1959, was contested by a host of parties. One of these was the Communist Party of Nepal (Unity Centre), a semi-clandestine far-left party led behind the scenes by Pushpa Kamal Dahal, *nom de guerre* Prachanda [the fierce one], with its visible cut-out, Samyukta Janamorcha [The United People's Front, or UPF] led by Baburam Bhattarai. These two exceptional men, both Brahmins from poor families in the middle hills, came to exert a major influence on Nepalese politics—though few could have seen this coming. UPF won only 9 seats in the new parliament, an insignificant number compared with Nepali Congress (110 seats) and the once-revolutionary Communist Party of Nepal (Unified Marxist-Leninist), or *Umalé* (69 seats). UPF seemed destined for the usual short shelf-life of Nepal's fissile ultra-left parties.

In 1994, Prachanda and Bhattarai formed the Communist Party of Nepal (Maoist) and boycotted the 1994 general election. The ballot box was not working for them; they decided to pursue a more violent route to power. As John Whelpton put it, the Maoists were

"…a relatively small group with little hope of competing effectively at the national level unless they were content to act a as a junior partner to the main force on the left, the UML (Umalé)."[9]

In 1996 they announced the inception of a People's War, centered initially in the Rolpa and Rukum districts of the mid-western hills, a poor, remote and infertile part of the country.

On the face of it, launching a Maoist revolution in the mid-1990s seemed absurd, given how discredited communism had become after the collapse of the USSR; even in China, the Maoist ultra-leftism of the Gang of Four had long been repudiated. The whole world, surely, had moved on.

The world of rural Nepal, however, had not. The Maoists' definition of Nepal as "semi-feudal" was accurate: the country had been closed off until the 1950s, backwatering the rural economy in a pre-industrial era defined by medieval technologies, land-hunger, ill-health and debt—much as China had been in the 1920s, when communism offered so much more to the peasantry than the violent class hierarchies into which they had been born. In Nepal, the poor were kept in their place through the double bindings of class and caste, locking whole ethnicities into the lower echelons of the socio-economic system. Classic Marxism focuses on class, but the Maoists recognized that ethnic discrimination was what rankled with so many rural Nepalis; from the outset of their campaign they professed to fight for the hill tribes and the ritually impure, the Janajati and the Dalits.

Their rebellion was assisted by the government's clumsy, brutal response. The casualty figures for the 10-year war totaled about 20,000 dead and missing, the majority at the hands of government forces. This helped give rise to an unprecedented sense of insecurity, reflected in the numbers of internally displaced (some 150,000) and the out-migration of

young men (those leaving for the Gulf and Malaysia rose from a couple
of thousand per annum in the mid-1990s to over 200,000 a decade later).
The Maoists were also brutal, but they were more selective and somewhat more predictable, targeting informers and unpopular "class enemies" (landlords, traditional money-lenders). Marie Lecomte-Tilouine,
who wrote about the Maoist "model village" of Deurali, a place she had
lived in for several years before the insurgency, noted that

> *"A majority of the population clearly suffered from the Maoist rule
> in 2005 and wished to be rid of it. I asked them why in this case
> they did not revolt collectively against it. The answer I got was
> that doing so would cause the red army to come in and 'cut out all
> our tongues.'"*[10]

To succeed, the Maoists didn't have to secure mass backing: nor did
they have to win on the battlefield, though at times they aspired to do
so. They needed to wear the state down, and thereby force the government to allow them back into the political arena on advantageous terms.

Because the 1990 Constitution left the monarch in command of the
army, King Birendra was able to engage in a peculiar dalliance with
Prachanda: clandestine talks took place in which each used the other
to stymie their common enemy—the parliamentary parties. Birendra
refused his ministers' requests to deploy the army against the Maoists,
leaving the fight to the woeful, ill-equipped police.

On June 1, 2001, though, King Birendra, all his immediate family and
six other royal relatives were murdered at a family gathering in Narayaniti
Palace, victims of a bizarre massacre. Some still insist that the murders
were planned by Birendra's younger brother Gyanendra—one of the few
royals absent that evening—but the true explanation seems more prosaic. The crown prince, Dipendra, was allegedly furious with his parents
because they opposed his wish to marry his girlfriend, Devyani Rana.
Enraged, and high both on alcohol and drugs, he came out of his room in
combat fatigues and first shot his father dead, then mowed down most of

the others in the room, including his sister, before stepping outside and there killing his mother and younger brother. He then shot himself, but lingered on in a coma for three days, during which he was—as succession laws mandated—proclaimed king. When, to the relief of many, he died, Gyanendra succeeded him.

This turned out to be a misjudged, fateful rule. King Gyanendra was brighter than his elder brother, and possessed the same ruthless instincts as his authoritarian father Mahendra. He saw little to respect in Nepal's floundering democracy and its bungled efforts to combat the Maoists, but at first he hedged his bets, both maintaining Birendra's secret dialogue and unleashing the army against them.

By 2004 the war was engaging large forces on either side, upwards of 20,000 Maoist fighters against double that number of Royal Nepalese Army (RNA) troops and police, and with no clear path to victory for either side. In early 2005 King Gyanendra finally lost all patience with parliamentary democracy. He had already dismissed several elected prime ministers, but he now declared a state of emergency, dispensing altogether with prime ministers and the Constitution, and heading up the government himself. He arrested several hundred politicians and civil society activists, and reintroduced press censorship.

This reprise of his father's 1960 royal coup discredited Prachanda's insistence on negotiating with the king, since it suggested that Gyanendra had no intention of sharing power with anyone. Prachanda decided to ramp up the war, and in April 2005 the People's Liberation Army attacked Khara army base in Rukum District—a base they had failed to over-run three years earlier, and which had since been further fortified. The attack failed, and some 250 Maoist soldiers died in the attempt. Chastened by this, and influenced by Baburam Bhattarai, the party changed tactics in October 2005 and committed itself to creating a Democratic Republic, as opposed to a People's Republic (i.e. a democracy rather than a dictatorship). Baburam, less charismatic than Prachanda, was a more considered thinker: he understood that global communism was on the retreat and must adapt, and that this meant entering the democratic electoral marketplace. Here was a real break with twentieth century communist orthodoxy, since it meant offering up Marxism as a commodity which the electorate might, or might not, choose to consume.

On the day King Gyanendra assumed direct rule, the Indian government had declared that

> *"India has consistently supported multiparty democracy and constitutional monarchy enshrined in Nepal's Constitution as the two pillars of political stability in Nepal. This principle has now been violated with the King forming a government under his chairmanship… we will continue to support the restoration of political stability and economic prosperity in Nepal…"*[11]

India's perspective on the Maoists was ambiguous: useful, but potentially dangerous due to the inspiration they provided to India's own Maoist insurgents. Now India decided to shoehorn them into Nepal's political system by brokering a Twelve Point Understanding between the mainstream political parties and the Maoists, and by supporting the negotiations that led to a Comprehensive Peace Agreement (CPA) in 2006.

Under the CPA, the Maoists formally agreed to re-enter democratic politics, dissolve the governments of the "liberated areas," and merge the People's Liberation Army (PLA) with the Royal Nepalese Army. In return, the mainstream parties agreed to the election of a Constituent Assembly that would rewrite the 1990 Constitution. The Maoists had always argued that a constituent assembly was needed if all of Nepal's different classes, castes and ethnicities were to be properly represented: it had been promised in 1951 under the Delhi Compromise that ended Rana rule, but reneged upon since by three successive kings.

Thus Gyanendra's impatience with everyone but himself had catalyzed an unexpected realignment, uniting the parliamentary parties, the Maoists and India against him. A few months later, in April 2006, the

Maoists and their new allies launched 19 days of nation-wide protests, the second *Jana Āndolan.* This forced the king to reinstate Parliament. Parliament then promulgated an Interim Constitution, which stripped the king of all his powers and privileges.

The Constituent Assembly was duly elected in May 2008, and at its first meeting voted to abolish the monarchy. On June 11, 2008 ex-King Gyanendra gave a press conference as he left the Royal Palace for new, more modest quarters on the outskirts of the city. He handed over the royal crown and scepter to the government of the Federal Democratic Republic of Nepal *"for safekeeping and protection for ages to come."* [12] Thus ended 240 years of Shah kingship—though not Gyanendra's aspirations to return to power, as his periodic statements and continuing links with Hindutva hardliners in India would attest.

Maoists in the Mainstream: 2008–The Present

The Maoists emerged as the largest party from the Constituent Assembly elections of May 2008, winning 220 of the 575 seats. India, according to Prashant Jha, had *"got it terribly wrong, predicting that the Maoists would fare a distant third."* [13] The prospect of a strong, non-deferential Maoist party now led India to see the army as the key bulwark against Maoist ambitions, and to worry that the merger of the PLA and army might be used by the Maoists to capture full state power. Also alarming were the overtures that now-Prime Minister Prachanda was making towards China, symbolized by his visiting Beijing before going to Delhi, in violation of long-standing tradition.

In the ninth month of his premiership, Prachanda dismissed the conservative, insubordinate Chief of Army Staff General Rookmangud Katawal, who opposed the merger of the two armed forces. India then lobbied the Maoists' coalition partners, who quit the government. The President of the Republic, assured of Indian support, stepped in and countermanded Prachanda's order. Prachanda, his troops inactive in cantonments, felt obliged to resign. India then helped cobble together a new government of 21 parties, headed by *Umalé*. Although the Maoists would return to power as a minority party in various coalitions (under Baburam Bhattarai's premiership in 2011-13, and under Prachanda's in 2016-17 and from late 2022 to mid-2024), the high-water mark of Maoist power and popularity had passed.

If the shifts in Indian support between the monarchy, the democratic parties and the Maoist revolutionaries seem bewildering, the logic appears consistent with its view of Nepal since India's own independence. Nepal is a vital buffer zone, and its desire to protect its sovereignty is perceived both as a security threat, and as an impertinence. Keeping Nepalese governments from becoming too independent, or too unstable, has justified continuous diplomatic meddling—almost as if the Nepali state is made of a type of plastic which, if left alone too long, grows cold, inert and no longer amenable to manipulation.

By the time of the 2013 elections for the second Constituent Assembly—mandated by the length of time it was taking to create a new constitution—the Maoists had lost a good deal of their appeal, and their share of the 525 seats fell from 220 to 80, behind both Congress and *Umalé*. By most accounts, the Maoist leaders had accommodated themselves quickly to the corruption of elite Nepali politics. They had initially employed ex-militia members as street enforcers under the Young Communist League, using selective violence to pursue 'people's justice' as well as to extort money from businesses. This might have started out as a way to raise funds for the party, but it soon became personal. *"The growing wealth of Maoist leaders invited much public derision,"* wrote Aditya Adhikari in 2014. *"Across the country, Maoist leaders had used their newfound influence to broker deals and capture government contracts."*[14] The Maoists' third-place 2013 electoral finish has persisted: in the 2017 and 2022 national elections (for the upper and lower houses of parliament and for the seven new provinces), they consistently polled below Nepali Congress and *Umalé* (the exception being in Sudurpaschim

Province, in the far west, where they were the largest party in 2017 and the second-largest in 2022).

Aditya Adhikari quoted Prachanda during the civil war as saying *"I have never been firmly committed to any fixed position,"*[15] and this flexibility has served him and his party well, keeping them close to the centers of power through alliances of convenience with their former enemies (including a three-year merger with *Umalé* and a 2022-4 coalition with Nepali Congress).

Apart from giving the high-caste leaders of the Maoists a seat at the political high-table, what did the Maoist revolution achieve?

The Maoists should be credited for ending Nepal's monarchy, and for Nepal's move towards federalism and the promise of greater regional and ethnic equality that such a system implies—as well as for constitutional provisions that now embrace proportional representation (forty percent of the seats in parliament), thereby increasing minority representation. Much of their social and economic agenda remains unrealized, though. Nearly twenty years after they laid down their arms, many of the promises they made as a rebel movement remain promises—particularly major reform of Nepal's land tenure system, and the economic advancement of the Janajati and Dalit.

The *Madhesh Āndolan* and the Road to Federalism

The Maoists tapped into latent ethnic grievances, and popularized the notion of a federal system based on ethnicity. In 2007, congruent with a growing belief in ethnic rights that Maoism had helped foster, hitherto-disregarded Terai groups rose up in protest at what they saw as continued neglect under the emerging post-monarchical state. For Tom Bell this *Madhesh Āndolan* was *"by far the most important development"* of the period.

"Madhesis, and many other communities, considered themselves the victims of discrimination and were, on average, poorer and less healthy than members of 'the dominant group'. The issue wasn't anywhere on the mainstream agenda, but it was ripe enough that the Maoists had drawn support for their insurgency by promising autonomy to marginalized people . . . when Madhesis rose up demanding their share in the New Nepal, everyone, including the movement's own leaders, was surprised by their intensity."[16]

Ethnic federalism became the least tractable issue facing the Constituent Assembly, one that invited a storm of opinion and defied clear consensus. Because Nepal's many dozen ethnic groups are dispersed so widely and are so intermingled, matching majorities to geographical areas would mean dividing the country into dozens, even hundreds of administrative areas—except in parts of the far west, where clear Brahmin-Chetri majorities exist (annoyingly so, since the ostensible purpose of ethnic federalism is to *lessen* Brahmin-Chetri domination). On the other hand, demarcating new provinces on the basis of administrative and/or economic coherence would immediately muddy any identification between peoples and land.

Endless implausible variants of the national map were prepared. Many Madheshis argued vociferously for one single Madhesh province that would cover the whole of the Terai. The new Constitution took nine years in all to write. When it did emerge, in 2015, the final provincial map was rushed through the Constituent Assembly. It divides Nepal into seven provinces; of these, only one consists solely of Terai land, while three others mix hill and Terai land tracts. Nor, in the end, can any province be said to favor any particular ethnic group, although the Terai-only province (Province No. 2, Madhesh) comes closest, with a population in which Madheshi and Tharu comprise about 93 percent, speaking Hindi dialects like Maithili, Bhojpuri and Bajjika as their mother tongue. This was not enough for many in the Terai, and 2015 saw further rioting and a blockade by the discontented of the main trade and transit points along the Indian border. This the Indian government at least tacitly approved of, ostensibly in political solidarity with the Madheshi, perhaps also because it offered yet another opportunity to keep the Nepali state off-balance.

The uneasy compromise between ethnic rights and state consolidation did not satisfy many people's ethnic aspirations, but it did acknowledge the most important deficit in inclusiveness, that of the Terai. With one exception, moreover, all the new provincial capitals are in the Terai, presaging an unprecedented shift in power to the lowlands. Federalism may prove an important counterbalance to the centralization that has characterized the state since its unification in the mid-eighteenth century, and which—since the civil war and the emergence of the Madhesh movement—now threatens the stability of the nation. Creating a federal system in any country is a massive challenge, though, and is made harder in Nepal by a grossly uneven spread of trained personnel and by the varied abilities of different provinces to support themselves: a problem reinforced by federal reluctance to grant the provinces adequate revenue-raising powers, and by erratic fiscal transfers from the center. Nor is it clear whether federalism will result in greater inclusiveness and stability, or if it will simply replicate the narrow elitism of Kathmandu politics at the provincial level.

Looking ahead...

Nepal's challenges are enormous: a population almost four times as large as it was in 1950 when the Rana regime ended, and with far higher popular expectations in today's communications age; a perennially moribund economy, the failings of which have been masked for the past twenty years by a major influx of remittance incomes; a limited natural resource base seriously threatened by increasing temperatures, drought, floods and landslides; a fractious political system in which the country's democratic inheritors have displayed little more public spirit than their autocratic predecessors; and a powerful, suspicious and meddling southern neighbor whose nerves will be further tested as Nepal tries to accommodate itself to China's growing power.

And yet the very factors that have kept Nepal a poor, marginalized and badly-governed state are also factors that have contributed to its durability and relative tranquility (using the post-independence history of violence in and among its South Asian neighbors as the comparator). Nepal's awkward location between two rising global superpowers is arguably the best guarantee of its continued independence: neither India nor China wants to provoke a war over Nepal. Its harsh and endangered terrain has, in today's globalized era, spurred a drain of resilient people out of the hills into the cities of the valley and the Terai and abroad, into more dynamic economic environments that have doubled real household incomes over the past twenty years (almost 3 million Nepalis now work in the Gulf and Malaysia). Even the narrow elitism of Nepal's powerbrokers has, for the most part, helped keep them inside a political tent in which the lure of state-derived rents outweighs the attraction of violence—as the post-war de-radicalization of Nepal's Maoists bears witness to.

Nepali elitism is also mutating. This was symbolized by the emergence of Rabi Lamichhane, who in 2022 founded a new party, Rastriya Swatantra [National Independent] that won 21 seats in the lower house in the 2022 elections—making it the fourth-largest political entity. Subsequently, Lamichhane served as deputy Prime Minister in a short-lived coalition with the Maoists in early 2024. He is a former TV journalist who earned a large following exposing government corruption and highlighting the exploitation of Nepali migrant workers in the Gulf and Malaysia, and his creative use of social media and centrist policies energized young Nepalis disaffected by the self-serving incompetence of the three mainstream parties (Congress, *Umalé*, the Maoists); in April 2025, though, Lamichhane was arrested on plausible charges of fraud and embezzlement, and is being held in jail pending trial. Another such exemplar is Balen Shah, the 35-year-old incumbent mayor of Kathmandu; he came to prominence as a battle-rapper on YouTube, and has earned both praise and controversy for his aggressive efforts to manage Kathmandu's increasing pollution, overcrowding and unlicensed building. The rise of such figures suggests that the populist path pioneered by media figures such as Ronald Reagan, Silvio Berlusconi and Donald Trump is beginning to take Nepalese forms.

May 2025

POSTSCRIPT
THE GEN Z UPRISING

Just as *The Leopard and The Moon* was going to print, Nepal erupted once again in street protest and violence—but protest of a new kind. Since 1950, all confrontations between the ruling authorities and those seeking their overthrow involved the monarchy, organized political parties and, in some measure, India. The Gen Z uprising of September 8-12, 2025 was spontaneous and essentially leaderless, a collective youth movement powered by the internet platforms Tik Tok, Viber and Discord, one that rejected *all* established political parties and business elites—and with India nowhere to be seen.

A month earlier, inspired by online protests in Indonesia, Nepali social media began ridiculing the vanity posts of elite 'nepo kids', evidence of growing anger at Nepal's self-dealing networks of businessmen and politicians. On September 4, the Nepal government blocked Facebook, Instagram, X, WhatsApp and YouTube, ostensibly because their parent companies had refused to register in Nepal. In explaining the reaction to this ill-judged move, mainstream Western media pointed to how much Nepali migrant laborers depend on social media to reach families at home; this perhaps underplays the fury a young population felt at the abrupt shutdown of an essential part of their culture.

The government ban threw gasoline on deep-rooted fury at the greed, theft and ineptitude of Nepal's political class. On September 7, *Hami Nepal*, a humanitarian NGO established after the 2015 earthquake, posted a call to the public to come out into the streets on the following day. On September 8, thousands of young men and women marched, initially peacefully, enraged by what they saw as an attempt to shut down criticism of elite corruption. When protestors broke into the grounds of the Federal Parliament, police panicked and used live ammunition, and by the end of the day at least nineteen protestors had been killed.

On September 9, in spite of a police curfew, much larger crowds gathered in Kathmandu and other cities across Nepal; these were no longer confined to the original Gen Z protestors, and included what Shubhanga Pandey describes as "*enforcers of political parties, as well as lumpen outfits allied to monarchists and Hindu nationalists*," intent on creating chaos.[1] The crowds attacked symbols of the state, setting on fire and/or trashing the Federal Parliament Building, the Supreme Court, the executive offices at Singha Durbar, and over 300 government buildings throughout the country. They also targeted the homes and properties of those deemed the most corrupt. The Kathmandu residences of the heads of the three major parties were torched, and Nepali Congress leader Sher Bahadur Deuba and his wife, Foreign Minister Arza Rana, were beaten up by protestors; communist leaders Prime Minister KP Sharma Oli (*Umalé*) and Prachanda (Maoist Centre) had to be rescued by army helicopter. Political party offices were destroyed, as were businesses identified with prominent crony capitalists: the headquarters of Kantipur Media, the Hilton Hotel and several branches of the Bhat Bhateni supermarket chain. Police posts were ransacked, and some 13,000 prisoners were sprung from jail (including Rabi Lamichhane, who later surrendered himself and is back in custody). Prime Minister Oli and his government resigned; the army imposed a nation-wide curfew. More than 70 died and over 2,000 were injured before order was restored.

For the next three days, Nepal experienced an unprecedented power vacuum while the Chief of Army Staff and the President of the Republic negotiated with Gen Z representatives, Sudan Gurung of *Hami Nepal* prominent among them. *Hami Nepal* launched an online poll on Discord to select an interim Prime Minister. The 73-year-old ex-Chief Justice

Sushila Karki, who had joined the September 8 protests, emerged as the favorite candidate. On September 12 she was sworn in as head of an interim government of technocrats without clear party affiliations. Parliament has been dissolved, and a general election scheduled for March 2026. Karki was strongly endorsed by Balen Shah, who declined to be considered for the post; many Gen Z/social media users believe he should be Nepal's post-interim PM.

While Nepal's Gen Z revolution is unique in Nepali history, it is also one of several recent internet-powered 'horizontal revolutions' in South Asia, with the clearest parallels found in Sri Lanka (2022) and Bangladesh (2024), where young urban protestors also toppled the ruling governments.

In May 2025, I summarized the arc of Nepali political history thus: "*Nepal's intimidating physical geography, the threats to its sovereignty posed by powerful neighbors, the successful domination of internal politics by high-caste elites: these are the persistent themes.*" Does this still hold?

Not quite so much as it once did, perhaps. The long shadows cast by India and China will continue to shape domestic politics, but Nepal's geographical isolation has been attenuated over the past two decades by the exposure of so many Nepalis to work abroad, and by the global communities of the internet: without these developments, the Gen Z revolution would not have taken place. Nor is Gen Z afflicted by the "fatalism" that Dor Bahadur Bista once saw as integral to the Nepalese character—that sense of powerlessness that leads to passivity, and to a sycophantic belief that survival and prosperity lie in the hands of remote masters to whom you must show unthinking loyalty [chākari].

The more intriguing question is whether high-caste elite dominance is under serious challenge—and this, so far, is unclear. Online Gen Z gives voice to all identity groups, yet seven of the nine interim government cabinet members that it helped select are high-caste, and none of them are Madheshis. There have also been calls to rewrite the 2015 Constitution; its proportional representation and federalist underpinnings have been questioned, and many favor the direct election of future Prime Ministers as a way of breaking the three-party monopoly on apex power. For all of its unsatisfying compromises and shortcomings, though, the Constitution does promote more equitable regional and ethnic power-sharing.

Sadly, the Gen Z uprising is a reminder that Nepal has failed to build trusted political institutions in the seventy-five years since the fall of the Ranas—nowhere an easy task. World Bank analysis shows that creating legitimate public institutions takes more than a generation under the best of circumstances.[2] In this era of short attention spans and impatience, it is unclear how long citizens will be prepared to wait.

Since the Arab Spring, social media has done extraordinary work in exposing abuse and mobilizing protest: but social media can also inflate citizens' expectations of what a government can achieve. The superficial equality of opinion that online platforms give their users means that many of those loudly demanding better government have little idea of what the state—any state—can realistically deliver. This "credibility trap" is a problem for all societies today. It is compounded when leaders fail to be honest with their citizens about what they can *not* do: a problem even in so-called "mature democracies" like the US and the UK, where institutions are well-established and relatively effective in providing services. This lack of political courage furthers angers citizens who already expect too much from their governments. The internet is also fertile ground for conspiratorialism, and this has helped push global political opinion to the right, towards the kind of magic solutions that would-be autocrats promise—if you will only surrender your judgment and your freedom of action into their hands.

Where will Nepal go from here? Will the discredited political and commercial elites find ways to return to power? Will the deposed King continue to build on an evident support base? If they are given power, will Nepal's younger leaders deliver cleaner and more effective government, or will they behave like their predecessors, promising much and taking more? And will online frustration and the violence it gave rise to prove to be the exception in Nepalese political life—or a foretaste of deep political instability to come?

October 2025

NOTES

Dedication

1 William Wordsworth, *Ode: Intimations of Immortality from Recollections of Early Childhood*, in *Poems, in Two Volumes*, 1807, Paternoster-Row, London, Longman, Hurst, Rees and Orme.

Author's Notes

1 Samuel Taylor Coleridge, *Specimens of the Table Talk of the late Samuel Taylor Coleridge*, 1835, London, Albermarle Street, John Murray, Volume I, September 22, 1830, p. 205.

Acknowledgments

1 William Wordsworth, *Ode: Intimations of Immortality from Recollections of Early Childhood*, op. cit.:
> *"But for those first affections,*
> *Those shadowy recollections,*
> *Which, be they what they may*
> *Are yet the fountain-light of all our day,*
> *Are yet a master-light of all our seeing;*
> *Uphold us, cherish, and have power to make*
> *Our noisy years seem moments in the being*
> *Of the eternal Silence ..."*

Prologue

1 William Manchester, *Goodbye, Darkness: A Memoir of the Pacific War*, 2002, Back Bay Books/Little, Brown and Company, New York, p. 395.
2 William Manchester, op. cit., p. 395.

3 Peter Matthiessen, *The Snow Leopard* [hereafter TSL], 1978, The Viking Press, New York, pp. 3-4.
4 TSL, p. 3.

Chapter 1

1 TSL, p. 37.
2 TSL, p. 40.
3 TSL, p. 298.

Chapter 2

1 Christina Rosetti, *Remember*, in *Goblin Market and Other Poems*, 1862, London, Macmillan and Co.
2 W. G. 'Max' Sebald, *The Rings of Saturn*, 1999, London, the Harvill Press, p. 24.
3 Music and Lyrics by Mark Knopfler, *River Towns*, on the *Tracker* album, 2015, copyright @ Will D. Side Limited.
4 W. G. Sebald, op. cit., p. 249.
5 W. G. Sebald, op. cit., p. 255.
6 T. S. Eliot, *East Coker*, from *The Four Quartets*, 1943, New York, Houghton Mifflin Harcourt Publishing Company, Stanza II, lines 95-96.
7 Meg Rosoff on *Art and the Unconscious Mind*, BBC, ArtsNight, Series 3, August 4, 2016.

Chapter 3

1 TSL, p. 33.
2 TSL, p. 37.
3 TSL, p. 32.
4 *Bhagavad-gītā As It Is*, undated, Bhaktivedanta Vedabase online Chapter 15, The Yoga of the Supreme Person, Text 1, https://vedabase.io/en/library/bg/15/.
5 *The Gospel According to Matthew*, Chapter 5, Verse 8, King James Version, 1611.
6 T. S. Eliot, op. cit., Stanza III, lines 138-141.
7 In his 2015 essay *How Discriminatory was the Muliki Ain against Dalits?*, published online by southasiacheck.org, Sujit Mainali gives the following example of where the *Muluki Ain*'s minute definitions and adjustments will take you: "*If an Upadhyaya Brahman … ejaculated his semen in the mouth of someone else's wife or made her swallow his semen ejaculated elsewhere, the punishment for him would vary based on the caste of the victim woman. (If the victim was an Upadhyaya Brahmin, the fine was 500 rupees; if an untouchable,*

100.) . . . If a man from the lowest caste group, i.e. Impure and Untouchable, ejaculated semen in the mouth of the wife of someone from higher caste than his or made her swallow his semen ejaculated elsewhere, the man is subjected to enslavement. But if the victim is also from impure and untouchable caste, then the perpetrator is subjected to a fine of 100 rupees."

8 Music and Lyrics by Adam Harrison, Nathan Ward Nicholson, Piers John Towler Hewitt and Todd William Howe, *Safe House* on the *Promises* album, 2013, Safe House lyrics © BMG Rights Management.

9 TSL, p. 41.

10 Jamon Van Den Hoek et al., *Shedding New Light on Mountainous Forest Growth: A Cross-Scale Evaluation of the Effects of Topographic Illumination Correction on 25 Years of Forest Cover Change across Nepal*, 28 May 2021, Remote Sensing, Multi-Disciplinary Publishing Institute, 13 (11), 2131, https://doi.org/10.3390/rs13112131.

11 TSL, p. 58.

12 TSL, p. 41.

13 TSL, pp. 58-59.

14 TSL, p. 3.

15 TSL, p. 61.

Chapter 4

1 TSL, p. 67.

2 Bradley Mayhew et al., *Trekking in the Nepal Himalaya, Walking Guide*, 2015, Franklin, Tennessee, Lonely Planet Publications Pty Ltd, Kindle edition, Day 6: Dhorpatan to Takur.

3 TSL, p. 74.

4 Nepal Central Bureau of Statistics, *Nepal Living Standards Survey 2010-2011*, Kathmandu, Government of Nepal.

5 Central Bureau of Statistics, *National Sample Census of Agriculture 1991/92 Nepal, Highlights*, January 1994, Kathmandu, His Majesty's Government's National Planning Commission Secretariat. https://nepalindata.com/media/resources/items/0/bHighlights.pdf

6 See, for example, *Worldometer*, updated continuously, https://www.worlddata.info/asia/nepal/populationgrowth.php#google_vignette

7 World Bank, *Personal Remittances Received (% of GDP)*, continuously updated, Washington DC, https://data.worldbank.org/indicator/BX.TRF.PWKR.DT.GD.ZS?locations=NP.

8 *"The poverty headcount, calculated at the national poverty line, was 42 percent in 1995, which gradually declined to 31 percent in 2003 and 12.5 percent in 2010."* World Bank, *Poverty and Equity Brief—South Asia—Nepal*, October

2020, Washington DC. https://databankfiles.worldbank.org/public/ddpext_
download/poverty/987B9C90-CB9F-4D93-AE8C-750588BF00QA/SM2020/
Global_POVEQ_NPL.pdf.

9 TSL, p. 80.

10 TSL, p. 79.

11 Bibhu Dev Misra, *The end of the Kali Yuga in 2025: Unraveling the mysteries of the Yuga Cycle*, July 15, 2012, on grahamhancock.com.

12 TSL, p. 93.

13 TSL, p. 92.

14 TSL, pp. 89-90.

15 TSL, p. 111.

16 NHS study referenced in Josh Bloom, February 11, 2016, *How Poisonous is DDT?*, American Council of Sciences and health online, https://www.acsh.org/news/2016/02/11/how-poisonous-is-ddt.

17 Google AI tells us that the term derives from the Sanskrit word *krośa*, which means "a call," and originally approximated the distance at which a human voice could be heard. Unsurprisingly, there are many variants of how far a *kos* can be, from 1.1 miles on up.

Chapter 5

1 TSL, p. 115.

2 TSL, p. 48

3 TSL, p. 48.

4 Siân Pritchard and Bob Gibbons, *A Trekking Guide to Upper and Lower Dolpo*, 2014, Himalayan Travel Guides, Kathmandu, Himalayan Map House, first Kindle edition, Tarakot-Laina Oder section.

5 Siân Pritchard and Bob Gibbons, op. cit., Tarakot-Laina Oder section.

6 Constantine Pleshakov, *The Tsar's Last Armada: the Epic Journey to the Battle of Tsushima*, 2002, New York, Basic Books, p. 273, Kindle edition.

7 TSL, pp. 92-93.

8 TSL, p. 93.

9 TSL, p. 93.

10 TSL, p. 4.

11 TSL, p. 97.

Chapter 6

1 David Snellgrove, *Four Lamas of Dolpo, Volume 1: Autobiographies of Four Tibetan Lamas*, originally published in 1967, Oxford/Cambridge, Bruno Cassirer and Harvard University press; this edn. 1992, Kathmandu, Himalayan Book Seller, p. 4.

2 Éric Valli and Diane Summers, *Dolpo: Hidden Land of the Himalayas*, 1987, New York, Aperture Foundation Inc, p. 4.

3 Kenneth Bauer, *High Frontiers: Dolpo and the Changing World of Himalayan Pastoralists*, 2004, New York, Columbia University Press, Historical Ecology Series, *Chapter 9, Perspectives on Change*, Kindle edition.

4 The Naxalite movement was named after the West Bengal village of Naxalbari, where a Marxist school teacher, Kanu Sanyal, organized a land redistribution program in 1967. Writing in China's People's Daily on July 5 of that year, the movement's ideological leader Charu Mazumdar declared that *"A peal of spring thunder has crashed over the land of India,"* and described the Chinese Cultural Revolution as an *"exploding moral atom bomb, from which splinters are flying to various parts of the world to start conflagrations wherever they land."* In 1970, Naxalite students set fire to cinemas showing *Prem Pujari* (Worship of Love), a potboiler which they construed as critical of China. Policemen were shot on the streets of Calcutta, and class enemies liquidated in their offices, shops and villages. The state and national governments had largely suppressed the movement by 1972; it reignited, however, in a plethora of armed movements up and down the eastern states of India. At their apogee in 2009-10, Naxalite-type movements fought in 180 districts in ten Indian states: the most extensive peasant revolt in the world at that time, although it is little known outside India. The founding Naxalite movement spilled into Nepal in the early 1970s, but the land confiscation program it inspired in the eastern Nepal Terai was quickly put down, and its leaders shot or imprisoned. This ineffective rebellion inspired the creation of two parties that have come to play determining roles in modern Nepalese politics: the United Marxist-Leninist Party (UML, or *Umalé*), a staple of post-1990 Nepalese democracy that has so far produced three prime ministers, and the Communist Party of Nepal (Maoist), which launched the ten-year Nepali Civil War and brought down the monarchy. The post-monarchy Maoists have held three prime ministerships, and were the principal drivers of Nepal's 2015 federal Constitution.

Chapter 7

1 Joseph Conrad, *Youth*, Blackwood's Magazine, Edinburgh, Volume 164, September 1898, p. 330.

2 TSL, pp. 33-34.

Chapter 8

1 TSL, p. 266.

2 See World Buddhism Association Headquarters, 2025, https://www.wbahq. org/hhdcb3/.

3 *Arts and Entertainment*, April 2015 (magazine now defunct).

4 *Arts and Entertainment*, op. cit.

5 David Snellgrove, op. cit., p. 140.

6 Music and Lyrics by Donovan Leitch, *There is a Mountain*, released as a single in August 1967, lyrics @ Donovan (music) Limited.

7 D. T. Suzuki, *Essays in Zen Buddhism, First Series*, 1927, London, Luzac & Company, p. 12, https://www.google.com/books/edition/Essays_in_Zen_ Buddhism/0MefAAAAMAAJ?hlen&gbpv=1&bsq=mountains%20as%20 mountains.

8 T. S. Eliot, *Little Gidding*, from *The Four Quartets*, 1943, New York, Houghton Mifflin Harcourt Publishing Company, Stanza V, lines 239-242.

9 Éric Valli quoted by Aseem Chhabra in *Journey into the heart of Nepal* (review of *Caravan*), April 1, 2000, rediff.com, https://www.rediff.com/us/2000/ apr/01us2.htm.

10 TSL, p. 4.

11 Quoted in Kenneth Bauer, op. cit., Chapter 8, *A Tsampa Western*, Kindle edition, citing Spotlight (*Caravan makes history by being the first Nepali film to be nominated for the Oscars*, 2000, Spotlight 19.32 (February 25 - March 2).

12 Kenneth Bauer, op. cit., Chapter 8, *A Tsampa Western*, Kindle edition.

13 Valli quoted in Kenneth Bauer, op. cit., Chapter 8, *A Tsampa Western*, Kindle edition.

Chapter 9

1 George B. Schaller, *Stones of Silence: Journeys in the Himalaya* [hereafter SOS], 1980, New York, The Viking Press, p. 231.

2 David Snellgrove, *Himalayan Pilgrimage*, 1961, Oxford, Bruno Cassirer; this edn. 2011, Bangkok, Orchid Press, p. 73.

3 SOS, p. 248.

4 SOS, p. 249.

5 See https://youtu.be/NvNMePltJ10, minutes 14:10-15:29.

6 You can find a number of von Fürer-Haimendorf's videos from the SOAS archive on YouTube: for example https://www.youtube. com/watch?v=nrnJFgkZhcU&list=PLTCcS6e700aOFeXYo_ wYXCze3Ik0H5Gi2&index=7.

7 TSL, p. 210.

8 TSL, p. 232.

9 TSL, p. 197.

10 SOS, pp. 262-263.

11 SOS, p. 252.

12 TSL, pp. 232-233.

13 TSL, p. 256.

14 SOS, p. 243.

15 SOS, p. 277.

16 TSL, p. 179.

17 TSL, p. 248.

Chapter 10

1 TSL, p. 170.

2 Matthew Arnold, Dover Beach, in *New Poems*, 1867, London, Macmillan and Co., lines 9-11.

3 TSL, pp. 27-28.

4 TSL, p. 36.

5 SOS, Acknowledgments, p. vi.

6 TSL, p. 150.

7 TSL, p. 149.

8 TSL, p. 146.

9 TSL, p. 149.

Chapter 11

1 T. S. Eliot, *The Dry Salvages*, from *The Four Quartets*, 1943, New York, Houghton Mifflin Harcourt Publishing Company, Stanza III, line 132.

2 *The Book of Isaiah*, Chapter 56, Verse 5, King James Version, 1611.

3 TSL, p. 36.

Chapter 12

1 Dor Bahadur Bista, *Fatalism and Development*, 1991, New Delhi, Orient Black Swan Private Limited, p. 4

2 Rabih Alameddine, *An Unnecessary Woman*, 2013, New York, Grove Press, p. 73.

3 Alfred Lord Tennyson, *Tithonus*, first published London, Cornhill Magazine, February 1860, lines 64-68.

4 *The Book of Genesis*, Chapter 1, Verse 21, King James Version, 1611.

Chapter 13

1 Sir Denys Roberts, *Family History* (unpublished), 2000, p. 65.

2 TSL, p. 298.

3 TSL, pp. 310, 313.

4 TSL, p. 298.

5 James Michener, *The World is my Home*, 1992, New York, Random House, p. 513: https://www.ebooks.com/en-us/book/1577376/the-world-is-my-home/ james-a-michener/?srsltid=AfmBOooDXyRrFcuLpMOH2nLYoUAndCnJ12L Tt5I4wOLIsFJXU7tOuH7h.

6 Joseph Conrad, op. cit., p. 330.

7 TSL, p. 298.

Chapter 14

1 Dawa Palden, *Saving Shey Phoksondo*, Nepal Times Buzz, 17-23 March 2017 #850.

2 SOS, p. 9.

3 Helpful as this insight is, its common attribution to *The Pilgrim's Progress*, 1678 (on Facebook and Instagram, for example) is false.

A Brief Political History of Nepal

1 Dor Bahadur Bista, *Khas of Chaudabisa*, Kathmandu, Himal Southasian, May 1, 1995, https://www.himalmag.com/cover/khas-of-chaudabisa.

2 Father Ludwig Stiller S.J., *The Rise of the House of Gorkha, A Study in the Unification of Nepal, 1768-1816*, 1975, Patna, The Jesuit Society, p. 45.

3 Nirmal Raj Joshi, *Divya Upadesh of Prithvi Narayan Shah with original text, modern Nepali text and English translation*, 2023, Ink Vault Publications online, p. 19, Kindle edition.

4 Father Ludwig Stiller S.J., op. cit., p. 139.

5 Mara Malagodi, *Nepal's Constitutional Foundations between Revolution and Cold War (1950–60)*, published online by Cambridge University Press, 16 February 2023.

6 The exact reference is no longer easily available, but see https://www. congress.gov/101/crecb/1989/06/29/GPO-CRECB-1989-pt10-4-1.pdf June 29, 1989, Vol. 135, Part 10.

7 Chandra Shekhar spoke in English. His speech was carried by a number of Indian newspapers, and a summary can be found in Lisa Choegyal and Michel Dunham's *The Nepal Scene, Chronicles of Elizabeth Hawley 1988-2007*, 2015, Volume I, p. 121. See also Chandra Shekhar: Selected Speeches 1990-91, https://archive.org/details/chandrashekharse00unse/ page/n1/mode/2up?q=nepal / https://nepalnews.com/s/politics/ chandrashekhars-role-crucial-for-consolidating-nepal-india-ties/. See also Rabindra Mishra, *India's Role in Nepal's Maoist Insurgency*, Asian Survey, Vol. 44, No. 5 (September/October 2004), pp. 627-646.

8 John Whelpton, *A History of Nepal*, 2005, Cambridge, Cambridge University Press: 4th South Asian edition printed in Noida, India, 2010, p. 201.

9 John Whelpton, op. cit., p. 205.

10 Marie Lecomte-Tillouine, *Political Change and Cultural Revolution in a Maoist Model Village, mid-western Nepal*, 2010, in *The Maoist Insurgency in Nepal*, ed. Lawoti and Pahari, Abingdon, UK, Routledge; Special Indian edition printed in New Delhi, 2015, p. 121.

11 Statement on developments in Nepal, Press Release, Feb 1, 2005 https://www.mea.gov.in/press-releases.htm?dtl/5841/ Statement+on+Developments+in+Nepal.

12 *Tied up by chains of tradition: Thus spake Gyanendra Shah, The Himalayan*, Jun 11 2008, https://thehimalayantimes.com/opinion/ tied-up-by-chains-of-tradition-thus-spake-gyanendra-shah.

13 Prasant Jha, *Battles of the New Republic*, 2014, London, Hurst and Company, Kindle edition, p 123.

14 Aditya Adhikari, *The Bullet and the Ballot Box*, 2014, New Delhi, Aleph Book Company, pp. 240-241, https://archive.org/details/bulletballotboxs0000adhi/ page/240/mode/2up.

15 Aditya Adhikari, op. cit., p. 153.

16 Thomas Bell, *Kathmandu*, 2014, Gurgaon, Random House India, p. 323.

Postscript: The Gen Z Uprising

1 Shubhanga Pandey, *Himalayan Uprising*, 3 October 2025, in Sidecar, New Left Review, https://newleftreview.org/sidecar/posts/himalayan-uprising.

2 See, for example, *Conflict, Security and Development*, the World Bank's World Development Report for 2011. A good way of thinking of institutions is as mediating devices—spaces in which people can argue their case and get a decision. It may not be a decision they like, but if enough colleagues and neighbors trust the institution, and if it is able to enforce its decisions, populations will tend to accept its verdicts. A law court is one such institution; so is a national budget; so too is an electoral law. When institutions with national reach are seen as legitimate (i.e. as sufficiently inclusive, accountable and effective), people have tended to rally behind them, and they have become accepted pieces of a mosaic of peaceful negotiation. That mosaic is the essence of a stable state. Creating legitimate institutions, though, takes time; progress is often reversed, and nothing is assured. The 2011 World Development Report measured this, and found that it takes *at least a generation* for mature, reliable institutions to emerge—when they do, that is. The International Country Risk Guidelines issued by the PRS Group, a geopolitical risk-rating firm, suggest that getting from

"Haiti to Ghana"—that is, achieving relatively modest improvements—took the *fastest* 20 countries 20 years to improve "bureaucratic quality," 27 years to achieve "control of corruption," and 36 years to "raise overall state effectiveness."

BIBLIOGRAPHY

Principal references

Matthiessen, Peter, 1978. *The Snow Leopard*, New York, The Viking Press.

Schaller, George B., 1980. *Stones of Silence: Journeys in the Himalaya*, New York, The Viking Press.

Books referred to or cited in the text

Attar, Farid ud-Din, 1177. *The Conference of the Birds*, translated into English in Farid ud-Din Attar, 1971. *The Conference of the Birds: A Sufi Fable*, Boulder, Shambhala Publications.

Acharya, Baburam; Siromani, Itihas; Yogi, Nataharinath, 2004 (reprint). *Budamaharaj Prithivi Narayan Shah ko Divya Upadesh*, ed. Prof. Acharya, Shri Krishna, Kathmandu, Law Commission of Nepal.

Adhikari, Aditya, 2014. *The Bullet and the Ballot Box*, New Delhi, Aleph Book Company.

Alameddine, Rabih, 2013. *An Unnecessary Woman*, New York, Grove Press, Kindle edition.

Arnold, Matthew, 1867. *New Poems*, London, Macmillan and Co.

Bell, Thomas, 2014. *Kathmandu*, Gurgaon, Random House.

Bauer, Kenneth M., 2004. *High Frontiers: Dolpo and the Changing World of Himalayan Pastoralists*, New York, Columbia University Press, Historical Ecology Series, Kindle edition.

Bista, Dor Bahadur, 1991. *Fatalism and Development: Nepal's Struggle for Modernization*, Hyderabad, Orient Blackswan Private Limited.

Bista, Dor Bahadur, 1995. *Khas of Chaudabisa*, Kathmandu, Himal Southasian, May 1, 1995.

Blaikie, Piers; Cameron, John; and Seddon, David, 1980. *Nepal in Crisis: Growth and Stagnation at the Periphery*, Oxford, Clarendon Press.

Bunyan, John, 1678. *The Pilgrim's Progress: From This World to That Which Is to Come*, London, Printed for Nath, Ponder at the Peacock in the Poultrey near Cornhil.

Byron, Robert, 1937. *The Road to Oxiana*, London, Macmillan.

Chatwin, Bruce, 1977. *In Patagonia*, London, Jonathan Cape Ltd.

Choegyal, Lisa, and Dunham, Mikel, 2015. *The Nepal Scene: Chronicles of Elizabeth Hawley, 1988-2007, in Two Volumes*. Kathmandu, Vajra Books.

Coleridge, Samuel Taylor, 1835. *Specimens of the Table Talk of the late Samuel Taylor Coleridge, in Two Volumes*, Albermarle Street, London, John Murray.

Conrad, Joseph, 1898. *Youth*, London, Blackwood's Magazine.

Conrad, Joseph, 1899-1900. *Lord Jim*, London, Blackwood's Magazine.

Dunham, Mikel, 2004. *Buddha's Warriors: The Story of the CIA-backed Tibetan Freedom Fighters, the Chinese Invasion and the Ultimate Fall of Tibet*, New York, Penguin.

Dunmore, Helen, 2010. *The Betrayal*, London, Fig Tree/Penguin Books.

Eliot, Thomas Stearns, 1943. *Four Quartets*, New York, Houghton Mifflin Harcourt Publishing Company.

Elliot, Geraldine, 1939. *The Long Grass Whispers*, London, Routledge & Keegan Paul Ltd.

Fisher, James F., 2017. *Trans-Himalaya Traders Transformed—Return to Tarang*, Bangkok, Orchid Press.

Govinda, Lama Anagarika, 1966. *The Way of the White Clouds*, London, Hutchinson and Co.

Haidt, Jonathan, 2013. T*he Righteous Mind: Why Good People are Divided by Politics and Religion*, New York, Vintage Books.

Hardy, Thomas, 1905. *Jude the Obscure*, London and New York, Harper and Brothers Publishers.

Jha, Prashant, 2014. *Battles of the New Republic*, London, Hurst and Company.

Kunwar, Laxman Singh, 2015. *Emigration of Nepalese People and Its Impact*, Kathmandu, Economic Journal of Development Issues, Vol. 19 & 20, No. 1-5.

Lear, Edward, 1871. *The Owl and The Pussycat*, in *Nonsense Songs, Stories, Botany, and Alphabets*, London, R. J. Bush.

Lecomte-Tillouine, Marie, 2010. *Political Change and Cultural Revolution in a Maoist Model Village, mid-western Nepal*, in *The Maoist Insurgency in Nepal*, ed. Lawoti, Mahendra and Pahari, Anup K, Abingdon, UK, Routledge.

Leigh-Fermor, Patrick, 1977. *A Time of Gifts: On Foot to Constantinople—from the Hook of Holland to the Middle Danube*, London, John Murray Ltd.

Lewis, C. S., 1955. *The Magician's Nephew*, London, The Bodley Head.

Mainali, Sujit, 2015. *How Discriminatory was the Muliki Ain against Dalits?* published online by southasiacheck.org, an initiative of Panos, South Asia.

Malagodi, Mara, 2023. *Nepal's Constitutional Foundations between Revolution and Cold War (1950–60)*, published online by Cambridge University Press, 16 February.

Manchester, William, 1980. *Goodbye, Darkness: A Memoir of the Pacific War*, Boston, Little, Brown.

Mathema, Kalyan Bhakta, 2011. *Madheshi Uprising: The Resurgence of Ethnicity*, Kathmandu, Mandala Book Point.

Mayhew, Bradley; Brown, Lindsay; and Butler, Stuart, 2015. *Trekking in the Nepal Himalaya, Walking Guide*, Franklin, Tennessee, Lonely Planet Publications Pty Ltd, Kindle edition.

Michener, James A., 1992. *The World is my Home*, New York, Random House.

Ogura, Kiyoko, 2004. *Realities and Images of Nepal's Maoists After the Attack on Beni*, European Bulletin of Himalayan Research 27, August 2004.

Palden, Dawa, 2017. *Saving Shey Phoksondo*, Nepal Times Buzz, 17-23 March 2017, #850.

Pandey, Shubhanga, 2025. *Himalayan Uprising*, in Sidecar, New Left Review, 3 October 2025, https://newleftreview.org/sidecar/posts/himalayan-uprising.

Pleshakov, Constantine, 2002. *The Tsar's Last Armada: the Epic Journey to the Battle of Tsushima*, New York, Basic Books, Kindle edition.

Pritchard-Jones, Siân, and Gibbons, Bob, 2014. *A Trekking Guide to Upper and Lower Dolpo*, Himalayan Travel Guides, Kathmandu, Himalayan Map House, first Kindle edition.

Rankin, Ian, 2015. *Even Dogs in the Wild*, London, Orion Publishing Group Ltd.

Regmi, Mahesh Chandra, 1971. *A Study in Nepali Economic History*, Delhi, Manjusri.

Schell, Orville, 2001. *Himalaya – Review of Caravan*, LA Times Film Review.

Sebald, W. G. ('Max'), 1999. *The Rings of Saturn*, London, the Harvill Press; originally published in 1995 as *Die Ringe des Saturn: Eine englische Wallfahrt*, Frankfurt am Main, Vito von Eichborn GmbH & Co Verlag.

Snellgrove, David L., 1961. *Himalayan Pilgrimage*, Oxford, Bruno Cassirer.

Snellgrove, David L., 1967. *Four Lamas of Dolpo*, Oxford/Cambridge, Bruno Cassirer and Harvard University Press.

Stiller, Father Ludwig S.J., 1975. *The Rise of the House of Gorkha, A Study in the Unification of Nepal, 1768-1816*, Patna, The Jesuit Society.

Stiller, Father Ludwig S.J., 1976. *The Silent Cry: The People of Nepal 1816-1839*, Kathmandu, Educational Publishing House.

Suzuki, D. T., 1927. *Essays in Zen Buddhism, First Series*, New York, Grove Press.

Tennyson, Alfred, First Baron Tennyson, 1860. *Tithonus*, London, The Cornhill Magazine, February 1860 ed.

Valli, Éric, and Summers, Diane, 1987. *Dolpo: Hidden Land of the Himalayas*, New York, Aperture Foundation.

Waugh, Alec, 1917. *The Loom of Youth*, London, Methuen and Co.

Whelpton, John, 2005. *A History of Nepal*, Cambridge, Cambridge University Press.

Whelpton, John, 2016 (second ed.). *Jang Bahadur in Europe: The First Nepalese Mission to the West.* Kathmandu, Mandala Book Point.

Wordsworth, William, 1807. *Poems, in Two Volumes.* London, Longman, Hurst, Rees and Orme.

Word Bank, 2011. *World Development Report: Conflict, Security and Development.* Washington DC, World Bank.

Other books on Nepal

Bates, Crispin, 1995. *Race, Caste and Tribe in Central India: The Early Origins of Indian Anthropometry,* Edinburgh Papers In South Asian Studies, Number 3.

Bond, Ruskin, and Gokhale, Namita, eds., 2016, *Himalaya: Adventures, Meditations, Life*, New Delhi, Speaking Tiger Books.

Caplan, Lionel, 1970. *Land and Social Change in East Nepal: A Study of Hindu-Tribal Relations*, London, Rutledge & Kegan Paul Limited.

Cognetti, Paulo, 2020. *Without Ever Reaching the Summit.* New York, Harper One/Harper Collins.

Cowan, Sam, 2018. *Essays on Nepal – Past and Present.* Kathmandu, Himal Books.

Edmundson, Henry, 2019. *Tales from the Himalaya*, Kathmandu, Vajra Books.

Gyawali, Dipak, 2003. *Reflecting on Contemporary Nepali Angst*, in *Understanding the Maoist Movement of Nepal*, ed. Thapa, Deepak, Kathmandu, Centre of Social Research and Development.

Hutt, Michael, 2004. *Monarchy, Democracy and Maoism in Nepal*, in *Himalayan 'People's War': Nepal's Maoist Rebellion*, ed. Hutt, Michael, London, Hurst and Company.

Keay, John, 2022. *Himalaya: Exploring the Roof of the World*, London, Bloomsbury Publishing.

Lawoti, Mahendra, 2010. *Evolution and Growth of the Maoist Insurgency in Nepal*, in *The Maoist Insurgency in Nepal: Revolution in the Twenty-First Century*. Abingdon, UK, Routledge, Special Indian Edition 2015 printed in India by Nutech Print Services.

Lhanlungpa, Lobsang P. (trans), 1979. *The Life of Milarepa*, Boston, Shambhala Publications, Inc.

Magar, Kshitiz, 2011. *Gandak Abhiyan (the Gandak Campaign)*, Kathmandu, Mangalesen Smriti Brigade, Fifth Division, the People's Liberation Army, Nepal.

Malla, Kumar, 2006. *Abhyasta Sipahi, Srasta ra Rato Tara (Trained Soldiers, Creation and Red Stars)*, Kathmandu, Janadesh 15 (10), 24 January.

Mottin, Monica, 2010. *Catchy Melodies and Clenched Fists: Performance and Politics in Maoist Cultural Programs*, in *The Maoist Insurgency in Nepal*, ed. Lawoti, Mahendra, and Pahari, Anup K., Abingdon, UK, Routledge.

Nickson, Andrew, 1992. *Democratisation and the Growth of Communism in Nepal: A Peruvian Scenario in the Making?* Journal of Commonwealth and Comparative Politics, vol 30, no 3.

Pradhan, Rajendra, 2002. *Ethnicity, Caste and a Pluralist Society* in *State of Nepal*, ed. Dixit, Kanak Mani, and Ramachandran, Shastri, Kathmandu, Himal Books.

Raeper, William, and Hoftun, Martin, 1992. *Spring Awakening*, New Delhi, Viking/Penguin Books.

Rose, Leo E., 1971. *Nepal: Strategy for Survival*, Berkeley, University of California Press.

Sill, Michael, and Kirby, John, 1991. *Atlas of Nepal in the Modern World*, London, Earthscan Publications Ltd.

Thapa, Deepak, 2003. *Erosion of the Nepali World*, in *Understanding the Maoist Movement of Nepal*, ed. Thapa, Deepak, Kathmandu, Centre of Social Research and Development.

Thapa, Manjushree, 2003. *The War in the West*, in *Understanding the Maoist Movement of Nepal*, ed. Thapa, Deepak, Kathmandu, Centre of Social Research and Development.

Upadhya, Rajib, 2020. *Cabals and Cartels*, Kathmandu, FinePrint Books.

Upadhya, Sanjay, 2002. *A Dozen Years of Democracy: The Games that Parties Play*, in *State of Nepal*, ed. Dixit, Kanak Mani, and Ramachandran, Shastri, Kathmandu, Himal Books.

Upreti, Bishnu Raj, 2010. *External Engagement in Nepal's Armed Conflict*, in *The Maoist Insurgency in Nepal*, ed. Lawoti, Mahendra, and Pahari, Anup K, Abingdon, UK, Routledge.

Van Den Hoek, Jamon; Smith, Alexander C; Hurni, Kaspar; Saksena, Sumeet; and Fox, Jefferson, 2021. *Shedding New Light on Mountainous Forest Growth: A Cross-Scale Evaluation of the Effects of Topographic Illumination Correction on 25 Years of Forest Cover Change across Nepal*, 28 May, Remote Sensing, Multi-Disciplinary Digital Publishing Institute, 13 (11), 2131.

ABOUT THE AUTHOR

NIGEL ROBERTS is a dual citizen of the UK and the USA. He grew up in East Africa, and has worked for over fifty years in international development, thirty of those years with the World Bank—initially as an agricultural economist, later as a resident representative and then country director in Nepal, Ethiopia, the West Bank and Gaza, and Australia. His last World Bank job was joint director of the 2011 World Development Report, which focused on global conflict. Since retiring, he has advised aid agencies and governments in Somalia, West Bank and Gaza, Myanmar, Afghanistan, Ukraine and Armenia. Living with his wife Sarah and his grandson Alex in Virginia, he writes regularly on Substack (as "ImperfeCt Contrition"), and has recently produced a film on the Bhote Khampa, a small tribe of nomadic traders in the remote far-western mountains of Nepal.